LIGHTEN UP,
GEORGE

Art Buchwald

LIGHTEN UP, GEORGE

951053

G. P. PUTNAM'S SONS
New York

G. P. Putnam's Sons
Publishers Since 1838
200 Madison Avenue
New York, NY 10016

Library of Congress Cataloging-in-Publication Data

Buchwald, Art.
Lighten up, George / Art Buchwald.
p.   cm.
ISBN 0-399-13667-3
1. United States—Politics and government—1989–   —Humor.
2. United States—Civilization—1970–   —Humor.   I. Title.
PS3503.U1828L54   1991   91-20265 CIP
814'.54—dc20

Printed in the United States of America
1   2   3   4   5   6   7   8   9   10

This book is printed on acid-free paper.
∞

THIS BOOK IS dedicated to all the people who never had a book dedicated to them. Please fill in your name and your Social Security number, and the dedication will be considered binding in any literary dispute.

CONTENTS

CONTENTS

CONTENTS

CONTENTS

CONTENTS

CONTENTS

CONTENTS

INTRODUCTION

ORIGINALLY I INTENDED that this book be about sex in Washington and how it affects the budget deficit. But after interviewing at least a thousand unnamed sources, I discovered that there was no sex in Washington, although there was an extremely large budget deficit.

The people in the nation's capital not only don't do it—they frown on anybody else who does.

The reason is that everyone, and I include those in the suburbs of Maryland and Virginia, prefers to watch Ted Koppel talk about Iraq than to bundle with each other. Washington public servants do not have time to sneak around or engage in hanky-panky, and despite what you have read in other kiss-and-tell books, this also applies to everyone who has ever lived in the White House.

Those engaged in formulating defense policy are so intent on giving the United States the biggest bang for the buck that they have no bangs left for each other.

When it comes to Congress, sex is not a subject to be discussed in either House. And yet there is always some well-motivated legislator searching for the perfect definition of pornography.

The Supreme Court has still to decide whether the Founding Fathers intended us to have sex or not.

It's not that sex is taboo; it just never enters anyone's mind that it is politically correct.

Without people's engaging in sex there can be no sex

scandals—and that's the way it has been in Washington ever since Frank Sinatra was driven out of town.

Once I eliminated sex as a topic, I sought other subjects of interest for my book, such as politicians screwing the taxpayer and raping the public trust. I searched in hopes of finding at least one dishonest official, but drew a blank.

Much to my amazement, I discovered that special-interest campaign contributions play little part in our legislation, and a man's position in the government has no effect on how he is treated by lawyers and lobbyists in this quaint utopia that we all call home.

Contrary to rumor, politicians cannot be bought by political action committees. The rule of thumb in Washington is that if you buy a table for a campaign prayer breakfast from a chairman of a committee, you should expect the chairman to go into the tank only once.

If you have no sex scandals and no political scandals, what kind of scandals are left to write about? It's impossible to say. The wonderful people who make up Washington are blessed to live in a community where no one can do any wrong.

So if you are expecting sleaze and dirty secrets, skullduggery and adultery, ad infinitum, you are reading from the wrong book. This one devotes its pages to what's good about America and what it means to live in a country where every man, woman and child has the privilege of bailing out the savings and loan bank of his or her choice.

I would like to give credit to all the anonymous sources for this book who were of tremendous help and encouragement when I was putting it together. Most of them know who they are—even though some of them have forgotten their own names.

If anyone objects to any material in this book, I will happily retract it.

LIGHTEN UP, GEORGE

HERE KITTY, HERE KITTY

"I'M TOYING WITH the idea of running for president of the United States. How would you like to be First Lady?" I asked my wife.

"Not while Kitty Kelley's alive," she replied.

"What can she do to you?" I said.

"Nobody wants to be the president's wife and show up on Kitty Kelley's computer screen."

"But you'd make a wonderful First Lady. What could she possibly write about you that would be negative?"

"Nothing until she talks to my 'good' friends."

"We've never smoked pot," I reminded her.

"You know that and I know that, but what's to prevent someone with a grudge against us from saying otherwise?"

"Who would do such a thing?"

"How about high administration sources who mow the lawn at Camp David? Suppose the White House pastry chef tells Kitty that I make my own clothes?"

"Look, just because Kitty Kelley wrote a tough book about Nancy Reagan doesn't mean she would write the same kind of stuff about you."

"Why not?"

"Because she needs a change of pace. I'm willing to bet that once you had Kitty over for tea, she'd treat you like an East Coast Madonna."

"I am so afraid that if you run for president, Kitty would discover that I make all the decisions in this family. You don't

17

even know whether to stand up or sit down when they play 'Hail to the Chief.' "

I laughed. "That's ridiculous. Everyone knows we're a team. Besides, who would tell them otherwise?"

"An embittered hairdresser, a member of the Joint Chiefs of Staff, a jealous salesgirl at Bloomingdale's. It just doesn't seem worth it to be the most powerful woman in America if people are going to throw mud at you to feed the public's insatiable appetite for gossip."

"I think that you are overreacting. But before I make my decision to run, I would like to ask you one question, so that it doesn't haunt us later on: Has Frank Sinatra ever been on the second floor of our house?"

For some reason this angered my wife, and she yelled, "He's never even been in the basement."

"So," I said, "we have nothing to worry about. Just stick with your story, no matter what the *National Enquirer* says."

She was adamant. "If you run for president and are elected, I will refuse to be the First Lady of the land."

"But where will you live?"

"Right here in our house. I'll fax my instructions to you about how to run the government. It's the only way to foil Kitty Kelley."

"I don't want to sit in the Oval Office without you faithfully at my side," I told her.

"Now you're making sense. No presidency is worth the paper an unauthorized biography is printed on."

"What if Kitty Kelley decides to write a book about you even though you aren't First Lady?"

"Why would she want to do that?" my wife asked.

"To follow up on the Frank Sinatra angle," I said.

SEVEN DAYS IN MARCH

CONGRESSIONAL HEARINGS WERE held on a bill that would require a seven-day waiting period before a person could purchase a gun. Witnesses were divided into two groups: those in favor of the bill because they either had been wounded by a gun or had had a relative killed by one; and National Rifle Association lobbyists and Justice Department officials who were against the bill.

I've never understood why anyone would object to waiting seven days for a firearm, so I sought guidance from Milton Hammer, a pistol aficionado who once told me at a picnic, "I may not agree with what you say, but I will shoot to death anyone who tries to stop you from saying it."

I asked Milton, "What is your objection to delaying the purchase of a gun for seven days?"

"It's too long. Have you ever had to hold your breath for seven days for something you truly wanted?"

"I know that a week is a lifetime—but maybe you could do something useful while you wait."

"Such as?"

"Community service. How about going into the slums to help the young people?"

"I'm not going into the slums. They might shoot me."

"Ah, there you have it. Why do they have guns in slums?

19

They have them because the shooters don't have to wait seven days to buy one. The law they're trying to pass is not aimed at honest, law-abiding Americans like yourself—it is to weed out people who purchase guns to do bodily harm to others."

Milton replied, "I once had to wait seven days for an electric train set when I was a kid. I vomited every morning. The Constitution says I can buy a firearm anytime I want to. That's because the Founding Fathers said that when someone wants a gun, they should get it *now.*"

"They just want the seven days to see if people have a criminal record, or if they are crazy. That's not asking a lot."

"So you say. But pretty soon they'll be checking on citizens who are prone to causing gun accidents. Do you think a seven-day check on John Wilkes Booth would have prevented him from shooting Lincoln?"

"No, but John Hinckley might have been prevented from shooting President Reagan."

"Well, tell me this," Milton said. "How come, if the seven-day registration bill is so good for the country, President Bush is against it?"

"President Bush owes a lot to the National Rifle Association, and he doesn't want to offend them. They could do him major damage in the election year if he starts supporting any gun control bills in this country. Bush wants a kinder and gentler America, but he also wants a tough America, and it cannot be accomplished if people have to wait seven days for delivery of a weapon to defend themselves."

Milton said, "I'm with him. No one in this country should be required to wait a week to shoot a duck."

"You're going to shoot a duck with a pistol?"

"If it was going to break into your house, wouldn't you?"

LEND ME A FORTUNE

As MORE AND MORE American institutions continue to founder, the little man keeps asking himself what the hell went wrong. A year ago we were assured that the banks could never be affected the way the savings and loan institutions were.

They made a mistake. How did it happen? Well, if you really want to know, we have to return to the go-go years of the eighties.

Mr. Stonehart the venture capitalist was walking down the street when he was tackled by Mr. Crabapple the banker. Crabapple held Stonehart's head in a grip and said, "How would you like to borrow seven million dollars to buy worthless real estate from a widow who lives in Florida?"

"I don't want to borrow seven million dollars," Stonehart yelled.

"Okay, then ten million. It's a much easier number for me to remember."

"Why would I need ten million when I don't need seven?"

"Mr. Stonehart, you never know when you may have a rainy day. Today you think you only need seven, but tomorrow your wife could find a nice Gucci dress on Fifth Avenue and you'd be glad to have the extra change."

"Maybe you're right. I must say that banks are certainly looking for business right now."

21

"That's because we have money to burn. If we don't spread it around, it will turn into mulch. Ha, ha, ha."

"Mr. Crabapple, would you ease up on my neck? How do you want me to pay back the ten million?"

"Very slowly. We'd rather you have our money and pay interest on it than for us to keep it in some teller's drawer where he'll have to stare at it every day. We'll work out a schedule for you. You must understand that this does not stop you from borrowing more than twelve million dollars from us for any junk bonds you would like to purchase."

"You're a really generous guy."

"When you're happy, we're happy. Banks are awash in cash nowadays, and if we don't loan you the fifteen million dollars someone else will."

"What fifteen?"

"The fifteen you're going to use to take your family to St. Moritz. We have a saying at the bank: 'No one ever got hemorrhoids from using other people's money.' "

"Why do they say bankers are tightfisted?"

"Charles Dickens gave us a bad name. The true story is that we loan to everybody—Donald Trump, Ivana Trump, Michael Milken and Bulgaria. We have a warehouse full of high-heeled shoes from Imelda Marcos. The more people owe us the better we are doing. We're known as the bank that never says no."

"What happens if borrowers don't pay back?" Stonehart asked.

"We've never had that problem. These are the boom-boom eighties, which means that anyone can walk out of the bank today with twenty million dollars."

"You'd let me have twenty million?"

"I gave it to Neil Bush and he didn't even thank me. You'd be amazed at the type of people we deal with. Do you know who was in yesterday? Sam Pierce, the former secretary of HUD. He wanted to borrow against all the public housing in the United States. You can't have better collateral than that."

And so it was that all the banks in the eighties extended themselves. Now it's the nineties and Stonehart can't repay Crabapple the $45 million he borrowed from him. He doesn't even like the man anymore.

BOOK SALE

FOR BETTER or for worse, many congressmen have entered into the book business. Both former House Speaker Jim Wright and Minority Whip Newt Gingrich admitted to marketing their books, but they denied any wrongdoing.

Wright and Gingrich are not the only ones in marketing. I went to visit Congressman Alamo the other day.

His secretary said, "The congressman is not here right now, but you are welcome to wait for him. Would you like something to read?"

"Thank you," I replied, "I would."

She handed me a paperback and told me, "That'll be twenty-five dollars."

"Twenty-five dollars!" I exclaimed.

"If you buy a hundred copies we can give you the bulk rate of nineteen ninety-five each."

"I'm not sure that I want to buy *The Collected Speeches of My Political Opponents*, by Congressman Alamo. What is he doing publishing the remarks of his enemies?"

The secretary explained, "Congressman Alamo used up all

his own speeches in his last four books, so he had no choice. Fortunately, they weren't copyrighted. If you'd like a complete set, we can let you have it for one hundred fifty dollars."

"What have the reviews been like?"

"The teamsters' union described him as another Tolstoy. The National Rifle Association said that his books will go down in history with *The Guns of Navarone*, and the National Association of Manufacturers bought one hundred thousand, for every member of its organization. If the congressman votes to bail out the savings and loan industry, we're going to have to go into another printing."

"Does Congressman Alamo print his own books?"

"Of course. He's involved with everything from cover designs to sales. He even goes to Finland every month to select his own paper. If you don't want the book, would you care for a magazine?"

"How much is it?"

"The same as the book—twenty-five dollars."

"How can that be? Don't people complain when you charge them so much for reading material?"

"The hot-coal industry never cares how much the congressman asks for his publications. When it comes to looking out for the coal interests, there is no price you can put on an Alamo creative work."

"I think I'll just sit here and wait."

"Would you like to visit Congressman Alamo's bookstore?"

"Where is it?"

"In his office. We had to put it there because we didn't have any room out here. You can go in and browse. Any publication you see is for sale, including the U.S. budget for 1989, bound in snakeskin."

"You are very hospitable," I told the secretary.

"We do our best to make everyone feel at home. Now if you'll excuse me, I have to pack five thousand books for the Killer Bee

24

Association. They want to give them as door prizes at all the state fairs."

"Maybe I'll read *National Geographic*."

"Do you want to pay cash or give me a traveler's check?"

"I have to pay to read *National Geographic*!"

"PAC money doesn't go as far as it used to."

THUMBSUCKER

THE THUMBSUCKER REPORT has just been released. Written by Dr. Alfred Thumbsucker, the report deals with the problems parents have communicating with their children, and the inability of those children to communicate with anyone.

"Most parents," Dr. Thumbsucker told me, "admit that they didn't have much luck with child-rearing, but they all have the same defense: 'Look what we had to work with.' "

"In your report, what do you consider the main barrier between children and their parents?" I asked.

"Rock music," he replied. "When teenagers turned to the Grateful Dead for all their needs, parents lost control over them. It is not generally known, but as soon as a child is born in the United States, the doctor inserts tiny Walkman speakers into the ears. The Walkman is activated when the doctor spanks the baby, and it remains on at full volume right through college."

"You're going to make the front pages with that one."

"As the child grows up he or she spends every waking moment listening to music, and tuning out on everything else. Parents were always under the impression that when a young person shook his head, he was answering either yes or no to a question. They had no idea that the kid was only keeping time to the Rolling Stones."

"Didn't it ever occur to parents that something other than thinking was going on in their offspring's head?" I asked.

"No, it didn't. Parents were happy to see their children snap their fingers, because it meant that they were still alive. Some teenagers found that the audio level of the Walkman was not strong enough for their rock music habit, so they put large radios on their shoulders to enhance the sound. They also installed loudspeakers in their bedrooms so that nothing else could be heard in the house.

"With so much electronic power at their command, it's no wonder that kids have been unable to converse in any spoken tongue. This is the reason that parents never get a response when they shout, 'Why don't you do what I tell you?' The child has no idea what his father or mother is saying."

"How can young people get by without communicating?"

"Most of them discovered early in life that no matter what they did, they would always be housed and fed. Knowing this, there was no reason for them to try to figure out what was going on in the world."

"At least they know what they want," I said.

"The generations of rock music fans, all of whom are still wired with Walkmans, are now becoming the labor force in this country. They are doctors, lawyers and oil tanker captains, but they all keep time to Bruce Springsteen."

"Did you interview a lot of people for your report?" I asked the doctor.

"I talked to many parents, but they were more confused than helpful. The children were something else again. Every time I asked a question, they rolled their eyes and clapped their hands. I would have been worried had I not known that each and every one of them had a Walkman implant."

"Then your findings are based more on your own knowledge than on what anyone said to you?"

"That is correct. But it does have substance. I have never met a child who listens more to his parents than he does to Michael Jackson."

STOOD UP

It was in all the papers. A young woman in Palm Beach, Florida, named Tomontra Mangrum, was stood up by her seventeen-year-old date, who had promised to take her to the high school prom. Tomontra did what any jilted woman would do—she filed a lawsuit to recoup the cost of her new shoes, her hairdo, plus the flowers for her hair.

Wait, there is more. The defendant, Marlon Shadd, says that he had fractured his ankle and had informed Miss Mangrum a week before that he would not be able to take her to the dance.

It must be obvious to anyone reading this that the only way this dispute can be resolved is to turn it over to the lawyers.

Something about this story was familiar. My mind went back to my youth, when the situation was very different from the one we have now. Those were the Roosevelt years, when many more men than women were stood up. I can remember at least ten, no, make it twelve, occasions when I arrived at a young woman's door only to be informed by her father that she had already left for the evening.

In those days, corsages did not grow on trees—nor did tickets to the Paramount Theater on Broadway. We're talking about five bucks for the entire package, but they were 1940 dollars, worth about $100,000 today.

Yet no matter how cruel the rejection, the last thing I would have done in that distant time and place would have been to sue the girl who wasn't there. The fact is, I respected her for seeing through me and for giving me a lower opinion of myself than I had ever had before.

It just wasn't *in* us teenagers to seek out a lawyer's help to resolve our lovers' quarrels. Most of us didn't even know a lawyer, which is more than can be said for the affluent kids of today, who usually have one attorney living on either side of them.

Instead of taking our case to court, we suffered, sometimes for weeks and, if it was serious enough, even a month. We wove fantasies in which we went off to join the Navy and came back in uniform, and then refused to dance with the girls who had broken our hearts. We never wanted monetary satisfaction, we only wanted the one who had wronged us to weep tears and beg forgiveness.

Those of us who grew up in the forties, fifties and even sixties did not wish for a black-robed judge to mete out justice against the person who had stood us up. We dealt with our sorrow alone.

So back to Miss Mangrum, who, I am sure, is quite lovely. Yet according to Marlon, she suffers from a communication problem. The reason her suit has today's parents unnerved is that young people are breaking dates all the time, and if they're going to be dragged into court for it, they'll never get their homework done.

In one newspaper I read that Marlon's mother offered to

compensate Tomontra for her expenses, but Tomontra's mother refused, saying that Marlon had to be taught a lesson.

What kind of lesson could Marlon possibly be taught, you may be wondering. He claims that he gave Tomontra notice and therefore is not responsible for her being left standing in the hall in her prom dress. I know there are many people who say Tomontra has no case, but that's the kind lawyers like best.

All over America teenagers are awaiting the outcome. The price of suing may be very high. The terrible thing is that if Miss Mangrum wins the fifty dollars, she will never know whether the boys who ask her out are inviting her for herself or because of her money.

SMILE, PLEASE

THE PRICE OF luxury goods is now so high that salespeople are unable to keep a straight face when they quote the cost of these items. Consequently, Angus Yates has started a school to train people how to handle this situation without breaking up. In his school Angus has a studio that resembles a section of a department store. Employees, whose tuition is paid for by the retail establishments they work for, sign up for six weeks. I was permitted to attend one of these classes. The students were lined up against one wall and Angus was sitting in a director's chair, holding a megaphone.

"Roll 'em," he yelled.

A student, playing the role of a customer, walked over to a counter and said to the salesman, "How much is this sweater?"

The student salesman looked at the tag and replied, "Eight hundred dollars." This was followed by an uncontrollable burst of laughter.

Angus threw down his megaphone. He screamed at the salesman, "What are you laughing at, dummy?"

"This sweater, sir. It's marked down to eight hundred dollars. Have you ever seen anything so ridiculous in your life?"

"It's not your job to make judgments. All you are supposed to do is close the sale. Eight hundred dollars may be amusing to you, but it is not funny to the man who pays the store rent. Now pick it up from the sweater part." He nodded to the student customer. The customer walked over to a sports jacket.

"Is this really a fourteen-hundred-dollar jacket?" he asked.

The student salesman bit his nails. "Yes, it is."

"Don't bite your nails," Angus told him. "The customer will think you're frightened."

"I am frightened. I know that I'm committing a crime if I take fourteen hundred dollars for that sports jacket."

"You're not. Fourteen hundred dollars is no longer a lot of money for a jacket. But you're the one who has to convince the customer that he deserves such a jacket because he's earned it."

"How do I do that?"

"By being blasé, and pretending that you sell three dozen of them a day. Mention the price the same way you would the cost of an order of French fries at McDonald's. You want your customer to believe that he has touched a sports jacket the likes of which he will never see again. Let's give it one more try at the jewelry counter."

The customer goes over to the jewelry counter and picks up a gold and diamond necklace. "How much?"

The student salesman looks at the price and then tries to talk. He can't speak.

Angus jumps up. "Tell him how much it is!"

The salesman says hoarsely, "You're not going to believe this, but the necklace costs forty-three thousand dollars."

"Why don't I believe it?"

"No necklace is worth forty-three thousand dollars."

"You don't know that!" Angus screams. "This is your last chance. I want you to tell that nice gentleman how much the jewelry costs and why he should buy it—all with a straight face."

The salesman made another attempt. "Sir, this necklace is a serious matter. Notice that I did not laugh when I picked it up, nor did the color drain from my face. I am happy to tell you, without smiling, that you can have it for forty-three thousand dollars, which is what my wife and I give to the Church every Sunday."

Angus shouted, "You're overdoing it. Just repeat the price with contempt in your voice. Hint that the customer could afford it if he wasn't so cheap."

"If he doesn't buy the necklace, what then?"

"Go back to the clothing counter. After the jewelry, the eight-hundred-dollar sweater will look like a steal."

THE BIG LOTTERY

THE LOTTERY IS now the last hope for all mankind, and the beauty of it is that so many players in this country believe they are born winners.

Joe Jarboe is one of them. He owes me fifty bucks, and he told me just last week, "As soon as I win the lottery I'll pay you back."

"I don't want to wait," I protested.

"It won't be long," he said.

"But Joe, millions of people are playing the lottery. What makes you think you'll win?"

"Because I have hunches that are almost supernatural. Take last month—the winning numbers were eight, seven, three, two, six, one. I played seven, eight, two, zero, three and nine."

"That's nowhere near the winner."

"Right. I learned a lesson. Never play zero on a Friday if it's raining. With just a little more concentration, I figure I'll be staring at a million dollars a year for the rest of my life. Then I'll be happy to pay you back."

"Joe, I think the reason you keep picking wrong numbers is that you're worried about the money you owe me. That's what is driving you crazy."

"You don't understand," he said. "I am determined to have a winning ticket. State lotteries are now the only way the government can provide its citizens with the American dream."

"You're living in a fantasy world," I told him. "Nobody wins the lottery except some porter from the Bronx who says he's not going to quit his job, no matter how much money they give him."

Joe wasn't listening. "I know my turn is coming up. I've been too close for comfort too often. Once I was off by just two numbers. Two months ago, if I had bet three instead of five I would have been on the *Today* show talking to Katherine Couric. I'm not the only one who thinks the lottery can save him. I have a friend who forgot to pay the IRS last year. He told them they would get their money after the next sweepstakes drawing."

"What did the IRS say?"

"They were happy because they were dealing with a winner. There is a woman who is selling her house in Hoboken, New Jersey, and moving to Princeton because she's sure she's going to split a ten-million-dollar prize with a bus driver in Bayonne. Next to God, the lottery is the only thing people have to live for."

"I understand that," I said. "But you couldn't do business in this country if everyone said they had to wait for their lottery money to come in."

"Why not? It's the easiest way to have a cash flow. You better watch out, or I may not talk to you when I win the sweepstakes."

"Joe, give me the fifty dollars."

"I don't have fifty dollars."

"Then what do you have?"

"I have a sign."

"What kind of sign?"

"I've had an itch under my left toe for a week. If this isn't a hunch that I am going to be a winner, then I don't know what is. You see, I am not like most people, who have no idea what they're doing. They shouldn't be playing, because for them the lottery is a sucker's game."

SUDDEN DEATH

IT WAS IN all the papers. A mobster had told *Playboy* magazine that Jimmy Hoffa, the former teamsters' union boss, was buried at the twenty yard line at Giants Stadium in the New Jersey Meadowlands.

The thug, a government-protected witness, stated that after

Hoffa was dispatched in Detroit, his remains were placed in an oil drum and shipped east. The drum was laid in the soft Meadowlands ground as support for the artificial turf.

The news came as a surprise to some sports fans who hang out at Clyde's in Georgetown.

Don Rogers said, "I thought Hoffa was buried under the highway between Grand Rapids and Kalamazoo."

"Nah," answered Steve Wells. "A friend of mine assured me his remains are under the starting gate at Hialeah. Hoffa liked horses."

Bob Boyd added, "The thing that makes me doubt the *Playboy* story is that Jimmy Hoffa was a Detroit Lions fan. Why would he want to be buried in New Jersey?"

"Maybe he didn't have any choice," Jim Morton suggested. "Perhaps they buried him in New Jersey to punish him."

"I never thought of that. Teamster gorillas can be insensitive. But why the twenty yard line?" I asked.

Rogers explained, "That's where all the action is. It's much more lively than the end zone."

Wells was shaking his head. "It just doesn't figure. The Giants are not that good a team."

Boyd said, "There could be other factors. Don't forget that at the time they buried Hoffa in the stadium, artificial turf was being installed. Look at all the money the teamsters saved on upkeep of the grave by burying him there. Teamster enforcers are always looking for ways to put a little extra into their pension fund."

"Is it possible that the *Playboy* story is a red herring, and Hoffa is really buried at home plate in Yankee Stadium?" I asked.

"That doesn't make any sense. Why would they bury him there?" Rogers wanted to know.

"That's where George Steinbrenner buried forty-six hundred Yankee managers. So the Mob might have thought that no one would look for Hoffa in that location," Wells told him.

"It's too far-fetched. I believe the mobster's story that Hoffa is now in a drum in Giants Stadium," Boyd declared.

"If that is true, it gives new meaning to the phrase 'sudden death,'" Wells said.

"You know what would be nice? If we all went up to the Meadowlands and strewed flowers on the Giants' twenty yard line," I suggested.

"While they are playing!" exclaimed Morton.

"It would be more touching," Rogers said.

"You've got to show me something other than the *Playboy* article before I'll believe that Jimmy Hoffa is resting in the Meadowlands. He could be anywhere—even under the Dallas Cowboys' locker room," Morton told us.

"They would never bury Hoffa in Dallas," Rogers asserted.

"Why not?" I asked.

"The Cowboys don't have a pass defense."

There was no consensus at Clyde's that evening on whether or not Hoffa was really buried in Giants Stadium. The problem, as we saw it, was that since everything else is buried in New Jersey, why not him?

TAKE ME OVER

THERE ARE SO many takeovers, mergers and leveraged buyouts in the United States that no one knows who owns what anymore.

I saw this with my own eyes the other morning when I stopped by Al & Rose's One-Stop Lunchroom on Route 312.

I ordered breakfast, and was sipping my coffee when the Japanese man on the stool next to me told Al he was putting too much butter on the toast.

"What business is it of yours?" Al wanted to know.

"My company, Nummi-Nummi-Summi Limited, bought your store yesterday."

Al was outraged. "They couldn't have. Rose and I are independent."

"It doesn't matter. We bought up every short-order store in America, including this one. Please take this with our compliments."

"What is it?"

"A golden parachute from Tokyo. It's just a small token we provide for each person we buy out."

"Just a minute," a man with a distinct English accent said. "I don't believe that Nummi-Nummi-Summi still owns this business. My firm, London Grabbers Associates, made a successful raid on Al and Rose's this morning. We bought the whole kit and caboodle for one billion dollars."

"That can't be true," the Japanese man retorted. "No one would offer to pay such a sum for this establishment."

"We're not going to keep it all. Our American subsidiary plans to spin off the stools in the lunchroom to the West Germans and just hold onto the convenience store."

Rose popped out of the kitchen. "Who ordered eggs, and who wanted the corned-beef hash?"

A Saudi Arabian businessman waltzed in with his entourage. He checked the tables and the condition of the jukebox, and then told one of his lackeys, "Call Shearson Lehman and have them make an offer to acquire everything."

"You want to own this place?"

"This and every building on Route Three-twelve from Baltimore to Atlanta."

"Now see here, my good man. Al and Rose's is ours. You have to deal with us for either the kit or the caboodle," the Englishman said.

"No we don't. It was sold this morning to the Tortellini Brothers. They put it on the market fifteen minutes after they gained control."

Rose asked, "Al, what's going on?"

"We're being bought and sold by every multinational in the Swiss telephone book. Our business is now worth three billion dollars, and there are buyers standing in line."

"Oh, yeah?" Rose said. "And if they take us over, who is going to cook the scrambled eggs and hash browns?"

"I don't believe they've thought that far ahead, Rose. They're only interested in the market value of our place."

The phone rang and Al answered it. He turned to the people at the counter and yelled, "It's Salomon Brothers. They want me to tell everyone here that they have a mystery client from Brunei who is willing to pay four billion dollars for the jukebox alone."

The bidding lasted for more than an hour. The Saudi businessman and the Englishman were getting ready to leave, when Al shouted, "You each owe me five bucks for breakfast."

The Englishman replied, "Everyone knows that people who deal with takeovers never carry cash. We'll send you a junk bond instead."

"HELP! HELP!"

I WAS PASSING an art gallery and went in to see what was going on. There were only three people in the gallery, including the guard. I glanced over the seascapes and then strolled into the next room, where I couldn't believe my eyes. On the wall for all to see was a giant oil painting of a nude lady eating an avocado. The title of it was *Bare-breasted Woman Contemplating Her Indoor Swimming Pool*, and it was by an artist named Loco-manni.

I was so horrified that I ran to the door screaming, "Help! Filthy pictures, pornography, dirty, dirty, dirty!" It didn't take long for my cries to be answered. People started to pour in from everywhere, many of them pushing me aside to get to the painting.

The mob stared in disbelief and then looked at the nude some more.

One man bellowed, "Call Jesse Helms."

Another said, "Get the vice squad."

Still another yelled, "I don't care who you call, but call somebody."

Visitors who couldn't get into the room were shouting to those already there, "Move out. We want to see the filthy pictures and be shocked too."

The guard attempted to keep order. "I can't understand it.

Nobody's been in this gallery for years. Now everyone wants to get in."

"You can't believe obscene art unless you see it for yourself," I told him. "Is it true that this show was sponsored by the National Foundation for the Arts?"

He replied, "Beats me. I only work here. I don't have nothing to do with what they put on the walls. You think that Mr. Helms is going to get me fired?"

"I hope so. He says that anyone who abets and encourages the dissemination of lifelike human bodies on a wall with taxpayers' money is showing contempt for him and North Carolina."

A Fine Arts Mounted Policeman pushed through the crowd. "There it is," an aide said, showing him the painting.

"Oh my God. It's a nude with no clothes on," the Fine Arts official gasped. "We didn't know. We gave the money because we heard it was going to be an exhibition of North Carolina tobacco butts. They didn't tell us they were going to display pictures of harlots."

The guard asked, "Are you going to shoot it?"

The mounted cop answered, "No, we're not permitted to shoot paintings we don't own. However, we can ask for the Foundation money back if we have a reason. Let me see the catalogue."

We all gathered around him as he riffled through the pages. "This is awful. The program attacks every great American senator connected with the art world. We're going to demand a refund of our ten thousand dollars immediately."

The taxpayers in the gallery cheered.

"Hang the curator," someone yelled.

"Run all art perverts out of town," a bag lady shouted.

The police official turned to me and said, "Thank heavens you discovered this masterpiece before any children came here on their Christmas vacation. It's a citizen's duty to report pornography whenever he sees it."

I responded modestly, "Or *thinks* he sees it. You people can't be everywhere."

Someone rushed in and spoke to the guard: "The line is six blocks long and getting longer. Everybody is afraid that you will take the dirty, filthy picture down before they can get a look at it."

DISNEY WORLD

I WENT ON a trip to Disney World, and what impressed me the most was the fun the parents were having taking their children there for a once-in-a-lifetime thrill.

I watched the beginning of the journey as I sat in the terminal waiting for the plane to depart for Orlando.

A mother was yelling at her four-year-old son: "If you hit your sister once more, I am going to check you in at the baggage counter."

To my left a father was shaking his boy. "Didn't I tell you to stay in your seat? I think I'll take you home right now."

The child obviously knew it was an empty threat, because so much money had been invested in the trip already. So he sat on the floor.

We boarded the plane. I counted 2.5 children for every adult. Two kids were hanging over my seat. One had a kazoo; the other a magic wand. The parents were unconcerned about what their offspring were doing to the other passengers. Their only worry was that the children might find the chocolate chip cookies stored in the hand luggage.

The father said, "If you touch that bag I'm going to tell Mickey Mouse what a rotten kid you really are."

That did it. The tears spilled all over me. It's tough, I thought, to go to Disney World thinking that you will be ignored by Mickey Mouse.

As the plane flew on I thought about all the love and planning that a father had spent on this family excursion, only to have it climaxed by his decision to bad-mouth his kid to every Walt Disney character in the book.

Down the aisle came a seven-year-old, returning from the bathroom. He didn't seem to be in a hurry, so his mother shouted, "Get back here this instant, or you won't see the Magic Mountain until you are eighty."

He weighed this statement very carefully and then apparently decided that it was just another example of his mother's losing complete control of herself, as she did every time they got on an airplane.

At that moment a small girl ran down the middle of the plane, sucking her thumb and dragging a wooden duck. Her father was chasing her. "For that you get no cotton candy, and you can't have your picture taken with the Seven Dwarfs."

I thought to myself, I can see what attraction Disney World holds for parents, but I just don't understand what's in it for the kids. The whole trip is one giant threat.

At the hotel, the scenario was repeated. One five-year-old child was warned that if he didn't straighten up and fly right, he would be chewed up by the porpoises at Sea World. Another was informed that he was going to spend the entire visit locked in his hotel room with a "Do Not Disturb" sign on the door.

A third, who lay on his stomach by the bell captain's desk, was told by his mother that all his souvenirs would be confiscated by the hotel manager and thrown into the parking lot.

Not since Dostoyevsky had I witnessed so much crime and punishment. It seemed as though all the children were ruining the wonderful vacation their parents had prepared exclusively for them.

The plane ride back was another story. The adults were too exhausted to threaten anybody. They had yelled at their kids for four days, and now they were so hoarse they couldn't speak. The children were marching up and down the aisles wearing their Mickey Mouse hats and holding Donald Duck quackers in their mouths. Occasionally a parent would raise a hand weakly and try to say something, but the words wouldn't come out. Many, who had vowed dire punishment on the way down, didn't even have the strength to fasten their seat belts.

HOW MUCH FOR A BIRDIE?

A LOT HAS BEEN written about power golf in Washington. Here is the darker side of the game which no one dares talk about.

What's going on in the U.S. Congress right now is nothing more than intense soul-searching and remedial hand-wringing. Up the Hill and down, the same question is being asked: How did some of our legislators go astray and lose their moral compass?

Before he became an encyclopedia salesman inside the Washington Beltway, Greg Peay was a door-to-door salesman for

House Speaker Jim Wright's book in Houston. Greg thinks he may have the answer.

"It all begins and ends with golf," he told me. "Assume that a newly elected congressman like Jimmy Stewart in *Mr. Smith Goes to Washington* arrives in the capital. The first invitation he receives is to play golf with a lobbyist high in government circles."

"Golf doesn't corrupt people," I protested.

"It does if you cheat," Greg said.

"Jimmy Stewart wouldn't cheat at golf!"

"He would if it was the only way he could lower his score. Here's what happens: Suppose his ball drops directly behind a large oak tree. Jimmy can't play it from there, so he kicks it to the side when no one is looking, and then he has a clear shot at the fairway."

I told Greg, "I imagine you would interpret that as cheating. What happens if someone sees him?"

"That's just the point," he answered. "Someone does see Stewart, but the fix is in and the lobbyist pretends that he didn't. When Mr. Smith realizes that no one will say anything if he kicks his ball, it opens up a whole new world to him. It isn't long before Jimmy forgets where he came from. He even picks up the ball and starts throwing it toward the pin on the green."

"If he does all these things, Smith is not the man he was when he came to Washington," I added.

"The lobbyists are devious. They'll let Jimmy Stewart give himself a three on a hole when he should have put himself down for a six. In Washington that's known as improving your game by lowering the score, with the help of people who need your vote. Once Stewart writes the wrong number on his card, the lobbyist has him in his pocket, not only for this game but for all future ones as well."

"Is there no end to the rot?" I asked.

Greg sighed. "Not really. Some lobbyists will even let Smith use an illegal golf ball."

"Do you think this is how all the legislators run into ethical trouble?"

He said, "It seems that the majority of congressmen who have gotten into the most difficulty took the first wrong turn when they sold their souls for a birdie on the fourteenth hole at Burning Tree."

"They should give the Mr. Smiths of this world a big raise so that they don't have to cheat at golf," I suggested.

"I agree. There's no end to what influence-peddlers will do to help a lawmaker with his golf game. I've seen them plunge naked into muddy water holes to retrieve a congressman's ball and throw it onto the green."

"I imagine that golf is an easier way of going into the tank than having a friend put you into an oil deal."

"The worst part of all this is that when Mr. Smith discovers that lobbyists do not insist on playing by the rules, he refuses to play with anyone else."

"Is improving his golf score the only payola Mr. Smith gets out of a golf game in Washington?"

"No," Greg said, "there's lots more. I was recently in a foursome and heard a lobbyist remark to a legislator, 'I'll buy twenty tickets to your political fund-raiser if you sink that one-foot putt.' And damned if the man didn't make it."

ACT OF GOD

IT WAS A tremendous storm—the worst in Washington's history. It caused tree damage, house damage and electrical outages the likes of which family legends are made of.

Once the storm blew out of town, the insurance adjusters blew in, and the serious storms between homeowners and insurance companies began.

I was over at Roy and Martha Thurston's place helping them clean up their yard when the man from Mutual of Deadwood arrived to discuss the Thurstons' claim.

He carried a beeper, a portable telephone and a fax machine. "The office likes me to keep in touch so that I don't give away the store," he said, chuckling. "So tell me, how are you trying to screw us?"

Roy was incensed. "We're not trying to screw you. All we want is compensation for the damage caused by this terrible storm."

"How can you be so certain that the damage was the result of a storm?" the adjuster asked. "It could easily have been caused by God."

"What's the difference?" Martha Thurston wanted to know.

"God moves in mysterious ways, but our company doesn't cover Him. If it's His fault, you have a fiddler's chance of our paying the bill."

"It couldn't have been caused by God," Roy said. "God would never dare hurt Chevy Chase."

"Can we just get down to specifics?" the adjuster pleaded.

"Okay. That tree up there was knocked over by the wind, and it crashed into my roof, leaving a ten-foot hole over the master bedroom."

"What kind of tree was it?"

"It was a three-hundred-year-old oak."

The man hit the button on his fax machine. After reading it he turned to the Thurstons. "Your policy doesn't cover damage from oak trees. Now if a Japanese bonsai tree had hit the roof, you would be in fat city."

"Why didn't someone tell me that when I bought the policy?"

"Any grade-school kid knows that. Do you have some structural damage from a falling Christmas tree?"

"Not that I know of."

"Too bad, because if you did we'd cut it up and cart it away free of charge," he informed them.

Thurston took the adjuster to the back of the house. "The wind blew my balcony away. You can see it hanging by one strut."

"I have only your word that it was the wind. How do I know that beavers didn't knock down the balcony?"

"We don't have any beavers in this neighborhood," Thurston protested.

"That's what everybody says," the insurance adjuster pointed out. "Then, as soon as I leave, the beavers come out and start chewing on every piece of wood around here."

"Aren't you going to pay for *any* of this?"

"I'm trying to find something. What happened to the glass door leading out to the patio?"

"A garden umbrella went flying through it on the way to our living room."

"Was it green or striped?"

"A green one."

"Too bad. We're only covering striped umbrellas this summer," the adjuster said.

"Well, that's it. You have been most helpful," Martha mumbled.

The adjuster told the Thurstons, "I'd like to do more, but how can I when it's all God's fault?"

ADVICE AND CONSENT, ETC.

IT APPEARS THAT almost half of the former Reagan administration has gone into the consulting business in Washington.

Are they doing anything wrong? Former secretary of the interior James Watt doesn't think so. Neither do any of the other people who are charging enormous fees to sneak their clients in through the back door of government. Yet the HUD scandals seem to have given the consulting business a bad name—at least that's what Horace Dipthong, a former White House aide, told me.

"We are providing a service. We know those in power and our clients don't, so we make the telephone calls."

"Some people think it smells," I said.

"That's because they are too cheap to use our services."

"How do you operate?" I asked him.

"Suppose you're a developer and you are trying to get a pile of money out of HUD. You're a nobody, and the people at HUD know it. You call up Jim Watt and say, 'I have a problem. I need money and no one in the housing department will tell me the time. Will you take my case?' Jim answers, 'Sure I will, because you are a great American and so am I, and you're going to give me two hundred thousand dollars for helping you.' You reply, 'That's a lot of money. Who are you going to talk to?' And he says, 'Would you believe the secretary of housing himself?' Now if that isn't worth two hundred thousand big ones, I'll cut down every tree in Yellowstone National Park."

"Watt is all heart," I remarked.

"I'm attempting to point out to you how we consultants in Washington earn our money. Only former appointees know what buttons to push."

"How do you manage to get such good results?"

"It's very simple. Every person now in power in this city was either recommended by us, trained by us or appointed by us. Practically all of Washington owes us a favor. We don't take advantage of it, and ask for something only when we're getting paid by a client."

"The present officials do seem eager to help."

"I hope so, otherwise the revolving door system would get stuck. People like Watt are the grease that makes our government go downhill."

"I assume that you do the same things as Watt does."

"Yes, but not as well. I could not have gotten Secretary Samuel Pierce on the phone—at least not on the first call. I don't do too badly. I have had clients who hired me to get them HUD money even though they hadn't decided whether to use it for building houses in Scranton or taking a trip to Rio de Janeiro."

"Did you get them the cash?"

"Has anyone ever failed to get money from HUD? We cleaned the safe out."

"Is it possible to get anything from this administration without hiring an ex-administration consultant?"

"Why would anyone try? God knows there is enough money to go around for everybody."

"So if I want funding from the feds, the easiest way is to call you."

He smiled. "It's the *only* way—unless you enjoy beating your head against the wall. Listen, everything we undertake is legal. We're the good guys in Washington. All we do is make the call verifying that you're a loyal American, and that it's okay for them to give you a check. The people in charge of doling out the money feel better that way, because then they know that the recipient is a safe risk. Who is going to question a Jim Watt client, after Watt guarantees that the guy is a one-hundred-percent patriot?"

"And for this Watt gets two hundred thousand bucks?"

"Well, he doesn't do freebies like Mother Teresa."

I PLEDGE ALLEGIANCE

JUST WHEN YOU think that everyone in this country is at peace with everyone else, the Supreme Court makes a decision that tears us apart. One Sunday in our backyard, Manchester suggested we all go down and set fire to the Court to protest its ruling that it is no longer a crime to burn the American flag.

I said it was too hot, and Manchester called me a closet flag-burner.

I told him, "I've never burned a flag, and I never intend to. If I did, I would burn Iraq's. By the same token, I have no reason to trash the Supreme Court on a lovely Sunday afternoon."

Manchester was livid and yelled that if the Supreme Court won't stop people from burning the flag, then American citizens should take the law into their own hands.

"How many flag-burners do you *know* personally?" I asked.

He replied that just because he didn't *know* any did not mean that they weren't out there.

"Have you ever seen anyone burn an American flag?" I yelled.

"No," he admitted, "but now that it's legal, every pervert in the country will buy one just to burn it."

I disagreed with him. "When it was illegal, burning an American flag was the strongest political statement a protester could make. Now, after the Court decision, it isn't considered a radical gesture at all. Do you think the media have any interest in covering an act that is the law of the land? I believe that the justices' ruling will cut down on flag-burning rather than encourage it."

"A flag-burner deserves to be executed," Manchester said, pouring too much barbecue sauce on the hamburgers.

"Fear of death never stopped a flag arsonist," I told him. "In the past, the thought of capital punishment convinced him that he would become a martyr. Besides, he knew that by desecrating the flag he could wind up on *The Morton Downey, Jr., Show.* To be successful, you have to commit the act in public. No one ever got famous for fifteen minutes by burning a flag in his bathroom. Since it is now legal and the burner will not be arrested for doing it, the protest is meaningless."

Manchester remained unconvinced. "Wait until the congressional elections. Any person who doesn't vote for a constitutional amendment will wind up in the gutter. We will put our politicians' patriotism to the test. We'll spread the word about which candidates love their country and which ones don't."

"I worry about that," I confessed. "There will be a lot of mud thrown in the next election over the flag issue."

"Good," Manchester said.

"Let me ask this question: How many flags do you think were burned in the United States last year?"

"Thousands?" Manchester suggested.

"You're wrong. There were fourteen, and of those, six flags were flying from houses that burned to the ground. So there is not a vast pool of flag-burners out there. Most of the American flag-burners these days are in Iran, Jordan and Cuba, and they don't care what the Supreme Court of the United States says."

Manchester, who had ruined the hamburgers by this time, declared, "If the Supreme Court justices don't like it in this country, they should go back where they came from."

THE LEFT STUFF

WE WERE ARM-WRESTLING with each other at Lefty's Bar and Grill the other night, when word reached us that lefties were an inferior species who were responsible for more accidents and premature deaths than any other group.

Lefty George was so outraged that he knocked over a bottle and spilled beer on his pants. "I knew it would come to this. They have nobody left to persecute, so they have decided to go after left-handers."

Lefty Eddie said, "Before I make any comment, I'll have to

study the report. Until then, I deny that I have any physical or psychological disorders."

"Why are you setting the tablecloth on fire?" Sam the Southpaw asked me.

"I am left-handed," I admitted. "And I am not ashamed to come out of the closet and say it. The report was obviously written by right-handed psychologists, who have persecuted left-handers since time began."

"Listen to this," Lefty Deardorf said as he read from his newspaper: " 'Left-handers are more prone to diseases and disorders than right-handers.' "

Lefty Cronheim yelled, "That's a stack of horse manure." He clutched the air as he fell off his stool.

We all turned to Fred the bartender. Since he owned the saloon, he was ambidextrous.

"Fred, do you think left-handers are more dumb than right-handers?"

He replied, "No. They are just slower. Look at Frieda over there. No one will dance with her because she has two left feet. Frankly, I have no problems with lefties unless they're the designated drivers."

"Do you really believe that we're accident-prone like the study indicates?"

"Not all of you," Fred said, "but I do worry about your reflexes. I heard on television that lefties always forget to put gas in their cars. It's something to do with genes."

Most of the left-handed people at the bar were edgy and dropping their pretzels everywhere. Several kept stooping to pick up the coins that constantly fell onto the floor through holes in their pockets.

Lefty Dowd cried, "Let's kill the right-handers before they kill us."

"How can we? There are no left-handed guns," I told him.

"We should have had the brains to figure that out," Frieda declared.

"That's just the point," Lefty Stanton moaned.

"Our brains work differently from other people's."

"But we're smarter than right-handers," I said. "So we can get them to do all our dirty work for us."

Lefty Cronheim announced, "Left-handers are better lovers than right-handers."

He had our attention. He explained, "I have heard this from many women who have been kissed from the right and from the left. Left-handers hold women as if they mean it."

Frieda asked, "What about left-handed women? Are they better romantically than right-handed ones?"

"Probably," I assured her. "But the ideal situation is if you put a left-handed woman with a left-handed guy. Then you'll really see the earth move."

VIVE LA RÉVOLUTION!

FRIENDS OFTEN ASK me if I can remember exactly where I was and what I was doing when the first shot of the French Revolution was fired. I recall it well.

I was working for *People* magazine at the time, and they sent me to France to do another feature on Marie Antoinette and her family. It was my fourth story about them. The reason *People* had such an interest in the French court was that every time we put Marie on the cover, sales soared.

I arrived at Versailles at about seven on a beautiful October morning in 1789 and was surprised to see such a large crowd out front. I assumed that they were tourists on an American Express tour, although they were shouting things like, "The royal family sucks eggs."

I told the guard at the gate that I was from *People*, and he let me in immediately. My magazine was read by everyone at the court, and the guards had a standing order to admit me whenever I came by.

The gatekeeper directed me toward the kitchen, where I would find Marie Antoinette. This was a break, because I had never photographed her doing any domestic chores before.

When I entered, I found the queen bedecked in a royal apron, attended by six ladies-in-waiting.

"What are you making?" I asked her.

"Brownies." She smiled. "I am sure it will quiet the rabble."

"I don't understand," I said.

She explained, "The mob has been shouting for bread all night long, but I'm not going to give them any. I know what the French need, and it's something sweet with chocolate in it."

I was snapping pictures. "This is wonderful. The photo caption will read: 'Queen Saves Her Throne in Versailles Bakeoff.'"

A guard came in and announced, "The mob has broken down the gates and will be inside the palace in a few minutes."

The queen told him, "Well, tell them I'm not ready. I hate it when the peasants become impatient."

The guard shrugged his shoulders.

"Where is the king?" I asked.

"He's sleeping in," the queen replied. "One of his advisors suggested that if he couldn't stand the heat, then he should stay out of the kitchen. I think I'll put a little powdered sugar on this batch."

"From your wig?" I exclaimed.

"Yes, it's a trick I learned from my German grandmother. You put the sugar inside the wig and then shake your head, and the powder falls out evenly."

The guard returned. "The mob is coming up the stairs," he cried. "They want to throw the entire family into the dungeon."

"They do now," Marie Antoinette said, "but after they taste my brownies they will be buying me furs and diamonds." She turned to me and asked, "Would you like me to stand by the stove with my Russian wolfhounds?"

I told her that would be great, but first I wanted a picture of her serving the brownies to the peasants. I didn't have to wait long. The crowd crashed through the door screaming, "Bread!" and the queen offered them brownies. To a man and woman, they sank to their knees and begged her for the recipe.

I didn't photograph Marie again until October 16, 1793, and as I was a foreigner, I had a front seat at her execution. On October 20, 1793, *People* ran its last cover photo of Marie Antoinette. It was a head shot.

THE FLIMFLAMMED MAN

THE REASON Ollie North didn't get any time in the Big House is that the judge believed Ollie was really a dupe of higher-ups in the U.S. government. In rounding up the usual suspects, the only superiors anyone in Washington can come up with are John Poindexter and President Reagan.

Not only was Ollie a dupe, he was also a pawn in the Iran-contra affair. He was a U.S. Marine who didn't know right from wrong, or good Iranians from bad ones.

That Ollie was flimflammed by people in the White House goes without saying. The how is something else again. This is the way I think it happened:

Some time back, when Congress voted against the United States' supporting the contras, President Reagan called Ollie into the Oval Office. Poindexter was also there, sending up large clouds of smoke that made it difficult to see the president behind his desk.

The president, reading from three-by-five cards, said, "Ollie, I consider you a hero."

"Why is that, Mr. President?" Ollie asked.

"Because by the time we finish duping you, your feet will be held to the fire but you will not cry uncle."

Ollie responded, "I'll do anything you want, because you are my commander in chief. Besides, I like this job. I can order around anybody in the country, and I get to work late with a small but good-looking staff of people who think the way we do."

The president was pleased with the answer. "All we'd like you to do is trade guns for hostages, collect money that will be deposited in Switzerland, where it will be placed in a paper bag and delivered to contras in Florida, who will see that it gets to Honduras, from where it will be taken to Nicaragua. Does that sound like much of a problem?"

"No, sir. That's something we did in the Academy every morning."

Poindexter puffed even harder on his pipe. "Ollie, all we are asking is that you be the fall guy."

"Sounds good to me. What's in it for me?" Ollie wanted to know.

Poindexter looked at a sheaf of papers. "A hundred-fifty-thousand-dollar fine, twelve hundred hours of community service and two years probation."

"What about a pardon?"

Reagan said, "I can't do that, or it will look as if I knew what you were up to."

Poindexter added, "As far as the judge will be concerned, you are an overzealous underling who exceeded his authority in a patriotic mission to rid Central America of communists. Because you are a sacrificial lamb to us in the administration, you will always be entitled to a standing ovation by those who believe that you should never have been involved in our dirty little scheme in the first place."

Ollie was overwhelmed. "You've done so much for me. Is there any way that I can repay you?"

Poindexter answered, "I may be tried for being your superior and giving you the orders to carry out the things you will do. I'd appreciate it if you denied any knowledge of my role in this affair."

Ollie said, "But if I do that, it means the person responsible will be President Reagan."

"Doesn't bother me," the president said, laughing. "Nothing in this job ever has."

WHERE THE MONEY IS

THE SUPREME COURT ruled that drug dealers, racketeers and others of that moral persuasion cannot use their ill-gotten gains to pay their lawyers when they get caught. The Court declared that money made from drug trafficking does not belong to the alleged criminal.

This means that many of our wealthy criminal lawyers are going to get cheated out of large fees, and clients may no longer be defended in the manner to which they have become accustomed.

"Is it right or wrong?" I asked.

Rich, a lawyer, told me that the Court's decision was wrong—dead wrong. "Every person in this country deserves the best defense money can buy, no matter where his legal fee comes from."

"What if it isn't his money? Suppose it's cash made in the underworld? Why should the person be allowed to defend himself with the funds he earned committing a drug crime?"

"Who can be sure that it's drug money? Maybe it comes from an uncle who worked in HUD. The government is trying to destroy the defense of people it doesn't like, and also drive lawyers away from their waterfront homes in Miami Beach."

"Are you upset because the Supreme Court is interpreting the Constitution, or are you more bothered because there is nothing left in the Brink's truck for you?"

"That is the most insulting question anyone has ever asked me. I want you to know that I would defend Noriega even if he couldn't pay me."

"You're kidding," I said.

"Okay, I'm kidding. What I don't like about all of this is that in the past the big wheels in crime and dope always came to us first. Now they're going to some dumb ambulance lawyer instead. If the client approaches us, the government will assume that our client still has some ill-gotten gains hidden away."

"Don't despair. The top crime figures are still going to have to hire you, even if it means borrowing on their mothers' Medicare insurance policies."

Rich was optimistic. "I hope you're right. I hate to think of someone going to jail just because he couldn't afford me."

"Is it easier to defend a man who can pay you than one who can't?" I asked.

"Yes, but I don't know why," he replied. "When I'm getting paid, I feel good all over. If there's no fee, I feel as if I've got Lyme disease."

"Will you still do a bang-up job if a person is indigent?"

"I don't know. I've never taken on anybody like that. Here's what I believe: When it comes to being defended, people should not have to explain the source of their money. Suppose that half of a defendant's income is derived from dope, and the other half from winning at bingo. I never question which part of his estate he's paying me from. I've had guys who paid me with suitcases of cash—and I've always assumed that it was from the sale of their Pete Rose baseball cards."

"If you can't get paid now by the bad people who are in trouble, how will you make your living?"

"I'm going to Texas to defend indicted savings and loan officers. Nobody would dare ask them where they got their money from."

MR. CLEAN

IT WAS AN environmental dream come true. The Exxon oil company announced it had completed its Alaska oil spill cleanup to everyone's satisfaction and would soon close up shop.

The man responsible for the Exxon success was Joe Sludge, who has personally shined ninety percent of all the rocks in Prince William Sound. Joe was in Washington to testify in front of a congressional committee, and I found him sitting by the Reflecting Pool, cleaning oil sludge from between his toes.

"No one thought you could do it," I said.

Joe replied, "I couldn't have done it without the help of the captain of the *Valdez* and his merry crew, as well as my superiors in the home office. A company like Exxon doesn't operate in a vacuum."

"Are you permitted to tell me how you won the environmental battle?"

"We just took a page out of Vietnam. We fought the good fight and then we said, 'The hell with it—we'll finish up next spring.' "

"How many rocks did Exxon polish up after the spill?"

"A lot more than anyone can imagine. But it isn't just cleaning them that we should get credit for. There are rocks around the sound you can eat a smoked salmon off of—that is, if you can find a salmon. But the main point is that Exxon gave it its best shot and now it's Mother Nature's turn to do some of the dirty work."

"Joe, everyone knows you have been diligent in saving the shoreline of Alaska, but you have to admit there wouldn't have been a spill if it hadn't been for Exxon. Shouldn't a neutral party decide when it's time to hang up the towel?"

"The only ones to judge such an important matter are the stockholders. After all, the cost of the cleanup is coming out of their pockets. Most of our stockholders care more about the environment than Exxon's critics."

"Why is that?"

"Because they have a vested interest in how much Exxon spends to clean up its mess. Unlike environmentalists, stockholders don't let sentiment interfere in tough crude-oil decisions. Exxon management could waffle at any time, but the pragmatic stockholder never will."

"I can see that the stockholders are less sentimental about Alaska's environment, but doesn't a nonnegotiable pullout jeopardize the good name of Exxon?"

"No, because the American people are fair. They know good spills from bad spills. *Valdez* could have been a disaster if we hadn't cleaned up the rocks. The Alaskan shoreline is far more spick-and-span now than it was before the spill. If Exxon hadn't had such a top-flight training program, the brave captain of the *Valdez* might have beached his ship in San Francisco harbor."

"Or perhaps in one of the Great Lakes," I added.

Joe said, "If you want the truth, the reason Exxon is signing off is that we're sick and tired of doing everybody else's laundry. I have personally cleaned rocks along the shore that were covered with oil I am certain did not come from our ship."

"If you were so sure, why didn't you just throw those rocks back in the sea?" I asked.

"Because Exxon doesn't operate that way. Our policy on oil spills has always been to clean every stone—with no questions asked. That's why we're known in the oil business as 'Mr. Clean of the Sea.' "

ROE VS. WADE

THE SUPREME COURT ruling on abortion did not have the calming effect on people that the justices for the majority opinion had hoped for. More Americans seem to want to kill each other in the name of "the right to life" and "freedom of choice" than ever before.

The day after the Court ruling, a group of typical U.S. citizens gathered around a bonfire on Cape Cod to cook frankfurters and eat potato salad.

We probably would have gotten through the evening, but one of the group declared, "May Roe and Wade lose their medical benefits in a Blue Cross computer."

"What did Roe and Wade ever do to you?" another person wanted to know.

"Roe and Wade kill babies," the first one asserted.

"Roe and Wade don't kill babies. It's the Supreme Court that kills laws that kill babies."

The man on the beach blanket said, "According to Justice Blackmun, we're facing a loss of liberty and equality for millions of women who will no longer have any say about what happens to their own bodies."

A professed right-to-lifer announced, "Women should think about Roe and Wade before they go to bed with a guy."

"Thinking about Roe and Wade doesn't prevent someone from conceiving. I know many girls who thought about Roe and Wade and still got pregnant."

"If women didn't make love, the Supreme Court wouldn't have to deal with this problem."

"If men didn't make love, the justices wouldn't have to decide when life begins," a nice lady snarled.

Another woman added, "Everybody knows that life begins when the guy says, 'How about it?' and the girl says, 'Okay.' If the Supreme Court is really concerned about unborn children, it would forbid people from bedding down with each other for pleasure."

"You can't police everyone. After all, there are millions of us and only nine of them."

I said, "What I don't like about this is that it has turned man against woman, and woman against politician, and politicians against their spouses. This country could return to the Vietnam War days, with people fighting in the streets and hitting each other over the head with 'Save Life' signs. The Supreme Court unknowingly has imposed a civil war on us. In order to save one child, the antiabortionists may kill sixty adults."

A man sitting next to me roasting marshmallows muttered, "And we will, too."

A pro-choice woman said, "Members of the Supreme Court indicate that they will soon rule against all abortions. But they won't say who pays for the child after birth. If they want to do justice to the unborn, they should set up a trust fund from their salaries for each unwanted child until the child is eighteen years old. That way, when a thirteen-year-old kid gives birth, at least she'll know that her baby will be provided for."

Another member of the group remarked, "I don't think abortion is anything to get too excited about. If we can all agree on it, why can't everyone else?"

"You're right," agreed the marshmallow roaster. "It may cause a difference of opinion among grown-up people, but *Roe versus Wade* is nothing to burn the flag over."

THE NEWS AND NOTHING BUT

TV NEWS IS getting more exciting than ever. The reason is that there has been a breakthrough. It is now possible to simulate a news story that is as good as or even better than the real thing.

The person who invented the SNS (simulated news story) is Arch McGarry, an independent TV special-effects producer who is now one of the most sought-after men in television journalism.

"Where did you get the idea to simulate the news?" I asked.

"I was watching an oil spill off California on the evening news. The film was so grainy that you had no idea what was going on. The thought occurred to me that I could simulate a better oil spill than that. So I went to my bathtub and with the help of my kids reenacted the spill and all the damage that followed. When I showed it to the producer at the evening news show, he was flabbergasted. Now whenever there is an oil spill in the world they use my film instead of the real thing."

"That's great. What other news stories have you simulated?"

"We do a lot of murders. In the past, TV news reporters were restricted in showing a crime of passion because their cameras usually got there too late to tape it live. They came to me with the problem, and with models I can simulate any crime twenty minutes before airtime."

"Do some people think they're seeing the real thing?"

"Most people believe they are. The advantage of simulation is that you can see a crime from start to finish, so you can get emotionally involved."

"Do you simulate political stories in Washington?"

"Yes, we do. The other day one of the networks heard that President Bush had playfully dunked Vice-President Quayle's head underwater a half-dozen times in the Jacuzzi at Camp David. They had no film of it so they asked us if we would reenact the dunking. We found two look-alikes and did the whole story. No one even knew it wasn't real."

"How about sports? Do you simulate football or basketball events?"

"Not yet, but we're working on it. So far we are sticking with hard news, such as train wrecks or Poland."

"You've simulated Poland?"

"We simulated what has been going on in Poland. We have a fellow who looks more like Walesa than Walesa, and we have the best Jaruzelski in the reenactment business. When we stage a fight between them, it's ten times better than what happened in Warsaw."

"Do you ever talk about Felix Bloch, the alleged spy?"

"I'm very proud to have been the first one to simulate the Bloch spy caper. To do it right I built the entire city of Vienna in our studios in Brooklyn. Not one news organization has ever done so much simulation on a story."

I couldn't dispute him. When I saw it I felt I was sitting in the FBI's suite at the Sacher Hotel. "Did you base the swapping of the briefcases on the real thing?"

"Everything we simulate has to have authenticity, or the networks couldn't call it news."

COMMUNISM DOESN'T WORK

"WHAT ON EARTH is going on in the Soviet Union?" I asked Sochek, my shoe repairman.

He replied, "All we are seeing is the expected. Communism doesn't work, and it never has. In addition, there doesn't seem to be any way for the communist leaders to switch to another system without losing their jobs."

"I grew up hating communists. If they disappear, I am really going to miss them," I told him.

"The Soviet people have had it up to here," Sochek said. "Gorbachev knows this, so he is hoping to change the system without toppling the entire party. One of the worst things is the corruption. No matter what is going on, someone always has his hand out demanding a bribe."

"Can Gorbachev make a difference to that situation?"

"No, but they will print his picture in the newspapers showing him in a crowd, *promising* that he will."

"Why did you leave Russia?" I asked.

"I was in charge of manufacturing shoes in Minsk. My responsibility was to get them made before winter set in. You have to know a lot of people to get shoes made in Russia. It was no fun, but I did it. I had only one major problem—I couldn't get any heels for my shoes.

"So I called the Lenin Rubber Heel Works in Pinsk. They said that they didn't have any heels at the moment, and told me I should call back in two years.

" 'How much will you take under the table for the heels you don't have?' I wanted to know. The manager told me, 'Four hundred rubles a heel. If you don't want them, the Smolensk Moccasin Cooperative will take all the heels they can get.' I paid him under the table for the rubber."

"Where did you get the money to pay him?"

"Anyone in Minsk who wanted a pair of shoes had to pay me under the table."

"Nobody could complain about that as long as they got their shoes."

"That's the problem," Sochek said. "They didn't get the shoes. Some big shot in Moscow ordered that my shoes be sent to his brother-in-law in Kiev."

"For which," I wondered aloud, "he was paid under the table?"

"This is why the system stinks. Even corruption doesn't work in a communist country. The bureaucrats are too corrupt to let it work. In a democratic society, if you bribe somebody, he stays bribed."

"Did you get into a lot of trouble because you couldn't honor your contracts for the shoes?"

"The party chief in Minsk attacked me on local television for letting Marx and Engels down. He claimed that I was one of the Brezhnev era's do-nothing managers, who deserved twenty years of hard labor in Finsk."

"That sounds serious. What did you do?"

"Just what any loyal Soviet citizen would do. I bribed someone in the Ministry of Emigration to get me out of the country."

"I'll bet you didn't mind paying that final bribe."

"It wasn't the last bribe. What makes you think that you can get on a Russian airliner for just the price of a ticket!"

"It sounds as if Gorbachev has his work cut out for him. In

order to change the communist system you have to change the people who are running the country. How do you get them out of office?"

Sochek's eyes lit up. "The only way is to bribe somebody else to do it."

GRANDMOTHERS, INC.

WHAT HAPPENED ON the Cape last summer was that more and more grandmothers seemed to be giving birth to grandchildren. From one end of the Cape to the other, grandmothers started showing up by the thousands on the beaches, carrying babies.

"Why this sudden influx of grandmothers?" I asked my friend Ruth, who was sitting on a blanket holding a one-year-old on her lap and wrestling with a two-year-old with her feet.

She replied, "The reason is that the need for grandmothers has never been greater. Daughters are depending on their mothers for more free help than they ever have in the past. With the demand so high, more and more of my friends are becoming grandmothers."

"Do you like being a grandmother?" I asked her.

"It's a living," she replied. "And it keeps me in touch with the family."

I asked her, "What is the most important thing a grand-mother must know how to do?"

"Baby-sit," she said. "No grandmother can justify her existence if she doesn't know how to sit with kids."

"Do you do it for money?" I inquired.

"Big joke. I don't even get gas money."

"Do you get bawled out a lot by your daughter?" I asked.

"Yes, I do. You don't know your daughters or daughters-in-law until they have children. They're always finding an excuse to pick on us. Let me give you an example. The other day I sat with my grandchildren for six hours and everything went beautifully. Ten minutes before my daughter came home, my grandson walked into the leg of a table, and he was screaming his head off when she walked in. I was sure she was going to charge me with child abuse."

"I wonder why daughters and daughters-in-law are so tough on their mothers."

"Because they know in their hearts the children love us more than they love them."

"It doesn't surprise me," I said.

"Don't repeat this," Ruth whispered, "but my daughter has no sense of humor."

"What mother does? How does your daughter show her displeasure?"

"She's always criticizing me. I give the baby either too much apple juice or not enough. I let them have too much sun or I keep them so covered up they'll be white like a sheet of Kleenex. I just can't seem to do anything right. I don't know what happens to a daughter when she becomes a mother, but it's a serious role reversal."

"Is that because she doesn't think her mother knows anything about babies?"

"Why would the mother who bore her know anything about children? She talks to me like I'm the village idiot. I took the baby into town this morning and bought him a lollipop. You would have thought I purchased a sugar-flavored cyanide pill. My daughter screamed at me, 'I told you he wasn't supposed to eat anything between meals except raw potato.' "

"Well, at least she cares what the baby eats," I said. I then asked her, "If you had to do it all over again, would you still be a grandmother?"

"What choice do I have? I'm the only real human being the grandchildren have."

ANCHORWOMEN

THE COMPETITION BETWEEN newspapers and television is getting fierce. Each one is stealing a page from the other's book. For example, when beautiful women became de rigueur on television news shows, it was only natural that newspapers would follow suit.

This is what happened the other day at a news meeting in the editor's office at *The Daily Beauregard.*

The managing editor said, "We're going to need a stakeout for the alleged spy Felix Bloch. It means standing outside his house all night long. Who should we send to cover the story?"

The news editor replied, "Maybe a six-foot blonde. That way, not only could she cover the story, but CNN might put her on the five-o'clock news."

"I was thinking along the same lines. What about Mary Strawberry? She writes like a dream, and she has deep blue eyes that you want to dive into. She's really the girl next door," said the managing editor.

"I was thinking more of Sara Williams. She has not only the looks but a sexy voice, so the people inside the house will eventually come out and talk to her."

The foreign editor disagreed. "I think you're wrong. This job calls for a sophisticated, well-dressed brunette. I don't think we're being sexist when we say that our readers expect us to send out the best-looking reporter money can buy. Gina Clooney is my candidate. Her legs always look great on a byline."

The features editor, a woman, said, "I think we might be putting a little too much emphasis on a reporter's looks. What if we send a man to do the stakeout?"

"So we send out a man and ABC sends out Diane Sawyer," said the news editor. "How is that going to look to the circulation department? I'm not saying we assign a woman to this story because she's a woman. I say we do it because she's a good-looking woman. In this dog-eat-dog world we're fighting not only Diane Sawyer, but Maria Shriver, Connie Chung and Lesley Stahl, and heaven knows how many others. It's TV's anchorwomen against our reporters, and I say we go with the best we've got. Therefore I propose we use Debbie Baumgarten, who was the Rose Bowl queen before she covered City Hall."

"If we assign stories to women according to their looks, there are going to be a few females on this paper who will never get out of the bullpen," the features editor said.

"We didn't start the beauty contest," said another woman editor. "But we can't ignore it either. After all, people are now getting used to receiving their news from someone who belongs on the cover of *Vogue*. NBC has an open checkbook for gorgeous anchorwomen. CBS has sent the word out that if you graduated from a good communications school and you're a size six they want to talk to you. Can we, as a newspaper, stick by the antiquated ways of the past and use women only because of their writing?"

The news editor agreed. "Not if we're going to stay in the news business. This readership survey just came in, and it shows that those interviewed want our reporters to look more like Deborah Norville."

The managing editor concluded, "There you have it. Let's get someone to stake out Bloch who looks at least like Cher. Who shall it be?"

The news editor answered, "Martha Chromosomes—but I'm not sure she'll go. Every time we give her a stakeout, she says we are treating her like a sex object."

A DOMESTIC BANG BANG

PRESIDENT GEORGE BUSH made a terrible mistake when he banned the importation of foreign semiautomatic guns into the United States. What he did was cut out the Italians, Israelis and Chinese to make sure the American people are supplied with semiautomatic weapons made in the good old USA. The trouble with this is that U.S. manufacturers can't meet the demand, and Americans now have to wait months to get the semiautomatic weapons of their dreams.

The New York Times reports that most domestic manufacturers are working seven days a week to meet the orders, and the demand for the guns is at its peak and going higher.

I confirmed this when I visited the Sudden Death Gun Company. The owner, Orville Bang, was sweating as he poured grease on the weapons that came off the production line. Between crates he told me that the semiautomatic business has never been better, and President Bush is a peach of a guy for keeping the foreign competition out of the U.S. market.

"The orders are pouring in," he told me. "We've proven that we can make a better product than the foreigners. Right now we're backed up until 1992."

"I always knew that semiautomatics were popular with the average person, but why the surge in sales at this particular time?"

"People are afraid Congress will ban semiautomatics altogether, and they want one hanging in their Land-Rover before some damn fool legislator takes it away from them."

"There must be more to it than that," I said.

"It could be a fad. Everybody wants a semi these days—from the squirrel hunter to the guy fighting a gang war in the barrios."

"But you can't sell semiautomatics to gangs, can you?"

"I should hope not, but a middleman can. The way I see it, the role of the gun manufacturer is to make guns, not war. We're the guys who turn out the weapons, and we're not responsible if they get into the hands of someone who wants to shoot up a schoolyard. That's why President Bush likes us. We can arm the nation with weapons that this country has to have to save it from the enemy."

"You mean the Russians?" I asked.

"No, I mean the other semiautomatic owners. Besides, if we can keep the gun-manufacturing business in this country, we can resolve our deficit problem overnight. All you have to do is tell the people in the U.S. there is going to be a shortage of an item, and they will immediately line up to buy it."

I said, "But in this case they were wrongly informed, because George Bush says they can have all the semiautomatics they want, as long as they are made over here. Why the panic?"

"If the gang wars get out of hand and more people are blown away by the guns, the president may have to take a stand and declare that semiautomatics aren't as safe as he originally thought. When that takes place, every one of us in the domestic gun business will be dead."

PARTY PARTY

THE MALCOLM FORBES megazillion-dollar junket to Tangier once again raises one of society's most pressing questions: Was it good or bad for the Nouveaux Riches? It came at a time when instant millionaires have been under tremendous fire for spending their money with gay abandon, while the middle class is trying to find the wherewithal to get its pipes fixed under the kitchen sink.

There is a lot more to this junket than the tabloids would have you believe. The Forbes bash was *really* designed to be a diplomatic mission of extreme urgency and importance.

This is how they tell it around the water fountains at the State Department: U.S. relations with Morocco had reached such a low point that neither country could be civil with the other. To make matters worse, Morocco had agreed to sell the Soviet Union 100,000 tons of Sahara sand, which because of agricultural failures had become a delicacy in Armenia and Georgia.

The president decided to send a high-ranking emissary to Tangier to try to get top-level talks going with Hassan, the king of Morocco. The natural choice was Henry Kissinger, who knows the king on a first-name basis. But Henry complained that because everyone recognized him it would be impossible to go to Morocco secretly. He needed a cover story.

"Why not have Malcolm Forbes organize a flying carpet for the rich and famous on his seventieth birthday?" he suggested. "I could be a guest on that. It would be a perfect cover because no one would guess I was doing anything more than romping with the Nouveaux Riches."

The CIA man liked the plan, although he objected to Forbes's being let in on it.

"Then I won't tell him," Henry said. "We'll have him think the party was his idea. We'll let him invite all the people who have it made, and they can play in Tangier while I take the king for a walk in the casbah."

"How many rich and famous do we need to make your presence credible?" Henry was asked.

"I figure a 747, a DC-8 and the Concorde ought to do it. We can expect flak from the press for my being part of a junket to nowhere, but I am used to getting flak for serving my country."

The CIA man asked, "How can we be sure all the rich and famous will agree to go to the bash?"

"Because the rich and famous are always worried that they will be in the wrong place at the wrong time. Once word is out that I am on the trip, everyone will fall in line," Henry told him. "To make this work, we don't want the rich, we want the superrich—people who fly to the Mayo Clinic to see the dentist."

"Once you get to Tangier, you will be whisked away to have a tête-à-tête with the king," the CIA man told him.

"That will come in time. I have to toast Malcolm and Elizabeth Taylor first, so as to assuage any doubts why I came. Then they can sneak me off to the palace."

"Good thinking," the CIA man said.

Henry smiled. "I will not fear to negotiate, or negotiate out of fear."

Everything went as planned, with one exception. When Henry got to Tangier the king up and left for other business in Rabat, and poor Kissinger never did have a chance to negotiate anything, except to make Tangier a duty-free port for any future parties the Nouveaux Riches want to give in Morocco.

How Lucky Can You Get

My wife is one of the luckiest women in the world. Don't take my word for it, ask all her friends. Late in the summer she tripped on a rock and broke her wrist. Ordinarily you would call this a piece of bad luck, but it turns out when she had the accident she did everything just right.

This is the way a conversation went the day after the accident:

"My wife broke her wrist."

"Was it the right wrist or the left wrist?" a friend asked.

"The left," I said.

"She's lucky it was the left. If she had broken the right it could be twice as inconvenient."

I agreed. "My wife has always been lucky when it comes to breaking a bone. It runs in her family."

Another friend, when informed about the accident, wanted to know if she fell forward or backward after she tripped. I said I wasn't sure that it mattered.

"Of course it matters," he replied. "If she fell forward it was the best thing that could happen, because otherwise she could have injured her back. By breaking her fall with her hand she saved injuring her nose. You have one lucky woman there."

"Don't I know it," I said proudly.

By this time word had gotten out about the accident, and experts on bones from all over the world were checking in.

One eyewitness told me, "I was five feet behind her when she fell. At that moment I said to myself, 'If she has to break anything, I hope it's her wrist and not her leg.' "

"You were thinking what I was thinking," I assured him.

"I'm a skier, so I know about fractures. Your luck depends on how you fall."

"Over the years she's always fallen right," I said.

The next-door neighbor called. "I heard your wife had a fall."

"Yes, she broke her wrist."

"I always look at the bright side. It could have been her hip. Some women are born lucky."

"It will be in a cast for six weeks," I told him.

"She's fortunate it didn't happen at the beginning of the summer, because you perspire under a cast and then you go crazy from the itch."

"That seems to be the consensus. Everyone is congratulating her that she didn't break it on the Fourth of July."

"The trick of any bone injury is to break it in the right place at the right time."

"How can you do that?"

"When you break something you have to be in close proximity to an orthopedic surgeon who isn't out playing golf when you need him. The real luck of falling down is to find the surgeon in his empty office playing solitaire."

"Our doctor wasn't even out fishing."

"Then she really is a lucky woman. I hope she realizes it."

"She does. She counts her blessings every time she falls."

IF I HAD A MILLION

IT HAS BEEN reported that Michael Milken made over $180 million in 1988. Michael is now having his problems with the feds, but he is still flying up there in the ozone with the super-rich. His name appeared on a list that included the highest-paid executives in America. (The lowest was Robert Haas, who earned a paltry $25 million in 1988.)

What can somebody do with so much money, except buy Grey Poupon mustard from the next Rolls-Royce? At some point the sublime becomes really ridiculous. I sought out one of the men on the top-money all-star team. His name was Net Gross, and his fortune came from manufacturing suspenders to hold up yuppies' pants.

I walked into his office as he was having his shoes shined. He waved me over to a chair.

"How do you feel now that everyone knows you made forty-five million dollars?"

"I still put my garters on one leg at a time," he said.

"Money hasn't changed you?"

"Why should it? Of course, I go first-class now. For example, this shoeshine is costing me fifty dollars. I could get one on the street for two dollars, but it wouldn't say anything about me."

"Is it really a better shine for fifty dollars than it is for two?"

"Most multimillionaires think so. The shine wouldn't seem worth much if it came cheap."

"But nobody knows whether you've had a two-dollar shine or a fifty-dollar one."

"I know it, and that's all that counts. It's the same with this shirt. It cost two hundred fifty dollars. That's what I used to pay for a suit when I started out in this business. With a shirt like this I feel as if the Lord and Merrill Lynch are watching over me."

"Besides the material happiness that money brings, what other good reason is there for you to earn so much?"

"It tells me exactly where I rank socially. More importantly, it shows where the wealthy stand in relation to me. It's hard for you to understand how important it is to me to take in more money than Malcolm Forbes. If I have more big bucks, I can ruin his breakfast."

"Then making a billion dollars is still the best revenge?"

"Yes, because when your income is in the billions, there are only about twenty guys in the world who can really screw you."

"Do you have any friends amongst the billion-dollar class?"

"Yes and no. I might gang up with T. Boone Pickens just to get a third guy. Then on Friday he might gang up with someone else to get me. That's why having money is so satisfying—you stick it to those who are trying to stick it to you."

"What else can you do with your fortune besides stick it to the other guy?"

"The really rich are the ones who put money into play. We spread it around, throw it on the table, toss it up and make sure that ten times more than we put in comes back."

"You must still be left with a lot that you don't know what to do with."

"That would be true if we didn't have to hire lawyers."

"Why do you need lawyers?"

"To tell us if it is legal to get a fifty-dollar shine."

EDUCATION FOR SALE

COLLEGE TUITIONS ARE going through the roof. Latest reports indicate it now costs $21,000 to send your loved one for a year to any respectable institution in the United States.

It is not the end of high tuition raises but rather the beginning.

Most educational experts predict that by 1995 the tariff for an average 150-pound male student or 110-pound female student will be $1 million a year, not counting admission to basketball games. Who will be the lucky students? Young people whose parents have made a killing in Time Warner stock or who own six or seven skyscrapers in a rezoned Central Park.

I asked Meyer Daniloff, a Regis Professor of Matriculation at Ivy League Normal, why tuitions were rising so fast. He replied, "All the universities in America are looking for a better class of student, and the only way we can get it is to raise the price of admission. We're tired of the grungy, unkempt, badly mannered students of the past, and the only way to get rid of them is to raise the rates. As the midget who sat on J. P. Morgan's lap once said, 'If you have to ask what college costs, then you can't afford it.' "

"Won't schools become boring if only rich kids can attend them?"

"They will at first, but pretty soon the students will get used to being with their own kind, and you will have a country club atmosphere that most schools at the moment seem to lack."

"Is there any way that middle-class students can find the wherewithal to attend college?"

"Of course. You don't think our society would keep them out just because they can't afford to go?"

"How can they do it?"

"They can buy a state lottery ticket, and if they win the lucky jackpot they can go to any school of their choice. But they have to pick all eight numbers before the registrar will accept them."

He continued, "The main advantage to the schools' raising tuition is that they get a fat-cat student who will eventually give to the alumni fund. The downside is that if it gets too expensive to go to college, fathers and mothers will not know what to do with their offspring when they reach eighteen years of age. Parents in the past could get rid of their children without looking cruel, by sending them to college. Now the children will have every excuse to stay in the house forever."

I said, "Without intending to, the colleges are making life miserable for the parents of middle- and lower-class kids."

"It's a difficult problem, but there is nothing you can do about it. There was always the fear that America would eventually price itself out of higher education. This is as good a time as ever."

"Will the students who pay the top-of-the-line fee get a better education?"

"I don't see why they should. We're not saying all parents have to come up with the tuition or else. All we're saying is that if a student chooses to become an airline pilot for a drug cartel just because he can't afford school, we are not to blame."

"Will you guarantee tuition is not going to rise more in just a few years?"

"Nobody can predict the future. But I'll bet Pete Rose anything that the price isn't going to go down."

MARINE REUNION

I WENT to a reunion of my Marine Corps unit, Fighter Squadron 113, in Pensacola the other day. All of us had fought valiantly in World War II. That's right, buster, World War II— and there are still a lot more of us around than most people think.

The guys set up a ready room in a suite at the Dunes Hotel, and that's where members of the squadron gathered to weave war stories and swap photos and souvenirs from the past. I grabbed a beer and waited for the lying to begin.

Schmitt was relating his war story when Frank Drury, one of the organizers of the reunion, came in, white-faced. "Shellack bought it."

"Where?" someone cried.

"At O'Hare Airport. Delta's computer went down and Shellack was left at the gate in tears."

"Couldn't they have put him on standby?"

"You know Shellack. He would only fly first class with a confirmed seat. He always maintained that standby was for dogfaces."

"Here's to Shellack," I said, raising my glass. "We'll always remember that Delta was not ready when he was."

Russ Drumm said, "Did I ever tell you about the time a shark stole my skivvies off a clothesline on Eniwetok?"

This sounded interesting, but the phone rang and Grundler answered it. He kept saying, "Oh, no. Oh, no." Then he hung up and held his head in his hands. "Andy Jones lost all his luggage coming into Kennedy."

John Lincoln threw his glass against the wall. "Why do they always lose the luggage of the good ones?"

"He had a hunch about this," I told them. "We were sitting together in the Denver terminal one day and he said, 'Last night I dreamed that my bags on TWA never made it to Boston. In case anything happens to me, I want you to see that my wife gets these claim checks.' "

We didn't seem to be making much progress with our war tales. I had one ready, but before I could begin, John Zoellner staggered into the ready room. His suit was rumpled, his shirt-tail hung out, and his cheeks were twitching.

He went straight to the bar, grabbed a bottle of cognac and began to drink.

"What happened?" someone asked.

"Tri-Continental had a flat tire. We sat on the runway for four hours and then the gate attendant discovered that the flight was overbooked. They made us slide down the chute and find our way back to the terminal in the dead of night."

Green said, "That happened to me once when I was traveling business class on Eastern. They announced that any passenger giving up his seat would get stock in the company. Everybody who got off went broke."

Zoellner took another swig. "I'm never going to fly again."

Drury grabbed him by his lapels. "No one chickens out at a Marine reunion. You're getting on the next USAir flight to Atlanta if I have to strap you to the 'No Smoking' sign myself."

The conversation turned serious. Kimak spoke up. "Question: Does anyone know why we fought the Japanese in World War Two?"

Bill Murray replied, "Everyone knows that. It was to keep them from flooding the United States with Toyotas."

Just then we heard the roar of engines, and we rushed out onto the balcony. A squadron of commuter planes was coming in from Tampa at sunset. Drury was looking through his binoculars and counting them: "One . . . two . . . three . . . four . . . five . . . My God, Chuck Woodbury's plane is missing. Call the tower."

Dufford called the tower. "What happened to Eight-fourteen?"

The controller told him, "Chuck blanked out after he ate the airline food over Biloxi."

A CRACK IN THE WHITE HOUSE

WHEN PRESIDENT BUSH was preparing to make his speech on drugs, he told his speechwriters he would like to hold up a bag of crack on television that had been obtained from a dealer in Lafayette Park, across from the White House. In this way the American people would be informed about how close drugs are to the Oval Office.

It turned out to be more difficult than anyone imagined. There aren't any dealers around Lafayette Park, mainly because it *is* too close to the White House. Therefore, no matter how hard the Drug Enforcement Administration tried, they couldn't arrange a buy from a dealer in the park.

The president was about to cancel his speech, when the DEA chief made a brilliant suggestion to two Bush speechwriters: "Why don't we find a dealer in another part of town, drag his butt to Lafayette Park and make him sell us the swag there?"

"Good idea," replied one of the speechwriters, "as long as the actual purchase is kosher."

The DEA chief and the two speechwriters started looking around town for the right man.

They went over to a large red Cadillac and spoke to the driver, who was wearing a diamond-studded mink coat.

"Pardon me," said one of the speechwriters. "Could you tell us where we could find a drug dealer for the president's TV speech?"

The red-Cadillac man smiled. "You want to put a dealer on television?"

"No, we want to put the dope he sells on television, in order to prove to the viewers how easy it is to buy the stuff across the street from the Oval Office."

Red Cadillac thought he had heard it all. "This is to help the president of the United States?"

"That is correct. The drug buy comes out of the president's entertainment budget."

Red Cadillac just shook his head. "Anyone who talks the way you people do has to be on the stuff already." He drove away laughing hysterically.

The threesome continued walking up the street. They saw a man making a sale in an alley and approached him.

"We have a proposition," the DEA man said, flashing his badge. "How would you like to sell us some of that white stuff in Lafayette Park?"

The dealer, his eyes bulging, told him, "I'm not selling anything. I'm just feeding Betty Crocker cake mix to the pigeons."

The DEA man persisted. "We want you to sell to us. The only hitch is that it has to be done in Lafayette Park, within snorting distance of the White House."

"I don't even know where the White House is. I've never been there. All my customers come to me."

The other speechwriter pushed forward. "Let me handle this." Then he turned to the dealer: "We're appealing to you as a great American. We need your crack to put on television so that all Americans can see how easy it is to purchase it in Washington. You'd be doing something very patriotic."

"You sure?" the dealer asked.

The speechwriter retorted, "As President Bush once said, 'Ask not what your country can do for you, but what you can do for your country.' "

"You must take me for a fool. Nobody sells crack to the White House without getting twenty years."

The DEA man replied, "Haven't you ever heard of a presidential pardon?"

I HAVE A SECRET

I NO LONGER HEAR people saying "Have a nice day." This salutation seems to have run its course, as has "Have a good one."

These greetings have been replaced by "Promise me you won't tell anyone what I'm about to tell you."

This is how a typical day went for me recently:

I was sitting in the kitchen eating my Cheerios and wondering how much Jane Pauley makes a year, when my wife said, "I'm going to swear you to secrecy. You have to promise on your honor that it will never leave this room."

I answered, "My lips are sealed, except to finish these last few Cheerios."

"The Marblewoods paid one million dollars for their house in Nantucket."

"What's wrong with that?"

"It was *her* money from her first marriage and, according to their prenuptial contract, the house is in her name."

"That's hot stuff," I agreed. I felt nervous walking around town with such information. Anyone could wrestle me to the ground and inject truth serum into me.

When I arrived at the office, I had a call from my sister Alice. "Don't tell Edith or Doris what I'm going to tell you: We're planning a trip to Alaska."

"I can keep *that* secret," I assured her.

The next call was from Edith. "Swear on the Bible that you won't say anything to Alice. They're taking a trip to Alaska. She thinks that I don't know, and I'm not going to let on to her that I know, if she doesn't want to tell me."

I waited for Doris's call. She said, "Mum's the word. Edith believes that she is the only one who's heard about Alice's visit to Alaska. I knew it before she did, but Alice made me promise not to tell Edith and you—and if you know what's good for you, you won't say anything to her children."

The part of my brain where I keep secrets was starting to fill up. A staff member at the *Boston Globe* bureau swore me to eternal silence about Tip O'Neill's assessment of Barney Frank.

At lunch a friend told me, in strictest confidence, that an important Republican was turned down for an ambassadorship after it was discovered that the large donation he had made came from HUD.

Even my taxi driver whispered, "I don't want to be quoted, and it's best if you leave my name out of this, but when Mayor Barry gave Washington the finger, he stuck himself in the eye."

As far as I can see, no one communicates with anyone else anymore without first asking the other person to cross his heart and hope to die.

On just one day I became the custodian of sixty-six secrets, most of which I was assured could blow the lid off the human race if anyone choked them out of me.

I don't know how many more I can keep, but I feel as if I've reached my limit. For me, one of the ways to deal with secrets is to unload them immediately onto somebody else.

For example, if George tells me some hot stuff about Joe, and I swear Ben to secrecy when I relate it to him, then it becomes Ben's problem and not mine.

Sealing another person's lips is now the main form of communication between people. Having said that, I would appreciate it if you kept the contents of this story to yourselves.

SEX CHANGE ON TV

EVERY TWO YEARS I put out a new book, and then make a tour of the talk shows plugging it. I can't do it anymore, because it is now impossible for someone who is not *really* weird to get on TV.

I discovered this when I walked into Lisa Johnson's office at

Putnam's and she said, "I've never heard anything so ridiculous in my life. The people at Phil Donahue's show say they are very sorry but they can't put you on the show unless you have a sex-change operation."

I laughed. "That's a good one."

She wasn't laughing. She looked at me and said, "We'll pay for it."

"Now Lisa, you know that I'm not going to have a sex-change operation just to sell a few books."

"That's your decision, but you'll never make the best-seller lists as a man."

"What about Oprah Winfrey?" I asked.

"We talked to her producer. This month they're only doing people who were physically abused by their pets when they were children."

"I had a dog who once bit me on the ankle. Any bulletins from Geraldo Rivera?"

"On his upcoming show he's featuring inmates who learned to cook key lime pie on death row."

"What about next Monday?" I wanted to know.

"He has a weeklong series on pimps and their grand-mothers."

"Count me out. I'm sorry Morton Downey, Jr., is no longer on the air. I would have thrown a chair at him."

Lisa said, "It's an entirely different ballgame this year. Everyone is in the ratings game and you have to be really far out to get on a show. Maury Povich, who used to be a great interviewer, will not have you on his program unless you've had kinky correspondence with a fax machine."

"What about the local shows?"

"They're no better. You're not going to get a plug on TV unless you are on the FBI's Ten Most Wanted list."

"It doesn't seem fair. Perhaps I could confess to a yearning to jog nude with the bears in Yellowstone National Park."

Lisa sounded harassed. "Our job is not to bemoan the state of affairs of talk TV, but to do something about it. We have to fulfill their production needs."

"I can't become a werewolf," I said.

"Maybe not," Lisa agreed, "but I had a tip that Joan Rivers is doing vampires who use steroids."

"You mean bloodsuckers in sports?"

"That's what I heard."

By this time Lisa was in tears. "How can I possibly get you on TV if your father wasn't even an Estonian war criminal?" she said, sobbing.

I tried to reassure her. "The sex change sounds the easiest, but I won't have it unless they promise to give me the full hour on *Donahue*."

"He'll only take you with Barbara Walters."

"Is she going to have a sex-change operation too?"

"She has to if she's got a book coming out."

VICTIMLESS CRIME

THE FIRST VICTIM of violent crime in this country is victimless crime. With all the mayhem that is going on in the streets these days, one can't expect the police to get too excited about a stolen pair of silver candlesticks or television set.

Vivian Andrews discovered this when the hubcaps were stolen off her Toyota.

Red-faced and steaming mad, she marched down to the Eighty-fifth Precinct and declared, "I wish to report a crime."

The sergeant was holding a drug pusher's head on his desk with one hand while he searched the man's pants with the other. Then he shoved him in the direction of another officer and said to Vivian, "What kind of crime?"

"Someone stole my hubcaps."

The sergeant looked at her to make sure that she wasn't kidding and said, "We don't do hubcaps."

"What do you mean, you 'don't do hubcaps'?"

"We stopped doing them years ago, about the same time we decided not to do anything about stolen television sets, car stereos and silver tea services."

"A crime is a crime," Vivian protested. "Those hubcaps mean as much to me as stolen cash means to a bank."

The sergeant threw a glass paperweight at a mugger who was being booked, and shouted, "Tell him to shut up." He then turned to Vivian. "Please don't think that the police are cold and heartless about hubcaps. It's just that we can't give them the same priority we give to a drug lord being gunned down in the street.

"In normal times we might even send someone over to fingerprint your car, and try and match the prints against every known convict in the city. But these are not normal times."

"What about the FBI?" Vivian wanted to know.

"The FBI can intervene only if the hubcaps are transported across state lines. They have problems too. They're using their entire force to guard Felix Bloch to see if he's a spy, and so they decided several months ago to cut back on solving hubcap crimes."

"You people really don't care about petty larceny anymore. All you're interested in is stuff that can put you on the evening news."

"That's not true. We're really falling behind these days, and if we rounded up every hubcap thief in town, we would never catch the few people who deserve to be locked up." With that the sergeant whacked a fly with his nightstick.

"So what are you going to do?" Vivian asked.

"Lady," the sergeant told her, "I am going to make out a report on your hubcaps and put it in a file with 'Stolen Fur Coats,' 'Credit Cards' and 'Punch Bowls.' "

Vivian was impressed. "Here's the form. When can I expect you to catch the thief and return my hubcaps?"

The sergeant looked at his calendar. "Let's see, today is Tuesday. I won't be able to get the entire precinct on the case until Wednesday. We'll put out an all-points bulletin this afternoon, so let's say we'll crack your case by Friday."

Vivian replied, "That seems more than fair. My friends warned me that with the increase in crime you wouldn't be able to solve the theft until next week."

WHAT TO DO

JACKIE MASON AND PANAMA, TAKE 2:

It was finger-pointing time in the Bush administration. Everyone was blaming everyone else for the Noriega fiasco. The president declared, "I'm not going to accuse anyone, because it would be an admission that I did something wrong. I'd like the 467th Damage Control Team to come up with a plan for getting rid of Noriega now, but I don't want any footprints leading to the White House."

A group of worried staff members descended to the bowels of the Executive Mansion. They assembled in the Situation Room to carry out the president's order.

A policy aide was the first to speak. "Why don't we pass the word to the Colombians that Noriega really works for the U.S. Drug Enforcement Administration and is snitching to Bill Bennett on everything the cartel is doing? Then we let the Colombian drug barons take care of him, pronto."

"It's too risky," responded a general. "For all we know, it may be true. God knows who the DEA has on its payroll."

A CIA man said, "Suppose we give Noriega a fatal illness and then he finds out that the government won't pay for any of his health insurance?"

A White House staff member added, "We mustn't have any rough stuff. All the world is watching to see if we can get rid of Noriega in a kinder and gentler fashion."

"Couldn't we capture Noriega and drive him insane by making him share a cell with Zsa Zsa Gabor?" asked a national security advisor.

The general said, "We can't. It violates the Geneva Convention."

Another White House staffer told the group, "Noriega is a man who likes money. Suppose we offer him Malcolm Forbes's yacht and the first three floors of Bloomingdale's?"

"That's not bad. But Noriega will want us to drop all charges against him in the U.S.," said the CIA man.

"No problem. If he pleads guilty, we'll give him two hundred sixty hours of community service making beds for Leona Helmsley."

"Wait a minute. I've got it," a young White House aide shouted. "Why don't we send Jackie Mason to Panama to work in Noriega's election campaign?"

"That's crazy," answered the general.

"Hear me out," the aide pleaded. "We'd drive Jackie around the country to warm up the crowd for Noriega. He could tell ethnic Panamanian stories like, 'How many Panamanian National Guardsmen does it take to screw in a light bulb? Two. One to screw it in and one to shoot it out.' Stuff like that. Pretty soon the whole country will turn on Noriega and he'll be booted out."

"Why would Noriega take Jackie to campaign for him?" the CIA man asked.

"Because Noriega can't win without the Jewish vote in Panama," a White House aide explained.

The NSC advisor agreed, "It does have merit. If Jackie can do a job for Rudy Giuliani, he can do the same for Noriega. Somebody get him on the phone."

The person came back five minutes later. "Jackie said he'd do it only if he can tell the truth about Panama."

"What truth?"

"That Panamanians couldn't dig a canal if their lives depended on it."

"Jackie said that?"

"Only as a joke. He wanted you to know that if he works for Noriega, he's going to tell a lot of good jokes about Central Americans."

"If he does, the Panamanians will kill Noriega," the CIA man remarked.

"So?"

THE HARD QUESTIONS

You ASK THE hard questions, and I'll give you the easy answers as to why the stock market just took a tumble.

"Why did it?"

"The prevailing wisdom is that the people trying to buy United Airlines couldn't get the financing they needed."

"What the *bleep* has that got to do with the stock market?"

"You will have to remain civilized if you want me to answer your questions. It all started when Marvin Davis, the billionaire who used to own Twentieth Century–Fox, tried to buy Northwest Airlines. He was unsuccessful, so he decided he would grab control of United Airlines instead. The management of UAL hated the idea so much that they got together with the airline's pilots and announced that *they* were purchasing the company. The price offered was seven billion dollars."

"Did they have seven billion dollars?"

"If you're going to ask stupid questions, I'll discontinue this briefing. Of course they didn't have seven billion dollars. They didn't even have seven billion baggage claim checks. Like everybody else they planned to go into the junk bond market and raise the money.

"This is the way the system works. You acquire a profitable company that you don't own, with money that isn't yours, and

95

drive it into the ground by paying unbelievable interest rates that you cannot afford."

"So what happened when the people who wanted to buy UAL couldn't get their seven billion?"

"The word was immediately flashed to Wall Street that United Airlines was not flying in very friendly skies. A twenty-four-year-old Wall Street trader named Sidney, fresh out of Wharton, saw the flash. He told his superior, Gloria, aged twenty-one, that he was worried because if UAL raiders couldn't get a lousy seven-billion-dollar loan in junk bonds, it meant the entire market was weaker than his assistants, Larry, twenty-two, and George, twenty-three, had been forecasting. Gloria panicked and ordered Sidney to sell five billion dollars' worth of securities which they were holding for the Septic Tank Workers' pension fund."

"How did Sidney do it?"

"He pushed a button marked 'Sell' on his computer, which lit up every pinball machine in America."

"It was Sidney who started the panic!"

"No, but he anticipated one. Everybody expects the market to go either up or down. They pay Sidney one million dollars to know this. They also expect him to be aware that the people who deal with the financial fortunes of the country panic easily. If it isn't Braniff Airlines today, it's United Airlines tomorrow."

"So Sidney sold his securities. What did he do with the money?"

"He bought stocks of other companies that Marvin Davis hinted he might be pursuing in the next two weeks."

"And those stocks went up?"

"No, they went down."

"Why was that?"

"I told you, dummy, because no matter what happened in the market, it all boiled down to the fact that United Airlines could not raise seven billion dollars. What makes this all so sad is that it could signal the end of junk bonds as we know them."

"You mean the takeover moguls will no longer be able to acquire healthy companies with other people's money and turn them into debt-ridden cripples?"

"I'm afraid so. We have a new saying on Wall Street: 'When Marvin Davis sneezes, the Japanese yen catches pneumonia.' "

THANKS FOR THE MILLIONS

A VERY WELL-DRESSED and extremely polite Japanese businessman came to see me in my office. He explained that he was on a search mission on behalf of the Fuji Wooji Electronic Company. "I would like to buy an ex–president of the United States," he informed me, "and I thought that with your background in the Orient, you could help."

I was indignant. "Our American presidents are not for sale."

"Mr. Reagan just visited our country for two million dollars."

"That amount was for the president's expenses and Nancy's wardrobe," I told him. "It was not to buy Reagan's unqualified endorsement of your country."

"He said some very nice things about Japan, including the fact that we could make better motion pictures in Hollywood than the Americans."

I reminded him, "That's only after the Sony people announced that they were going to start production on *Bedtime for Banzai.* The president has always been an admirer of Japanese movies. He saw *Tora! Tora! Tora!* three times."

"You're wandering from the problem," my visitor chided. "The company which brought Mr. Reagan over is our biggest competitor. We have lost face because they sponsored him. We must find a person with the same stature, influence and cheerfulness as President Reagan. Do you have any suggestions?"

"We have three other living ex-presidents, but I'm not sure that any of them would go to Japan for a lousy two million bucks. It's not a lot of money for an American ex-president."

"Then why did Reagan do it?"

"I'm positive it wasn't for the dough. Perhaps his astrologer suggested that it was an auspicious time to travel. What the Japanese have to understand about our presidents is that they cannot be purchased like the Empire State Building or a shopping mall outside of Pittsburgh."

"Then why did President Reagan accept the money?" he persevered.

I replied, "If he hadn't, somebody else would have. Reagan did not sell out. He only said out loud what most Americans think—that the Japanese are wonderful people, they make great products, and we're glad that they won the war."

"Did it ever occur to you," he asked, "that President Reagan did himself harm by allowing the Fujisankei Communications Group to take him over to Japan? As competitors, we consider it a great insult to the Japanese nation that he would sleep on Fujisankei's futons. Reagan is president to all the Japanese people, and not just to one communications outfit."

I told him, "If what you say is true, Reagan is a Japanese problem, not an American one."

"Well, who would you recommend we sign up?"

"What about Oral Roberts, the TV evangelist?"

"Why Oral Roberts?"

"He needs the money."

"No, we want someone more presidential."

"How about Donald Trump? He is not an ex-president, but he likes Japan very much and has announced that he is in the process of buying it."

I LOVE NEW YORK?

TOM BROKAW HAD to apologize to New York City for knocking the town during a news broadcast. I am going to talk about New York today, but I have no intention of following his example. The reason for this is that New Yorkers never offer me an apology, so why should I apologize to them?

Here are some random notes about the Big Apple that I jotted down on my last trip:

The first thing a visitor notices is that all the people on the street are talking to themselves. The assumption is that they are mentally disturbed. This is not the case. The people talking to themselves are the sane ones—it's the New Yorkers who talk to each other who are crazy.

New York City has won the Nobel Prize for Potholes. What makes the potholes so special is that they are not only in the streets but also on the sidewalks. In New York a person has twice as much chance of breaking an ankle when walking than he has when he's riding in a bus.

It is not generally known, but each New Yorker averages eight fights a day with total strangers. The fights are mostly verbal, and only in rare cases do they become physical. When he returns home at night the family is waiting to find out how many he won. This is how it goes:

"So Dad, how did you do with the fights today?"

"I won five and lost three."

"Not bad for an old man."

"Who are you calling an old man? Show me another New Yorker over fifty who can still win the Big One in the subway."

"Who did you beat, Dad?"

"I went up against a cab driver who drove right through a puddle and splashed water all over my pants."

"Did you give him a piece of your mind?"

"No, he sped off. Another cab came along and had to stop for a red light, so I yelled at that driver instead. You should have seen the look on his face."

"Bully for you, Dad."

"Later on I was waiting to make a telephone call at a public phone box on Broadway. I stood for ten minutes while some guy made obscene telephone calls to his ex-wife.

"He hung up, and I was about to take the receiver, when this little old lady pushed me aside and grabbed the phone. Being a New Yorker, I said as polite as can be, 'I think I was waiting longer, shorty.' Do you know what she did? She gave me the finger."

"A little old lady did that to you at a public phone booth?"

"They'll do it anywhere they can. So I lost that one. Next I went into a big department store to buy a pair of socks. The guy at the sock counter was nibbling on the neck of the girl selling cologne. 'Please,' I said, 'all I want are some socks.' The girl sprayed cologne into the salesman's ear. I got impatient and shouted, 'I want socks!' The guy didn't move, but the store detective came over, shoved his chest against mine and said, 'Can't you see the man is on his lunch hour?'"

"Fifteen years ago you would have won that one, Pop. Salespeople can smell it when a customer is over the hill and doesn't have any fight left in him."

"My greatest victory came after I saw a mugging this afternoon, ten feet away from me."

"Why was it such a triumph?"

"The mugger got away, so no one asked me to be a witness."

GIVE ME THE TRUTH

THE FIRST CASUALTY in the war of the sexes is truth—or at least the truth as we know it. One of the arguments that wives constantly use against their husbands is: "If *I* don't tell you the truth, who will?"

The only sensible response to that is: "So what?"

I was witness to such a discussion on the beach one day.

Susan Allen said to her husband, Paul, "Your problem is that nobody tells you the truth."

"What's wrong with that?" Paul asked.

"It means that you think you can get away with murder. I'm the only one who levels with you."

Paul wanted to know: "Who anointed you Goddess of Truth?"

"That's what wives are for," Susan said indignantly. "We see husbands as they really are—warts and all."

Paul protested, "Men don't want the truth—ever, and they certainly don't wish to hear it from their wives."

"I suppose you expect us to behave like cheerleaders."

"Exactly. We want you to swing your pom-poms back and

101

forth, kick your legs and spell out H-U-S-B-A-N-D in the middle of Yankee Stadium. Is that asking too much from someone who provides you with extravagantly beautiful towels from Macy's?"

"Every male has to have one honest person in his life to tell him when he has no clothes on."

"Maybe so, but it shouldn't be the person he's married to. The trouble with wives is that they don't just tell husbands about one thing that's wrong with them—they have to list *every* fault. It's a litany of booboos, from forgetting to put gas in the car to mixing up the names of the new Polish leaders.

"The worst part is when you correct me in front of other people, rather than when we're alone. This is not something for a woman to do while searching for the bluebird of happiness."

Susan said, "The fact that you won't take my criticism means that you can't accept criticism from anybody."

"There," yelled Paul, "you're doing it again. You're criticizing me for being unable to take criticism."

"I'm not doing anything of the kind. I am just making a statement of fact. If there were anything wrong with me, I would expect you to call my attention to it. That's what marriage is all about."

"Marriage is not about that at all. Show me the license which allows you to tell me when I am making a fool of myself in public."

"I don't have a license, but as your wife, I have been given the right to let it all hang out. I know husbands who would kill to be told when they are using the wrong fork at a dinner party."

"This may surprise you, but I didn't want to hear that. Neither did I wish to know the correct way to hang up my pants when I lost money on the stock market. You think I like to know the truth about myself, but you have to believe me when I say that it's not something I yearn for."

"A wife can't get close to her husband unless she tells him what he's doing wrong, even if it's just in conversation."

"There," screamed Paul, pounding his head, "you're doing it again!"

CAMPAIGN TRICKS

DIRTY EDDIE, campaign manager for Howard McClintic, was packing up his literature and campaign signs.

"I am proud of the fact that it was a clean political campaign," he told me. "Race never played a role in the contest. Not once—even when we said that our opponent went to school with Willie Horton."

"But McClintic is white, and so was his opponent."

"All the more reason for not mentioning the race issue. At the beginning of the campaign, McClintic announced that he would not introduce color as an issue. He stuck to his promise."

"With that statement, he made it an issue."

"McClintic never made it an issue. His opponent, Glockenspiel, did when he attacked McClintic for bringing it up in the first place."

Dirty Eddie continued, "When we started out we decided to take the high road in the campaign, even if it meant losing."

"Is that why you ran a TV commercial of Glockenspiel beating up senior citizens in a public park?"

"We felt that the voters had a right to know what turned Glockenspiel on. Was it less fair than the other side showing our guy in a raincoat flashing in front of a McDonald's?"

"I am curious about how you managed to get film of Glockenspiel and Noriega riding in the same seat on a Ferris wheel."

"It's incredible what you can do with a computer these days."

"Dirty Eddie, I know you ran a clean campaign, but there are some who feel that you spread stories about Glockenspiel which weren't necessarily true."

"Like what?"

"Like the time you said that he had to take steroids before he could go out to campaign."

"We only mentioned it when *they* claimed that McClintic was a compulsive gambler and bet on his own race. We weren't looking for low-down things to say about the other side, but you have to fight fire with fire or your election will go up in smoke. We had a lot of dirty stuff that we didn't use."

"Such as?"

"Glockenspiel has one of the highest cholesterol counts of anyone running for office this year."

"Why didn't we know that?"

"He keeps his cholesterol results in a numbered Swiss bank account."

"Dirty Eddie, it seems to me that the last two weeks of the campaign were the worst. Both sides took off their gloves. After what we saw, are you still trying to tell me that you ran a clean campaign?"

"I'd bet my life on it. We were entirely issue-oriented."

"Was that why you leaked the story about your opponent being the serial killer of Gladly Heights?"

"We didn't say that he was. We just raised the question. That what's political campaigns are all about. If someone running for office is a serial killer, the public has a right to be informed. We didn't claim that he was unfit for the job."

"Dirty Eddie, what are you doing with all that stuff you're packing away?"

"Saving it for the next election. Politicians will pay anything to find a squeaky-clean campaign manager like myself."

RED IS DEAD

THERE WERE WINNERS and losers when the Berlin Wall fell. We saw the winners on television. The losers were nowhere to be seen. Among them were Karl Marx, Friedrich Engels and Vladimir Lenin—the architects of the communist system which fell on its kiester with a thud heard around the world.

The three men were hiding out and refused to speak to reporters. Lenin's wife announced that her husband was disgusted with the way things were going and was leaving on a train for Switzerland.

"What went wrong with communism?" I asked her.

"My husband feels that the Central Committee did not respond to the Regional Party Committee's demands concerning the way the District People's Committee operated. When bread became more important than local party study groups, the people turned their backs on all of our five-year plans. My husband is furious with Karl and Friedrich because they should have seen this coming and not left him holding the bag."

"Is communism dead?" I wanted to know.

"Is Stalin dead? The problem was never East Germany or

West Germany or even Bulgaria. Communism was a political philosophy based on the theory that if you have three bureaucrats for each worker, you can double the beet crop for your borscht."

"What did Comrade Lenin suggest for Russia if communism didn't work?"

"There was always one democratic economic solution: Shoot everyone who questioned the system."

Lenin, Engels and Marx were not the only big losers when the Wall fell.

The entire U.S. military industrial complex was in despair.

A bitter defense contractor had told me, "If the USSR tilts toward the West the way East Germany and Poland have, there will be people in the U.S. claiming that all these billion-dollar weapons are unnecessary. Everyone seems to forget that if they tear down the Berlin Wall, we will need more bombers than ever to stop the Albanians from overrunning Western Europe. The time to spend defense money is not when our enemies are preparing for war, but when they are disarming for peace. The military industrial complex has never been fooled by a fresh government in Poland."

Another victim of the end of the cold war is Lucifer Grummdart, a fundamentalist preacher who headed up the most active anticommunist organization in America, known as the Anti-Pinko Grass-Roots League. Lucifer used to collect millions of dollars from Texas millionaires who wanted to prevent a commie takeover of the Panhandle. With the threat of communism weaker than at any time in the last fifty years, Lucifer's fund-raising sources have dried up.

Grummdart is now looking for free-lance American communists who can testify on TV that, although communism is sinking behind the Iron Curtain, it is growing in this country. It's a desperate effort on Lucifer's part because all the anti-Red organizations in America are looking for a few good communists. According to the CIA, there are only three card-carrying Bolsheviks in the United States to go around, and they're informers for the FBI.

The final loser of the counterrevolution in Eastern Europe was President Bush. When an aide informed the president of the collapse of the East German government, Bush exclaimed, "Golly gumdrops!"

The aide cleared his throat and said, "That's the good news. The bad news is that they want you to give them five hundred fifty billion dollars."

THIS LAND IS *THEIR* LAND

ALL RIGHT, so the name Radio City Tojo Hall doesn't grab you—nor is the Kamikaze Ice-skating Rink at Mitsubishi Center on Fifth Avenue your cup of tea. Don't get mad at the Japanese. Everyone has a right to be in the real estate business these days.

When the news of the Rockefeller Center sale was announced, each family in the United States dealt with it in its own particular way. Nancy Sharp stared at Peter Jennings reading the evening news, and then threw a lamp at the television screen.

"*What* is going on?" she screamed.

Her husband, Fred, was fiddling with his Sony VCR, mixing

himself a daiquiri with a Toyota blender and thinking of when to get his Nissan tuned up. Nancy's cry brought him back to reality.

"Why would the Rockefellers do that to us?"

"It's just business," Fred said. "If they didn't buy it, the Ethiopians would."

Nancy protested, "It shouldn't be allowed. It's part of our national heritage, like Disneyland or Sea World."

"You have to understand, my dear, that everything in America is for sale. People must have money if they are to achieve happiness."

She shook her head. "Not the Rockefellers—they're filthy rich."

"That's what you think," Fred told her. "Did it ever occur to you that there could be many poor Rockefellers scattered among the wealthy ones?"

Nancy remained unconvinced. "Rockefellers *can't* be poor. That's why they're called Rockefellers."

"Well, smartie, I happen to know that there are Rockefellers who are as poor as church mice. They would just as soon have a basket of Japanese yen as see their name on a building in New York. The word on the street is that the church mice forced David and Laurance Rockefeller to sell everything to the Japanese, including Bryant Gumbel, Jane Pauley and Deborah Norville."

Fred's wife was distraught. "Rockefeller Center is our shrine, the same as St. Peter's or the Mosque at Mecca. It's where people go to see the Rockettes kick up their legs, and watch ordinary Americans dance on the tops of tables at the Rainbow Room. It doesn't belong to the Rockefellers—it belongs to you and me."

Fred put his hand on his wife's shoulder. "Don't worry, I'm sure the Japanese have ice skaters just as good as ours."

"Why did the Japanese have to be the ones to buy the Center?"

"They have a lot more money than Nicaragua. Even Donald Trump is too strapped to close a deal on the place."

"How come the Japanese are so rich?"

"It's simple," Fred replied. "Everything you see in this room was manufactured by them. Thanks to us, Tokyo is drowning in U.S. dollars. But man can't live on dollars alone. The Japanese then transfer the money back here and purchase American real estate with the same dollars. The whole world is buying up this country with our money."

"Before I agree to all this," Nancy Sharp said, "I want to know who is going to run Radio City Music Hall."

"I heard a rumor that Ronald Reagan has been asked."

"Why?"

"Remember Reagan's trip to Japan? You don't think that he went over there for nothing, do you?"

TRUE OR FALSE?

TRUE OR FALSE: The main reason for deregulation of the airlines was to make the business more competitive.

Donald Trump, who keeps giving away free rooms in Atlantic City on his shuttle flights between New York and Boston, has raised the one-way fare from $99 to $119. That's okay, since it's his airline.

Here's the rub. As soon as he did it, Pan Am, his only shuttle competitor, announced that it was raising its fares from $99 to $119—not $118.99, not $120, but $119. Because of this odd coincidence I looked for a Pan Am ticket agent to find out what happened.

109

She was wiping her computer with a chamois cloth.

"I would like to ask you why Pan Am raised its fare to exactly match Donald Trump's."

"That's a good question. My understanding is that Pan Am was going to raise its fare first. Donald Trump heard about it and beat us to the punch. People say we followed suit, when in fact Trump was dragging behind us."

"How did you arrive at a hundred nineteen dollars?"

"It seemed like a nice figure that we could live with. It was neither too high nor too low. It was exactly what people expect to pay for a pleasant ride in a beautiful airplane."

"And yet," I added, "some would say that each side subconsciously agreed to charge the same amount rather than compete against the other."

She tapped on her computer and said, "It doesn't show that on my screen. Frankly, we don't care what Donald Trump does. After all, he's our competitor."

"If you are competing, why not make it a hundred fifteen instead of a hundred nineteen?"

She went to her computer again and then looked up. "That doesn't make sense."

"Why not charge less than Trump and steal all his business?"

She smiled patiently. "Because he would then lower his price to undersell us, and pretty soon a fare war would break out with blood all over La Guardia Airport. Pan Am is an honorable airline and would never do anything to lower prices in order to take business away from another carrier."

"So you stick to your twenty-dollar increase and they stick to their twenty-dollar increase, and the only one who gets speared is the passenger."

"You have to try and understand what airline competition is all about. Sure, we want to hurt the competition, but we can't afford to do it if they are going to hurt us. Let me give you an example. If we hadn't raised our fares right after Trump did, he would have had to lower his fares back to where we were. That way he'd be out twenty dollars, and so would we. By meeting his raise, we sent a message to him that we will compete with him dollar for dollar."

"Are you planning on raising your rates again?"

She kept hitting her computer on the side to make it work. Then she answered, "Not in the near future. But I'm sure that if we did, Mr. Trump would not be far behind. Why are you asking so many questions?"

"Because I have a feeling that you people aren't serious about the free enterprise system."

"We're more serious than the antitrust division of the Justice Department."

"Will Trump and Pan Am really compete on fares?"

She smacked her computer again and a large word came up on the screen—it was TILT.

MAIL DAY

THE MAIL HAS been piling up, and it's time I got some of it off my desk.

Marianna Beck writes: "Dexter Manley, the Redskins' lineman, has been suspended by the football commissioner for life, which they say means that he can apply for reinstatement in one year. I'm not sure that I understand this. Please explain it to me."

Dear Marianna:

In the world of sports, when you are suspended for life, you have to sit on the bench for twelve months. At that time the commissioner will decide whether or not you can return to the game. If athletes who were banned for life could not reapply in a year, they would become very disgusted with the system and go into some other profession.

Julian Hoffar from Alexandria, Virginia, had the following question: "I am a big sports fan and watch all sorts of games on television. I think that the networks do very well except for one thing. The announcers never tell you the score. Is there any reason for this?"

Dear Julian:

Before announcing a game, all sportscasters take a blood oath not to reveal the score, because it will take away the suspense from fans who have tuned in late. In place of a score, announcers tell you where a player was born, how many tattoos he has on his body, what he eats for breakfast, and how much he makes doing commercials for car dealers. The networks support the secrecy pact and maintain that the score is nobody's damn business but that of the sponsors who pay to broadcast the games.

Carolyn Shuck writes: "President Bush vetoed a foreign aid bill because it provided funds for a UN birth control program for the People's Republic of China. Is he bonkers?"

Dear Carolyn:

The president is as sane as anyone else in Washington. He feels that it would be a mistake to allow Chinese women to become pro-choice when they should be having all the babies they possibly can. The population of China is now one billion, three hundred twelve million and six. Were American foreign aid money spent for birth control, China's population would be reduced something awful. Mr. Bush feels that nobody could live with the knowledge that American tax dollars were to be used to drive down the number of children born in China.

This one comes from Rita Gamphor in Denver, Colorado: "The Defense Department is talking about reducing its budget for the next four years by $160 billion. It is estimated that the bailout for the savings and loans institutions will come to $160 billion. Why doesn't the Defense Department give the money directly to the S&Ls and cut out the middleman?

"By the way, what happened to the officials who lost the $160 billion?"

Dear Rita:

There is a lot of misunderstanding about the S&Ls. We are not bailing out the institutions themselves—we are bailing out the citizens who put their money into them. The men who are responsible for the debacle are now in either Sun Valley or Hawaii licking their wounds. Not only were many of them leaders of their communities, but also they have given tons of money to U.S. senators and congressmen. These factors are often ignored when people criticize them for their mistakes.

"Dear Sir: If we do not want to give the $160 billion to bail out the S&Ls, who can we bail out instead?"

Poland.

STORE FOR SALE

I WENT CHRISTMAS SHOPPING one day at Blackdale's department store.

"Can I help you?" the salesclerk asked.

"I'm looking for a present for my wife. Is there anything on sale?"

"We have a nice buy on the store," he told me.

"What do you mean, 'on the store'?"

"The whole place is for sale. We were planning to mark it down after Christmas, but since Bloomingdale's is on the market, as well as Saks, we decided to reduce the price now."

"I don't want a store," I said. "I was thinking more of a nice woolen sweater."

"We have those, of course, but if you purchase Blackdale's you can get forty percent off anything on the fourth floor, which includes women's running shoes."

"I don't understand it," I responded. "You work in the home furnishing department. Why are *you* trying to sell Blackdale's?"

"Every employee in the store has been ordered to unload the establishment any way he or she possibly can. Management feels that there has to be a live one among all of its customers. If you buy it, we'll throw in our branch store in New Jersey as well. You don't need to put anything down for three months."

"I'm curious about something. Why is Blackdale's being sold?"

"It's the same old retailing story. Five years ago a Canadian company bought us, and then it was taken over by the Australians, who then sold the place to Siamese twins from Singapore.

"The deal depended on huge loans, which had to be paid back with the cash flow from our store. When the new owners took away our daily receipts, we didn't have any money left to buy merchandise. Without stock we had no cash flow, and when the owners went broke they put us up for sale."

"That's awful."

"We call it modern retailing, or nouveau cannibalism."

"Anyway, it's not my problem. Please direct me to the sweater department."

"I'll tell you what I'll do. If you acquire Blackdale's, we will issue you a gold credit card, and we'll paint the walls on the main floor any color you want."

"I'm not interested in purchasing a department store. If the former owners can't make a go of it, how can I?"

"They were all sleazeballs. They intended to sell off the store, escalator by escalator, until there was nothing left. They were interested only in making money by burying Blackdale's. You look like a man who cares about the survival of a retail store."

"I am, but I'd just as soon get my wife an electric skillet," I told him.

"I know what you are thinking. You'd rather have Saks or Bloomingdale's. It would be a mistake. You're never going to beat a location like this. Our traffic is twice as heavy as theirs, and we have an upper-bracket clientele that any bankrupt store in America would kill for. We'll even gift-wrap the entire men's department for you and deliver it on Christmas night."

"I still think a skillet would be more useful."

"The thrill of owning an electric skillet lasts only a few days. A bankrupt department store is forever."

I didn't say yes to the man, and I didn't say no. I'm thinking it over. Blackdale's costs more than I really can afford, but then again so does everything else around Christmastime.

THE RATINGS FELL DOWN

THE GOOD NEWS was that millions and millions of people in the Eastern bloc were freed from communist oppression. It was the most significant story since World War II. The bad news was that the television ratings in the United States were way down. Freedom may have its moments, but it doesn't sell Kellogg's cornflakes.

With the heat on, the network news divisions began calling their staffs together.

The president of the Rambo Network, whose assistant kept feeding him Rolaids, stared out at the group. "Okay, who was the wiseguy who said that tearing down the Berlin Wall would make a good news show?"

There was dead silence in the room. Finally the anchorman spoke up. "I thought it might be interesting. Americans had seen the Wall standing for so long, I imagined that they would enjoy watching it being torn down *live.*"

The president asked, "Do you know what the rating was on that? It was two point one. We used to have a six share of the audience. Two point one is lower than the polo game we covered with Prince Charles from Karachi."

The executive producer from the evening news tried to smooth things over. "Everybody makes mistakes. On paper, the end of the Wall seemed like a good idea. It just so happened that

116

more viewers tuned into *I Love Lucy*. Does that make over-throwing communism a bad idea?"

The president said, "It is if you overdo it. What about the liberation of Czechoslovakia? For four nights we showed Czech citizens dancing in the streets of Prague, and we wound up in the sewer."

A writer added, "We were covering history. It was television's finest hour."

"Tell that to the guys who own this network, and who also have a light bulb factory in Schenectady. Look, I'm a news-man and I know a story when I see one, but I'm not going to put on Bulgaria if nobody will watch it. When are you all going to learn that a *little* freedom on television can go a long way?"

Another producer asked, "Do you want us to cut back on Gorbachev too?"

The president replied, "No, his ratings are still okay. I wouldn't want to have him on every night, but the guy does have charisma. Now the research staff, who were immediately alerted after the Nielsen disaster, have come up with some guidance on what we can do to beef up the audience.

"They are suggesting that we downplay any future stories on countries freeing themselves from communism. We don't have to accept all of their ideas, although the light bulb boys like them. They also think that we should go out and find some shooting wars instead. The TV audiences would rather see people being killed than watch them being liberated."

"What if Albania declares itself free?"

"I don't think that's any of our business. Nobody in America knows where Albania is. I'm not asking you to fudge the news, but you have to remember that if nobody watches the show, we're all out of business.

"The fall of the Berlin Wall is a perfect example of over-playing a story. After a while, the only ones who were inter-ested were those who lived near it. John Q. Viewer in Amarillo couldn't care less—and that's the guy who is buying our sponsor's light beer."

The producer said, "So you don't want us to call them like we see them."

The president told him, "Call them any way you want to, but I have to answer to a higher authority. My bosses want to know why this network is providing upbeat news from Europe, which is producing lousy ratings, at a time when their light bulb business needs all the downbeat news it can get."

THOSE WERE THE DAYS

DURING AN ADDRESS to his people, Romanian president Nicolae Ceauşescu promised that he would lead them back into what he called "the golden dream of communism."

Like most of us, I didn't know that there was such a thing. So I spoke to a Romanian Gypsy violinist who plays at the Georgetown Tea Room down the street.

"Do you remember living in the golden dream of communism?" I asked.

"I remember it well," he answered. "We lined up in one town to buy a chicken being sold in the next town. When they announced that they had run out of fowl, we stamped our feet and sang songs to Papa Lenin and Uncle Stalin."

"It sounds like a meaningful time for the Romanian people."

"None of us would have missed it. We didn't have to worry

about anything under communism because our leaders did all the worrying for us. During the golden dream, one day drifted into another, and every Romanian couldn't wait to get up in the morning."

"Were there secret police in the golden dream?"

"There were, but they weren't exactly secret. They used to come to the door at night and tap lightly, and ask if they could get us a cup of warm milk. They were always fun to have around."

"What else can you remember from the golden dream?"

"There was respect for Lenin and Khrushchev. Khrushchev once declared that without Romania there would be no people's paradise behind the Iron Curtain."

"Was he drunk when he said it?"

"Let's say that he wasn't dead sober. Everyone in Moscow loved us because we never wavered from the party line and we spit in the face of Western imperialism."

"I don't imagine that there were too many original ideas during the golden dream."

"None, but we had something better. Every person who didn't think was permitted to put his name on a waiting list for a new Bucharest apartment."

"That must have been worth keeping your lips sealed for."

"What made the golden dream work was that if the party didn't make something happen, the army would. Our leaders turned us into true believers."

"I'm still not clear about what makes a communist golden dream."

"The dream is golden when everybody goes about his business and keeps his mouth shut while the leaders live in a style only capitalists are accustomed to. We knew that we were living the dream, because we couldn't buy any shoes and socks, and there was no oil or gas to heat our homes. We prayed to the glory of the revolution and called for the downfall of the United States. We managed to do all of that with only one television station."

"It must have been the best of times," I said. "Why did you leave?"

"Everything was too cushy. I was afraid I was getting soft. I feared that if I succumbed to the attractions of the golden dream of communism, I would finally get an apartment and be stuck there forever."

"Where is this golden dream now?"

"It went west with Nadia Comaneci."

THE NEW GAME PLAN

A NEW GAME PLAN for Dan Quayle has been worked out. President Bush gets to praise Mikhail Gorbachev and Quayle gets to criticize him.

"We're working both sides of the street," my White House source told me. "In that way we keep the American conservatives and the communists happy."

"It's hard to read Bush's lips and watch the vice-president speak with a forked tongue at the same time," I confessed.

"Bush likes it that way. Besides, nothing that Quayle says is going to hurt the president's policy," my source said.

"Who made the decision for Quayle to beat up on Gorbachev?"

"The way I heard it is that Quayle went to see Bush in his office one day and complained that he had nothing to do.

"Bush said that he would let him light the Christmas tree on the Mall. Quayle informed him that Marilyn Quayle felt he should do something more vice-presidential, like warn the country of the Red Menace.

"The president said that events were going along nicely in the Eastern bloc and he wasn't sure that this was the right time to question Soviet foreign policy.

"So Quayle had a tantrum on the Oval Office rug and screamed that the Soviet Union is a totalitarian country and an even bigger danger to the world than Bulgaria."

"I didn't think that Quayle cared that much for foreign policy," I said.

"He persuaded the president that he could rattle sabers between golf games," my source went on. "Bush would be the aye-sayer and Quayle the nay-sayer of the administration, and when the right got mad at Bush, he could feed them Quayle. It's a beautiful way of convincing the country that the White House has everything under control."

"Does Quayle dislike Gorbachev?"

"Yes, because he heard that Gorby said he was a pipsqueak and a lightweight. Gorbachev once told his staff that he would never get into a boat in Malta with Quayle. The important thing is not that Quayle suggested he oppose the president, but that Bush accepted it. The president has agreed to be criticized by his own vice-president to further the cause of right-wing jingoism in the United States."

"So can we expect more criticism from Quayle on Bush's foreign policy?"

"Dan is very excited to be allowed to take on the issues. There are a lot of people out there who don't like the idea of all those commie countries getting their freedom, but Quayle is the only one in the administration who believes that it's a trick. Once he took the hard-line stance, Barbara Walters's show even booked him.

"President Bush has yet to reveal whether Dan Quayle bugs him or not. Since he was one himself, Bush knows how tough it is for a vice-president to keep busy. Therefore he is grateful that Dan has something to do. The president has put out the word that people are not to jump on Quayle just because he is marching to a different drummer."

"Or singing a different tune from the same songbook," I added.

"Something like that. The plan is to continue with Quayle attacking Bush to appease those who are mad at Gorbachev. The conservatives feel that the president is much too liberal, but that Quayle is about right. Remember this, communism may be dead in Europe, but anticommunism is very much alive in this country."

"How do you know this?"

"Ever since Quayle started Gorby-bashing he has received more invitations to give dinner speeches than President Bush."

THE NUCLEAR FAMILY

I DON'T KNOW IF the nuclear family has arrived or not, but conversations at holiday get-togethers are very different from what they were in days gone by. When relatives used to meet at Christmas, it was to exchange news about each other. Nowadays they give bulletins about strangers.

"Oprah Winfrey has lost two more pounds," cousin Alice announced. "Pass it on."

"I read in *Parade* magazine that she gained three," her sister Edith countered.

"Well, according to the *National Enquirer*, every time Oprah gains weight, they adjust the camera lenses so that she looks thin," Waldo, an in-law, declared.

Joanie, my sister-in-law, was ready to drop an atom bomb. "I heard that Elizabeth Taylor eats a cheesecake every night. Ho, ho, ho!"

"Where did you hear that?" I wanted to know.

"It was in *The Star*, which is sold in supermarkets—so it prints only the truth."

"Sometimes *The Star* makes things up," Aunt Fusty told her. "I have a rule that if *The Star* prints something and the *National Enquirer* doesn't confirm it, then it's suspect."

I tried to get the family on track by asking, "What's going on in your homes?"

Cousin Sue said, "Zsa Zsa Gabor is seventy-two years old. They found a schoolmate of hers to confirm it. There's also a rumor that she wants to do all of her community service at Elizabeth Arden's."

I spluttered, "Enough already. Don't you people have news from your own families? We haven't seen each other for a year."

There was silence.

"Leona Helmsley stands to make a lot of new friends," cousin Paul continued.

"We all know that," cousin Alice said. "It was on *Entertainment Tonight*."

My niece Maureen added, "Jane Pauley has vowed to reclaim her couch from the *Today* show."

"Do you think that NBC pushed her out the window?" cousin Edith wondered.

"*Us* magazine reported that the NBC executives had no choice but to get rid of her because she was thirty-nine years old."

I tried again.

"So is anyone in this family graduating? Is anybody getting married, and can we expect any babies this year?"

Everyone ignored me.

Cousin Pat said, "Princess Di gave Prince Charles an ultimatum. It was either her or polo. He's now sleeping in the stable with his horse."

"Where did you read *that*?" cousin Edith wanted to know.

"I didn't read it," Pat replied. "I made it up so that I could join in this conversation."

I decided on one final attempt. "Why is this family so fascinated by strangers?"

"Because they are more interesting than we are," cousin Edith declared. "Do you know anyone in this room who can match the charisma of Nancy Reagan?"

My brother-in-law said, "Donald Trump sleeps with a night light."

"How do you know that?" I asked.

"I stopped by the store before I came here. I read the whole story in *The World*, which was displayed on a newspaper rack next to the canned tomatoes."

THE SPY WHO

THE OLD MEN from the intelligence agencies drifted into the Café Mozart in East Berlin. They were all there—Smiley from MI-5, Rostov from the KGB, Fouquet from the French Sûreté, and Woodhouse from the CIA, among others.

Smiley ordered a cup of tea. "Does anyone know who'd like to buy the plans for the Warsaw Pact defense of the Northern Corridor?" he asked.

"Forget it, Smiley," Rostov told him. "There's no market for defense secrets anymore. The cold war is over and Moscow is giving away Warsaw Pact plans, not buying them."

Woodhouse said, "I know a Czech mole in Margaret Thatcher's cabinet if anyone is interested."

Smiley shook his head. "No one cares about moles in London. They're a dime a dozen, and what damage can they do now? Let's face it, men, we are no longer essential. The cloak-and-dagger days are over."

"That's the way it is whenever the cold war melts down. As soon as the war starts, it's Ivan this and Ivan that, but when the killing stops, they tell you to shove your stolen blueprints in your shoes and go home," Rostov complained.

An East German secret-service man named Kraut joined in the conversation: "I was in the department for thirty years. I caught more traitors trying to climb over the Berlin Wall than any other government official. Now I am going to lose my pension because there is no Wall. I ask you, gentlemen, Is that fair?"

"Oh, shut up, Kraut," yelled Fouquet. "You were a butcher, not a spy."

"What's the difference?" Kraut wanted to know.

Smiley said, "It's too late to cry over spilled milk. We're all in the prime of our careers. Surely someone has a use for us in these terrible times of *perestroika* and *glasnost*."

Woodhouse answered, "I doubt it. Every country that has declared independence wants to trade military secrets for bread and cheese. I was offered the complete plans for a brand-new Soviet submarine the other day, and Washington wouldn't let me buy them. Apparently the CIA had used up its entire espionage budget on tickets to the Moiseyev Ballet."

Fouquet added, "The worst aspect of all this is that beautiful foreign women are no longer attracted to us."

"I noticed that," Rostov said. "Women used to find us glamorous, but now they're much more taken with Eastern bloc economists."

Woodhouse began to reminisce. "I had a girl in Leipzig, and I told her that I'd come back for her when I rescued her boyfriend, East Germany's greatest mathematician. I heard from her the other day. She and the mathematician are going to open an H&R Block office in Leipzig. She was sorry that they didn't need me anymore."

Smiley was sucking on the lemon from his tea. "There is no reason to go home. If I tell people that I was a spy for MI-5, they just laugh at me and say, 'That was dumb.' "

"It's the same with the Americans," Woodhouse said. "Nobody wants a cold-war warrior when the saber-rattling has stopped. I think I'll stay in East Berlin and operate a radar trap for people driving over fifty-five miles an hour on the autobahn."

Fouquet concluded, "There's just not much for me to do.

Maybe I could work for an Eastern bloc credit company. If there is going to be peace, there has to be credit card fraud."

Smiley was called to the phone. He came back white-faced. "It was John le Carré. He told me he is going to drop me from his next book. Spies who come in from the cold aren't selling anymore."

ANSWER THE QUESTION

ONE OF THE big breakthroughs in television news is that it is now possible to conduct an entire interview without having the subject of that interview answer a single question. Developed at the Sam Donaldson School of Communications, this method is being used by anchormen and anchorwomen all over the country.

Here's how it goes:

"Mr. Secretary. Your department intends to spend two hundred fifty million dollars for development of underwater underwear for the Navy. In light of our present fiscal situation, can you explain why you are asking for these funds?"

"It is my opinion . . ."

"Please answer the question yes or no. Did you ever go out on a date with Barney Frank?"

"I resent that question. I wish to be emphatic about this . . ."

"You appear to be beating around the bush, Mr. Secretary. If you don't want to respond, I can't make you."

"What was the question?"

"Do you plan to take the Fifth Amendment rather than testify about what happened when you and Sam Pierce had a joint
bank account in Chevy Chase?"

"May I answer that?"

"Of course. That's what you're here for."

"I have never—repeat, never . . ."

"Just as I thought, Mr. Secretary. You've been toying with us
since you came on the show. We ask you a simple question and
you pretend that you're deaf. Shall we go on? Did you have any
idea that Jackie Mason was going to get into so much trouble in
New York City?"

"No, I didn't."

"How can you say that, when ethnic politics is your specialty?"

"That's not true . . ."

"Mr. Secretary, we're starting to run out of time. Would you
please get to the point."

"I *am* getting to the point."

"Let that go for a moment and we'll discuss the Stealth
bomber's frequent-flyer program."

"I don't know anything about the Stealth bomber."

"You didn't say that when you went to the president and sold
him on refitting five more battleships."

"You've got me mixed up with someone else."

"Can I assume from your response that once again you are
refusing to answer the question?"

"Can I speak?"

"Yes, but make it short."

"You have taken everything I've said and . . ."

"That's about all the time I can give you, Mr. Secretary. I
want to thank you for being on the show and shedding so much
light on such a variety of subjects. Now after this break I'll sum
up with my partner, Roland Lockjaw. . . .

"Roland, didn't you find the secretary evasive?"

"Very much so. He came here determined not to say a word and he stuck to his game plan. I am amazed at what few insights he had about the situation in the Brazilian rain forests."

"I guess the only thing we can assume is that the secretary is in more trouble than anyone realizes."

"How do you figure that?"

"Well, several times he tried to answer my first question while I was already asking the second one. People don't do that unless they have a great deal to hide."

ROCK WARFARE

THE LATEST SECRET military weapon from the American arsenal showed up in Panama when U.S. military forces tried to drive Manuel Noriega out of the Vatican embassy by blasting him with rock music all day long. While it failed to achieve its goal, it is now believed that the tactic resulted in a lot of hard-of-hearing Panamanians.

The idea of using rock music to dislodge ex–heads of state and other sleazy enemies was thought up by the Psychological Warfare Division at the Pentagon. It was actually the invention of a senior staff member, Colonel McArthur Wolfpack. Colonel Wolfpack got the idea after he had been driven out of his home by his son's repeated playing of the Grateful Dead's "Skeletons in the Closet."

I spoke to Colonel Wolfpack as he sat ramrod straight on top of four loudspeakers at Andrews Air Force Base.

"Any casualties?" I yelled at him.

"We lost three microphones and one woofer, but we knocked out four Panamanian National Guardsmen, three nuns and a papal nuncio."

"Any damage to Noriega's eardrums?" I asked.

Wolfpack said, "He's starting to feel the pressure. We're going to fire off the Rolling Stones' top ten tomorrow, and if that doesn't make him surrender, nothing will."

I shouted up, "Are we to assume that rock warfare is the wave of the future?"

"It's a proven deterrent. We know that no grown-up can survive four hours of Led Zeppelin. We believe that any tin-horn dictator will come out with his hands high rather than listen to three Jefferson Airplane singles."

"What about the Geneva Conventions, which forbid the playing of loud music around a diplomatic mission?"

"We don't recognize the Geneva Conventions. Noriega is a thief and a drug dealer, and we will torture him with U2's *Rattle and Hum* no matter what world opinion is."

"If rock music is such a successful weapon, why is Noriega still in the Vatican embassy?"

"The CIA reports that he may have taken earplugs in there with him."

"Why didn't the CIA know this at the beginning?"

"They were watching the back of the building. Noriega came in through the front. But we're not worried. We have more rock records in stock than Noriega has earplugs."

"The Vatican has officially complained about the noise, and Washington announced that they might knock it off."

"That's typical of Washington. They give us the rock war weapons and then they chicken out to Rome. If they just let us play one Madonna platter, we will have Noriega sticking his fingers in his ears and running naked down the streets of Panama City."

Wolfpack told me that many countries are interested in rock war but the United States is worried that the weapon is too powerful to be allowed to fall into the hands of foreign governments. "Can you imagine what the Libyans would do to us if they could play Michael Jackson at high volume in front of an American consulate?"

"Are you going back to Panama?" I asked the colonel.

"Yes, as soon as we add two more boom boxes to our amplifiers. We shall return, and this time we're going to knock Noriega out of bed with Bruce Springsteen's greatest hits if it kills us."

HOCH, HOCH, HOCH!

W<small>AY BACK IN</small> the beginning of time, before the Berlin Wall was built, there was rubble, and it was possible to go from West Berlin to East Berlin across the sea of rocks without having anyone stop you.

In May 1951, I paid my first visit to Berlin.

It was May Day, and I was drawn to East Berlin because it was the main way-station on the road to the evil empire. All I tell you here is true. Every Western intelligence agency has pictures of me to prove it.

131

There were no signs to the May Day parade, so I followed a crowd of people, assuming that they were going in the right direction. I walked through the jammed, narrow streets for eight or nine blocks, and then we all turned as one and came out onto the Unter den Linden, East Berlin's answer to Fifth Avenue.

As soon as we made the turn, the undisciplined stragglers suddenly spread out neatly in files, banners were unfurled, and hammer-and-sickle flags went up—I was smack in the middle of my first communist May Day parade.

Marching alongside me was a platoon of brownshirts from the young Communist Party. I eyed them nervously as I tried to figure an escape. Before I could make any plans, a ten-year-old brownshirt handed me a red flag which I waved furiously in the air.

People chanted as we marched. First we all screamed, "Death to Eisenhower!" and then I heard the word "NATO," and I shouted, *"Hoch, hoch, hoch!"* This infuriated the ten-year-old and his friends because apparently I was cheering the fact that NATO was taking over the world.

It didn't take me long to get with it. I had to because East Berlin policemen and their dogs lined the curb and the only safe direction to go was forward.

I yelled for the destruction of all Wall Street warmongers, Konrad Adenauer, Yugoslavia and the Rockefellers. I also waved my red flag in salute to Lenin and Stalin and, of course, the East German five-year plan.

I did this under the strict gaze of the ten-year-old, who kept whispering to his comrades every time I stumbled. I took my cue from his cries of *"Hoch, hoch, hoch!"* especially when the USSR was mentioned over the loudspeaker.

We finally arrived at the Tribune of Honor, where the East German premier, the mayor of East Berlin and every damn communist behind the Iron Curtain were reviewing the troops. I had no choice but to give it my best shot, and I shouted, "Burn all the Army PXs in Germany!" As I walked past the stand, I was sure that I was starring in a movie called *An American Goes to East Berlin*, produced and directed by the CIA.

We continued down the Unter den Linden another five blocks before disbanding. I figured that if the brownshirts were going to beat me up they would do it at that time, but they seemed to have gotten used to me. I offered to give the red flag back to the ten-year-old but he refused to take it. I guess that I had proved myself as a good communist when I called for the destruction of all U.S. nuclear bombs—not once, but five times. In any case, the kid handed me a piece of sausage which he had taken out of his pants pocket.

That was about forty years ago, so the boy must be fifty years old today. With the wall coming down, the memory of the East Berlin parade came back to me. I wonder what happened to that young kid? Did he turn into a hotshot Communist functionary, or did he sour on the system after a half-dozen May Day parades? Did he come out of the cold last week to see the glitter of West Berlin, or did he sit in his dank apartment and curse the darkness?

Most of all, I wonder if he ever asks, "What happened to that stranger who marched in our parade and, when it was over, broke into an unbelievable sprint to the West Berlin border?"

THE GRADUATION SPEECH

THIS HAS BEEN a very exciting year for the Miss Wellesley Graduation Speaker Competition. The graduation ceremony itself will be held June 1. As most of you know, the winner was Barbara Bush, who scored a 9 in the cap-and-gown category, and a 10 in the bathing suit contest.

Runner-up was Hilda Marton of Los Angeles, who played the violin and harmonica at the finals. If anything should go wrong with Mrs. Bush's plans, Hilda will fill in as speaker.

"Congratulations," I told Hilda. "It's quite an honor to be the runner-up in the Miss Wellesley speaker's contest."

Hilda said, "I've dreamed about it all my life. I have a great message to impart to the young women of America, and I hope that Mrs. Bush gets delayed by Mrs. Gorbachev so that I can make the speech."

"What are you going to tell them?"

"I intend to say that there is a lot more happening in people's kitchens than there is on the floor of Bloomingdale's."

"There has been criticism that Mrs. Bush got where she is only because of her husband. Do you believe that this is fair?"

"It's the opposite. President Bush is where he is today only because of Mrs. Bush. Women like the First Lady perform amazing tasks, when people think that they are not doing anything at all. My message to the Wellesley graduates is: To be a success, do your own thing and your husband's thing as well."

"Won't their husbands be mad?" I asked Hilda.

"Not really. Manipulating men has always been a Wellesley strong suit."

"The students will be happy to know that."

"There are some graduates who don't want to listen to a speaker unless she has made her mark as chairman of the board of *The Washington Post*. Whether they like it or not, most of the Wellesley graduates will have babies. It's important that they hear this from someone like me who has driven a station wagon in a car pool than from a person who invests money for a teachers' pension fund. I am going to make the point that we all have choices, but you can't go skinny-dipping with a two-window office on the fortieth floor of a Wall Street building."

"You really gave this graduation speech a lot of thought."

"That's my job as a runner-up speaker. Mrs. Bush and I come from a generation of women who put our children and husbands before ourselves. The present generation, which happens to be made up of our children, thinks that we're crazy. Yet our kids wouldn't be able to do one darn thing if we hadn't ironed their skirts in the basement."

"I'll bet the Wellesley girls would hate to hear that. Do you think Mrs. Bush will say it?"

"No, she's too polite. She'll probably tell them that they have a right to think anything they want to, which I feel is a mistake."

"I don't imagine it will go over very well if you keep telling them to be good wives."

"I'm not asking for a standing ovation."

"Have you spoken to Mrs. Bush about the contents of your speech, in case she doesn't make it?"

"I tried once, but she was playing in the garden with the grandchildren."

"No wonder Wellesley students are mad at her."

"HELLO, BOB"

LIKE SO MANY other people, Robert Shoun acquired a cellular phone in 1990. This came as a surprise to his friends because Shoun hates phones and he never answered his calls in the past. There is no doubt that Bob is enjoying his new toy. I know this because he called me four times in one day.

"How is everything with you?" he wanted to know.

"That's a stupid question, Bob. Why are you calling?"

"I got this new car phone and I have to ring somebody."

"You never telephoned when I needed you," I told him. "Now I hear from you all the time."

Bob became defensive. "Can I help it if I prefer to call from my car? I just don't like doing it from the office."

"If you have to talk to someone, why don't you call your wife?"

"She isn't taking my calls anymore. She took her telephone off the hook two weeks ago."

"Surely you have some business buddies you can get in touch with," I said.

"I do," he answered. "But most of them are putting me on hold. They figure anyone who calls from a car phone doesn't have much to do. Give me a break—talk to me for the next three blocks."

"I ran out of things to say after you went through a red light on K Street last week. Bob, you should have thought about how many people would answer your calls before you bought the telephone."

"I did, but the ones I counted on let me down. You would think they'd be eager to converse with someone who is gridlocked in front of the White House."

"They are, but sometimes your phone fades out on them, Bob, and that can be very annoying."

"Who told you that my phone faded out?" he asked.

"Michael Kahme. He said that every time you ring him up, you pass a dead spot and he can't hear a word you're saying."

"He's just making it up. I am known to everyone because of the clarity of my calls."

"Bob, I have to go. Joe Califano is calling me from his car and he gets nervous when I leave him hanging."

"It's okay with me. I'm going to be busy. I have to dial the weather service, and then nine-one-one, and after that the eight hundred number to order cut-rate Pavarotti records."

"You'd be better off forgetting the phone and listening to your radio."

"You don't understand—a cellular phone has to be used. I keep looking at it and I know that there is someone out there waiting to hear from me. Maybe I'll call information in San Antonio."

"Do you know anyone in San Antonio?"

"No, but it would be nice to find out how many Shouns live in Texas."

"Tell me, Bob. Have you ever made a call that couldn't wait until you reached the office?"

"I don't think so, but I've made many to people who were terribly impressed when they found out that I was calling from my car. Once you have a phone in your automobile, others respect you for who you really are."

"That's probably true. Can I go now?"

"Okay, but you better take my car number if you get the urge to talk to me."

"Why would I want to do that?"

"To thank me for using AT&T."

WE'RE BROKE

AN ASSISTANT SECRETARY OF STATE entered the State Department's kitchen and said, "Old Mother Hubbard, we need five billion bones for East Germany."

Mother Hubbard replied, "My cupboard is bare. Hungary cleaned me out last week."

The assistant secretary sounded grim. "Nation after nation is achieving independence, but they can't do it without bones. Have you looked carefully?"

Mother Hubbard told him, "I know a bare shelf when I see one. If I were you, I'd inform the next country asking for bones that it is barking up the wrong tree."

"We can't do that," the assistant secretary said. "We've been telling the people of every enslaved country that if they break the chains that bind them, we will supply them with everything needed to become a democratic nation."

"Look, I just store the bones. I don't make them. Before the White House tells Bulgaria to jump over to our side, they could at least check to see how many bones are left in the cupboard."

The assistant secretary became agitated. "What's going on today is bigger than a breadbasket. We thought that only one country would liberate itself this year—and perhaps another country would do the same next year. How could we have known that they would all torch their governments at the same time? If you don't have any bones in the cabinet, do you have *anything* that Romania can chew on?"

Old Mother Hubbard went to the cupboard and opened the doors wide. "Do you see something that I don't? And why the pressure?"

"Guess who's coming to dinner? Lithuania, Estonia and Latvia."

"You're kidding."

"And Chile."

"Tell Chile to cool it—at least until we find some bones for Panama. Why don't we just issue junk bonds to the liberated countries and charge it to Bloomingdale's?"

An intern came in and announced, "Mr. Assistant Secretary, the Polish ambassador is out in the hall. He says the president promised Lech Walesa six billion bones when he toasted him at the White House. He was wondering if he could have them now."

The assistant secretary responded, "I was there, and the president promised no such thing. Why is it that every time some freedom fighters liberate themselves, they come to us for aid?"

Mother Hubbard added, "Someone should tell Poland that knocking off communism does not guarantee them a Rose Garden. In any case, when it concerns bones, I'm not going to give any to El Salvador. Doesn't the president know that the cupboard is bare?"

The assistant secretary said, "He does and he doesn't. Every time we tell him we have no bones, he says, 'We would if we cut the capital gains tax.' "

Mother Hubbard sounded upset. "Do you know what really

gives me nightmares? I am so afraid that someday you will come into the kitchen and inform me that the Chinese have overthrown their leaders and we have to give them bones."

"I don't see that happening soon," the assistant secretary assured her.

"I'd trust you more, but you are the person who declared that the Berlin Wall would never come down," Mother Hubbard reminded him.

"Can we talk about Central America?" the assistant secretary asked.

"We can talk about it as long as we don't have to give them any bones," Mother Hubbard warned.

"But we must. Those countries aren't going to come over to our side for peanuts."

BAG BANKERS

THE DOPE WAR continues. On television I saw a whole bunch of bankers who were accused of laundering millions and millions of dollars in narcotics payments.

Their hearing was held in Tampa, Florida, although the bank was located in Luxembourg, with branches in Miami. Alas, all the bankers plea-bargained. The Justice Department's deal was that there would be no fine and little jail, particularly if the bankers agreed to testify against Noriega.

Dope bankers' friends everywhere rejoiced at the news. Manuel de Colombia, spokesman for the Drug Launderers of America, declared, "These are good people. They wear nice clothes and own beautiful boats. You cannot hold them responsible for the drug trade."

"Why not?" I asked him.

"Because those who launder dope money never see the dope. They have nothing to do with it. They only move dollars from one place to another. It's just business."

"And yet," I added, "there wouldn't be a drug trade without launderers. They make it possible. Surely they should serve a little time when they get caught."

Manuel shook his head. "I can't believe my ears. You want a banker to do time just because he takes cash deposits from agricultural interests in Colombia?"

I replied, "Suppose the money comes from cocaine. Do you believe that the bankers should still be let off?"

"It's impossible to run a bank in Florida if you keep asking about the source of the money. Besides, a bank that deals in narcotics earnings can lend a lot more to its legitimate customers than one that doesn't."

"Do you think that the government has a right to make deals with bankers who launder drug profits?"

Manuel said, "It not only has a right, it has a duty to see that they don't go to jail. If we sent every banker who was involved in dope sales to the slammer, there would be no one to manage the drive-in teller stations. These people are among the classiest in the country. You won't find a finer group anywhere. They not only play good golf, they give to the blood bank. Are you going to ask them to do time simply because they had interests in international commerce?"

"Yes, I am. I hope and pray that anyone involved in the sale of dope will wind up cleaning prison toilets for the rest of his life."

"Did it ever occur to you that these bankers could nail Noriega?"

141

"Frankly, no. But I would think that the bankers could do more damage to the country than the pipsqueak from Panama. If you let the bankers off free, they'll go straight back to the laundromat. I'd rather *they* take a poison pill than Noriega."

Manuel was starting to worry that his message wasn't getting across. He tried again. "Is it so hard for you to understand that maybe society needs money launderers to turn bad money into good money? Perhaps the proceeds did come from selling dope, but before the bankers got through with it, they were financing condominiums in the Everglades. I know most of those launderers personally, and I would trust them with my sister."

"Provided your sister was a courier for a drug cartel in Peru."

"We have a saying in the drug-banking business: 'You wash my money and I'll wash yours.' "

SPACE FOR SALE

WHAT I LIKE about today's magazines is that it is no longer possible to tell the difference between the editorial copy and the advertising.

With the sophisticated computer techniques at their disposal, publishers are constantly challenging the readers. They are doing this with "advertorials," which seem to be the wave of the future.

The other day I was reading a story in a newsmagazine about the king of Morocco.

"This is some king," I remarked to Hyman Bixby, an editor of the magazine. "Your reporters think he's hot stuff."

"Not *our* reporters. That's an advertorial," he told me. "It was paid for by Morocco. It says so at the top of the page."

"I can't see anything at the top."

Bixby handed me a magnifying glass, and after five minutes I found the words "Special Advertising Section." "By gum, it does say 'advertising.' It looks exactly like editorial copy."

"Well, it isn't. Do you think that we'd sell our independent news reporting for money?"

"I hope not," I said. "On the other hand, if you hadn't drawn my attention to it, I was all set to buy Moroccan savings bonds immediately after reading the story."

"The purpose of advertorials is to give the person in the news an opportunity to tell his side of the story. In that way we present two opinions for the price of one, and we make a lot more money besides."

I asked, "Doesn't it bother you that the editorial people have lost control of the copy in the magazine?"

"Now you're being picky. Look at the Exxon *Valdez* oil spill. In the past, the oil companies could not defend themselves. Thanks to advertorials they have as good a chance of vindicating themselves as the environmentalists do."

"How does the reader know whether the advertorial is telling the truth?"

"There isn't enough money in the world to make us go into the tank for the king of Morocco, or any other member of a royal family. An advertorial enables us to cover areas of the globe that we cannot afford to staff. In the case of Morocco, our readers will always prefer a seven-page paid spread about it to no news at all about North Africa."

I said, "I guess the trick of an advertorial is to make the warning so small that no one can read it."

Hyman confided, "Our dream is to reduce the word 'advertising' to such tiny print that people will need a microscope to read it. At present, ninety percent of our subscribers can't tell the difference. It's interesting to see the reaction of readers who are unaware that it is a paid spread. Most of them want to nominate the king of Morocco for the Nobel Peace Prize."

"Do readers like advertorials?"

"We're not sure, because they don't know that they're reading them. Some are confused when they learn that Qaddafi is really Abraham Lincoln in drag. The reason we get away with it is that Americans would rather read good news than bad news, and all our paid supplements are upbeat. Publishers who accept advertorials in their magazines are interested in only one thing."

"What's that?"

"The bottom line."

PARENTS IN FEAR

"GOOD MORNING, EVERYONE. Welcome to TV's *Fighting with Phil*. Today our topic of conversation is parents who are afraid of their children. We have with us Horace Plankton, Stanley Pluto, Andrea Peaches and Sally Peters. All of whom suffer from kiddophobia—the fear that their offspring will not love them.

"Horace, when did you first realize that you were afraid of your children?"

"When my son was four years old and I told him not to climb up on a ladder. He kept doing it and I screamed at him. His face turned red and he burst into tears. At that moment I said to myself, 'My God, what have I done?' I've been afraid of him ever since."

"What about you, Mr. Pluto?"

"I have always had this secret fear that if I do anything to discipline my daughter, she will reject me as a loving parent."

"And this causes you great anxiety?"

"Yes. If I once thought that she was withholding her love from me, I wouldn't be able to sleep at night."

"Andrea Peaches of Great Neck, Long Island, has three sons and has been afraid of all of them since they were born. What seems to be the problem?"

"Well, Phil, I don't like to see kids sobbing—I never have. The minute one of my sons chokes up, I am certain that *I* have done something wrong."

"How old are they?"

"Thirty-four, thirty-five and thirty-seven. The one I worry about the most is my thirty-seven-year-old. When he was young he used to hide under the stairs and refuse to come out. It frightened me so much that I lowered milk and graham crackers to him so that he didn't think I was a terrible mother. He still looks hurt when he sees me."

"Stanley Pluto. What makes you fearful?"

"My son, Alan, is very sensitive and has a terrible temper. He wouldn't talk to us when we asked him to eat his oatmeal. His mother and I didn't press him because we were afraid that our relationship would never be the same."

"Sally Peters. Over the years you have suffered from your fear of children. Can you tell us what it all means?"

"My father was afraid of me when I was young. If he wouldn't let me watch television, I threatened to tie myself to the water heater. Naturally, I felt as if I had a lot of power. When my kids started growing up, I realized they were pulling the same tricks on me that I had played on my father. I told them I wasn't buying it, so they began doing worse things, like putting the baby in a shopping cart and running through the middle of the parking lot."

"Is your husband afraid of your children?"

"He's afraid of the boy—I am afraid of the girls."

"We will now take some telephone calls. Yes, Peoria."

"I'd like to question Mr. Pluto. My kid is six, and I think he knows I am frightened of him, because every time I tell him not to hit his brother he does it anyhow. Is there some way of controlling his behavior without my son thinking that I don't love him?"

"It's very hard to convince a six-year-old that you care for him after you have yelled no at him several times. The first words a child learns to say are: 'You don't love me.' Most parents will cover their ears rather than hear their offspring say that."

"And now another caller. Hello, Redford."

"My question is to Mr. Plankton. Is it possible to be a good parent and not worry about whether your children love you or not?"

"In some countries it's possible—but not in America."

FAX

THE MOST IMPORTANT new word in the English language is "fax." It refers to a method of sending paper by telephone. For example, if I want to shoot you a story from this book, I put it into my fax machine and it is transmitted to your fax machine in seconds.

Because the United States shuffles more paper than any other country on the planet, the fax machine has changed the way we deal with problems.

This is all you hear in offices these days: "Will you fax me that report? . . . I'll fax you my objections and then you fax everything to the client in San Francisco."

The trouble with faxing papers is that people judge how hard you are working by the amount of faxing that you do. In most offices, those who fax only every hour are thought to be less productive than those who fax every fifteen minutes. John O'Connor is one of the great faxers of Washington. He has a fax in the office, one at home and one in his car. During his lunch hour he thinks nothing of faxing the U.S. budget to a friend in Singapore.

"You were an early faxer before it became popular. Does it discourage you that everybody is doing it now?" I asked him.

"The more the merrier," he replied. "Don't forget, it takes

147

two to fax. Excuse me, I have to fax an anniversary card to my wife."

"Doesn't she mind getting her anniversary greetings by fax machine?"

"Why should she? It's on her desk right away."

"Is there a knack to faxing?"

"Like everything else, there are good faxers and bad ones. A good faxer knows exactly how to insert the paper so that the print comes out nice and clean at the other end. Some people are born faxers—lawyers, for example. They can service two clients on two different telephone lines at the same time and charge them both the full fee. Doctors are starting to fax throat cultures to each other, and people are even sending love letters on the machine."

"Why?"

"When you're in love you want the whole Bell system to know it."

"Do some people in your office fax more than others?"

"Damn right they do, and it's costing us a bundle. There is a guy here who faxes all the baseball scores to his bookie in Las Vegas. We have a woman who transmits Ann Landers's column to everyone in her aerobics class. We're looking at an electronic revolution that will change our lives. Today we're faxing paper—someday we could be faxing people."

"You mean we'll be sending people by telephone?"

"It's well within the realm of possibility. The world is getting smaller thanks to the fax machine. First we communicated by Morse code, then by voice and now by paper. Tomorrow we may place our kids in fax machines and send them to camp."

All the time O'Connor was talking to me he was inserting memoranda into one machine and ripping off messages from the other one.

"The trick," he said, "is to fax more outgoing material than you take in."

"How do you do that?" I wanted to know.

"Fax everybody. My greatest moment as a faxer was when I sent an entire manuscript to a publisher I had never met. I tied up his line for nine hours because there was no way he could turn his machine off."

POOR DEMOGRAPHICS

ONE OF THE things bugging network TV executives is that too many older Americans are watching television. This is causing havoc with the advertising community, which puts great store in demographics. The word in the advertising suite is that young viewers buy products—older ones watch *People's Court*.

As much as they like them personally, TV businessmen cannot making a living off citizens who follow the silver fox. What advertisers fear most is that their shows will suffer from "poor demographics."

Alf London, with whom I play checkers in Lafayette Park, said, "I know I am nothing more than a statistic, but dammit, why must I be considered an over-the-hill one?"

I told him, "Well, Alf, the networks have to deliver a young audience if the advertiser is going to buy the time—and viewers with poor demographics don't even pay for the studio lights. Having weak purchasing power is worse than having bad breath."

"What makes them so sure my demographics don't measure

up? Some of us with baggy trousers have a ton of money to spend. Why, we could watch Connie Chung one day and clear out Macy's the next."

"They don't count individuals when they play the demographics game. The ratings companies throw everyone into the pot, and then decide which are the good advertising prospects and which ones are the bad."

"It doesn't seem fair."

"I think that network executives are never fair—they even include their own mothers on the list of lousy spenders."

"Where is it written that although we don't have the same purchasing power as Mr. and Mrs. Yuppie, we can't buy all the panty hose they sell on *Monday Night Football*?"

"No one ever said that people with inferior demographics should not watch television—you're just not supposed to let anyone know you're doing it. The advertiser puts on a program to sell his product. He doesn't need senior citizens who sit there like couch potatoes on their wallets."

"So why don't they run an advisory at the bottom of the screen saying, 'This program is not suitable for viewers who just wait for the sales. Senior citizen discretion is advised'?"

"You are not very sympathetic toward the networks. They don't like to deal with below-par demographics any more than the sponsor down the street. But you can't spend millions of dollars on programming that appeals only to people with bad feet."

"The reason seniors watch so much television is that they don't like to leave the house," Al yelled. "We may not buy as much stuff as the baby boomers, but at least we have never turned our backs on *I Love Lucy*."

"I don't know why you're taking all this personally. You may not be the most popular group on the marketing-research hit parade, but nobody is trying to prevent you from watching TV. All they are saying is that they don't figure you to be in the market for Guess? jeans."

Alf was still irritable. "I wish you wouldn't keep saying that. Maybe we don't buy ski boots, but we're on American Airlines flights to visit our grandchildren every chance we get."

"Forget I brought the subject up. I am the last person to tell someone else he has poor demographics."

"I never miss *60 Minutes*," he said. "Is that good or bad for a show?"

"It's good for the show, but the advertiser couldn't care less."

I AM NOT AND NEVER HAVE . . .

"THE MOSCOW COMMITTEE ON UN-SOVIET AFFAIRS will come to order. I call Misha Obolensky as a witness."

"I am ready when you are, Mr. Chairman."

"Misha, are you now or have you ever been a member of the Communist Party?"

"No. I just went to a few of its dances."

"Misha Obolensky, I have in my hand the names of fifty million members of the Communist Party. Would you please tell us if you know any of them?"

"I don't recognize the names, but then again, I live in the suburbs."

"A likely story, Misha. Our records show that on May first, 1985, you marched in a May Day parade with the Lenin Daughters of the Revolution. Do you deny this?"

"It was an accident. I was looking for the GUM department

store and I wound up at the head of the march. It was a terrible thing to do, but how was I supposed to know that all the people in the parade were fellow travelers?"

"You should have known. Moscow was full of Communists at that time."

"Mr. Chairman, it was my wife who made me go to Communist Party meetings. She told me that if I did, we would get a larger apartment and be allowed to shop at the Party store."

"Are you denouncing your wife for being a Communist?"

"I would like to very much. Her first name is Lara."

"Misha Obolensky, you don't get off just because you denounced your wife. We want names of other people in your cell. You owe it to us to provide a list of Reds."

"You will have to torture me before I reveal the names of the traitors I associated with."

"Misha, we can hold you for contempt of the Presidium."

"Why didn't you say so? Here is a list in alphabetical order. All of them said nice things about Joseph Stalin at one time or another."

"This committee is trying to ferret out every Marxist-Leninist in the Soviet Union. We cannot do it until mealy-mouthed pinkos like you tell us what took place at your meetings."

"What happened at a Communist Party meeting? We laughed, we sang, we partied, and we played spin the proletariat."

"You made no speeches about the world order of socialism, and burying the West?"

"It was just cocktail conversation. You know how Reds are when they get together and have nothing to talk about."

"Would you care to give us details of what else your cell discussed?"

"What cell? It was a club—we went to soccer games and Lenin's tomb. Believe me, Mr. Chairman, we had nothing to do with the revolution whatsoever."

"If you didn't, who did?"

"The Trotskyites. They're the ones who imposed a one-party system on the motherland. My members were for the Democratic Party. I swear it on my wife's head—would you like her address?"

"Misha, did you ever put microfilm in a pumpkin in your garden?"

"I think I may have once. They were nude photographs of Comrade Brezhnev, whom we all hated and feared. Having pictures of him doesn't make me a Communist."

"It doesn't make you a Lithuanian either."

DOING TOUGH TIME

IT'S BEEN A tough time for people involved with Irangate. General Richard Secord was sentenced to two years' probation for his role as one of the architects of the infamous arms plot.

Most people were shaken by the harsh sentence. The next one was even tougher. Albert Hakim, another conspirator, was given two years' probation and a fine of $5,000. He was punished further by being told that the only money he could keep from the plot was the $1.7 million he had deposited in Switzerland.

"Why the cruel and unusual punishment?" civil libertarians wanted to know.

"We are trying to teach a lesson to everyone who flouts the

law," the Lord High Chief Plea-Bargainer in the Justice Department informed me. "When people see what North, Secord and Hakim got, they will think twice about diddling with the law of the land."

"Be honest. Didn't you roll over and make a deal with Secord and Hakim so that they would testify against Poindexter? Isn't he the last link in the chain that leads straight to the Oval Office?"

"If we had made a deal with both of them, why would we insist on such harsh probation? The Justice Department doesn't make deals with people who plead guilty to high crimes and misdemeanors."

"The rumor on the street is that you're always willing to make deals—no matter what the felon does. There is a story out that you will drop charges against Noriega if he turns state's evidence and testifies against Fidel Castro and Daniel Ortega."

"There is no truth to that at all," he assured me. "We do not plea-bargain with prisoners of war. Noriega will be given all his rights according to the Geneva Conventions, where, incidentally, he has all his money. He will then receive the sentence he is entitled to, depending on his name, rank and serial number."

"I believe you," I said. "Suppose Noriega ratted on Imelda Marcos. Would that get him tickets to the Super Bowl?"

"We make deals only if a person can lead us to other people. Now, if Noriega wanted to tell us what he knows about Leona Helmsley, we might start talking about putting him in a minimum security lockup. But he's going to have to give us more than her old IRS 1040 returns. It'll be hard for Noriega to plea-bargain with us when we've told the whole world that he's Mr. Big."

"Suppose Noriega demands that every American secret be produced at his trial. Will you plea-bargain with him just to shut him up?"

"We will never be reasonable with anyone who puts the

government in an embarrassing position. The Justice Department must prosecute those who resort to lawless behavior, whether they take money from the Iranians, the contras, or a savings and loan bank in Albuquerque. If we're going to be tough on North, Secord and Hakim, then we have to be just as tough on Noriega. After all, we started a war to get him."

"Speaking of war," I said, "has it ever occurred to you that since Noriega is a prisoner of war, he is entitled to a ticker-tape parade?"

"He's not going to get one. We didn't give one to North, Secord or Hakim, and Poindexter won't get one either, even if he blows the whistle on Ronald Reagan."

"Why not?"

"Because a ticker-tape parade could give people the wrong idea about those who violate the law."

THE JUNKYARD

I ARRIVED HOME AND waited for an opportune moment to break the news to my wife. It came between the lentil soup and the meatloaf.

"Drexel Burnham went down the toilet."

She dropped the mashed potatoes.

"How could they? They're not a savings and loan."

"It's worse," I told her. "Drexel deals in junk bonds, and if it dumps them all on the market, Wall Street will lose its sense of humor. We have to find a way of keeping Drexel afloat so that the pension funds and brokerage houses won't go under."

I could see her getting angry. "If they were called junk bonds, why did people buy them in the first place?"

"Because they paid more interest than the dowdy run-of-the-mill bonds, which have no sex appeal. Investors need adventure as much as anybody else."

"I don't understand why we needed junk bonds at all."

"The sharks needed them to raise money so one raider could buy another raider's company. Take R. J. Reynolds Nabisco. No one could have bought it if Drexel Burnham hadn't raised the money to make the deal. Without junk bonds, takeover artists would never make a living. Unfortunately, Drexel got stuck with so many bonds of its own that it had to file for bankruptcy. This means that if Drexel owes you anything, you get ten cents on the dollar."

"Why can't the government bail out Drexel?" my wife asked.

"They won't, although they have good reason to. The government is among the biggest holders of junk bonds," I told her. "They picked them up from all the savings and loans they took over. The S&L safes were stuffed with bonds. But so far there is no bailout."

"Where was the government at the beginning, when Drexel floated all the junk bonds?"

"It couldn't interfere," I said, "because you have to allow the system to work until someone proves that it doesn't."

"I read where people like Mike Milken made millions selling the Drexel bonds."

"Possibly he did, but we can't hold him responsible for the nosedive. He took his money up front."

"I absolutely refuse to worry about one more financial institution whose main product is greed," she declared.

"You mustn't talk that way. Junk bonds made America what it is today. We can't turn our backs on Drexel Burnham because its paper is worthless. As Americans we must say, 'We didn't like what you did, and we didn't understand why you did it. Yet we're ready to forgive and forget your mistakes, because bailing out companies is what Americans do best.' "

"You really want me to say that?"

"That or something like it. You have to think of junk bonds as meatloaf. As long as someone wants meatloaf it has great value. But the minute no one wants it you can't even give it to the dog."

"Is that my lesson in banking for this evening?"

"All I'm trying to do is prepare you for the day when George Bush announces, 'I am asking every man, woman and child to contribute to the Drexel Burnham Meatloaf Relief Fund.' "

She had the mashed potatoes poised to throw.

"All right, already. Don't help Drexel Burnham dig out from its junk bond mess! But remember this—if Mike Milken winds up sleeping in the park with the bonds as blankets, you will have to live with it for the rest of your life."

PREDICTIONS

PRESIDENTS OF THE UNITED STATES are not the only ones who hire soothsayers to tell them what the future will bring. Large corporations also sign up former cabinet officers and foreign-policy experts to warn them what to expect around the globe.

These experts don't come cheap, but they're worth it. From Moscow to Mandela it's been one triumph after another for global consultants.

Occasionally there are misunderstandings. I was sitting in the anteroom of Heinrich Applebaum's Made-to-Order Quality Predictions, when Willard Dergen, CEO of Stardust Avionics, charged in. He wanted to know why he hadn't been informed about the overthrow of the old regime in Czechoslovakia, and its replacement with a playwright, after he had paid Heinrich a fee of $750,000.

Heinrich smiled, as he usually does when stuck in a corner, and replied, "We didn't want to bother you with something so insignificant. Czechoslovakia is such a little country, it can't affect anything."

Willard spluttered and said, "Why did I have to find out on CNN that Romania was about to fall, and its leader be executed? Your job is to let me know who is going to get killed in Romania."

"Willard, we didn't want to go off the deep end until our CIA sources confirmed it for us. One thing we don't do at Applebaum Predictions is fax a client for the sake of faxing him."

"This may sound strange to you, but I don't like to spend two million dollars a year and not even know about the fall of the Berlin Wall. Why didn't you people inform us that the Wall was going to be torn down?"

"The East Germans gave us their word that the Wall would stay forever. But they double-crossed us to suck up to West Germany."

"Why didn't your firm predict the collapse of communism in East Germany?"

"We don't Red-bait. Nobody could have seen that coming. If we had told you last year that there would soon be only one Germany, you would have asked for your money back. Weren't you surprised?"

"I pay you so that I won't be surprised. How come I didn't hear from you when Bulgaria went under?"

"We told you that there is a surcharge for information about events in Bulgaria. Willard, were we or weren't we right on Poland?"

"You were as right as *Time* magazine, which was where I first read the story. What have you been doing about the Soviet Union?"

"We're very interested in it. There are many significant things going on there right now, and when we find out what is happening we're going to make a report to all our clients."

"I have to know *now*. If I can't figure out what the Soviet Union is doing, I won't be able to decide how much business the Defense Department is going to throw my way. You owe it to me to give me the scoop on daily events in the Kremlin."

"Willard, we have a report on Raisa Gorbachev's dressmaker that will make your hair stand on end."

"When do I see this intelligence?"

"As soon as we get the leather-bound report with your name engraved on it back from the printer's. It's a gorgeous presentation if I may say so myself."

"Give me something today that I can go back to my board with to justify your outrageous fee."

"The South Africans are going to release Nelson Mandela from prison."

"They already did that."

"They did?" Heinrich was truly surprised. "Nobody tells me anything."

HOLY *PERESTROIKA!*

I WAS GLUED TO the set when Tom Brokaw did his *A Day in the Life of the White House* for NBC. I knew that it would be a tough show on Bush, but I wasn't prepared for so many surprises. First, the TV audience was given an exclusive look at the Bushes' pet dog, Millie, which has never been seen on television before.

In addition, we saw the president's "brain trust" calmly, and with dignity, carrying on the nation's business. We found out that President Bush likes not only children but also the San Francisco 49ers.

It would have been a perfect, reassuring documentary as to how well the White House works—except for one glitch. At the beginning of the show we saw one of the president's men placing a call to Gorbachev in Moscow. But at the end of NBC's day—it hadn't come through. The NBC producer, Tim Russert, told Tom Shales, the *Washington Post* television critic, that White House telephone calls to Gorbachev normally take a day to complete.

"Holy *perestroika!*" I said to no one in particular. "What kind of world are we living in when a missile can make it to Moscow in twenty minutes, and President Bush needs twenty-five hours to get a telephone call through to Gorbachev?"

I spoke to a top communications man at McDonald's to find

out why it takes so long for the White House to make contact with the Kremlin.

He told me, "Well, to begin with, there are no telephone books in the Soviet Union. So when the president asks the operator to raise Gorbachev on the phone, she has to call information in Moscow. In the past there was no trouble getting the number, but because he is getting so many obscene calls from Lithuania, Gorbachev now has an unlisted number."

"Wouldn't the CIA have it?"

"Yes, but unfortunately the CIA has an unlisted number too."

"It seems to me that Gorbachev would want instant contact with the U.S., and vice versa. These days a lot can happen globally in a short period of time."

"Everyone is aware of this, and there have been efforts to speed up the calls. The problems aren't mechanical. They are more related to protocol. President Bush's secretary will not allow him to pick up the phone until Gorbachev gets on first. Gorbachev's secretary refuses to let Gorby pick up the phone until Bush gets on first. It's impossible to put both men on the phone at the same time."

"That's the kind of stuff Brokaw should have told us," I said.

My McDonald's man explained, "The other problem is that every time Bush calls, he is informed that Gorbachev is in a meeting. Every time Gorby rings Bush, he's told the same thing about Bush. It's very hard to catch two superpower leaders when they're *not* in a meeting."

"Maybe we should present Gorbachev with a cellular phone as a gift, and he can call Bush from his car. Even world leaders like to telephone from their automobiles," I said.

"On paper it sounds like a good idea. The truth is that Gorby's advisors are deathly afraid we would catch him in his car when he's least prepared for arms reductions.

"The biggest obstacle we have had to deal with lately is that, in their last economy drive, the Kremlin fired its night telephone operator. They have replaced her with an answering machine. We can only leave thirty-second messages on it, so President Bush is not able to get much business done. For example, Mr. Bush cannot say on the machine, 'Mr. Gorbachev, because of a navigational accident, there are five hundred B-2 bombers flying in your direction. Please ignore them. Their real targets are the Mediterranean fruit flies in Pasadena.' "

"Is there any effort being made to patch up the communications rift between the two countries?" I asked.

"The only hope we have is if each leader buys a Stealth beeper."

PUFF-A-PET

It's BEEN A bad time for tobacco companies. First, it leaked out that they were developing a cigarette specifically to appeal to black people. When that idea ricocheted, they began concentrating on a cigarette for the young blue-collar white woman. The cigarette, named Dakota, was being test-marketed to see if it would appeal to ladies without a high school diploma.

This news did not receive the public welcome that the cigarette manufacturers hoped it would. As a matter of fact, Health and Human Services secretary Dr. Louis Sullivan assailed it. So the tobacco companies have now gone back to the drawing board to try to find another group that might pick up some of the slack in the smoking business.

A meeting was held in the offices of smoking materials consultants Ploughwright and Ploughwrong, who specialize in programs to further cigarette consumption in the United States.

Ploughwright addressed an industry mogul named Ziggy Slick. "We think we've found the answer to the problem. We'll make a cigarette for pets. It's an untapped market. Our surveys indicate that there are over two hundred million dogs in American homes, and only a handful have ever known the joys of smoking."

Slick said, "How the hell do you get a dog to light a cigarette?"

Ploughwrong answered, "Who says the pet has to light it? It can just eat it. You don't care what anyone does with a cigarette as long as it is consumed."

Ploughwright added, "We have given it a name that any dog will recognize. How do you like Fetch? We also plan to add a stick on the package in the center of the target. That way the dog will never mistake it for Lucky Strikes."

Slick was dumbfounded. "It's going to take more than a stick on a package to get a dog to go for a cigarette."

"Right. That's why the product has to have a strong advertising campaign. We have a TV commercial now that will blow your brains out. It shows a dog bringing in a package of Fetch to his master. The master takes two out of the pack and puts them in the dog's mouth—and lights them. Then the master takes one of the cigarettes out of the dog's mouth and puts it in his own mouth. Everyone remembers the scene when Paul Henreid did that with Bette Davis."

Slick said, "Dogs don't watch TV commercials."

"Are you kidding?" yelled Ploughwright. "They're glued to the set all day long. The latest Nielsen ratings show that more canines than people are looking at network shows. We've got this whole thing worked out, Mr. Slick. We have to move fast, before the other tobacco companies decide to go after the pet market too."

Ziggy sounded unconvinced. "Look, we got burned on the cigarette aimed at the black smoker, and we didn't do too well with the proposal to appeal to dumb girls who are only looking for a good time. What makes you think that we won't be criticized for promoting a product intended for four-legged animals?"

"Because," countered Ploughwrong, "we're promoting free choice. We are not suggesting that dogs have to consume tobacco. We're saying that it should be up to the animals themselves—not to some bureaucratic humane-society official who keeps telling them that cigarettes are dangerous to their health."

Slick said, "Haven't there been laboratory tests with pets that indicate that after they smoke cigarettes they get cancer?"

"The tests are inconclusive. Most of the dogs who became ill from smoking were also hit when they chased motorcycles down the street without wearing their helmets."

SWEET AND *L'EAU*

I'M GLAD IT came back, because I am one of those people who took the Perrier recall to heart. The reason for this is that I don't drink during the cocktail hour, and I am dependent on Perrier to keep me in the mainstream of a party.

I discovered that when my hostess, or the waiter, asked me what I wanted to drink, I got instant respect as I responded, "I'll take a glass of Perrier with just a squeeze of lime." Talk about provoking awe. Everyone jumped as soon as I gave the order. It was not always like this.

Before Perrier became the national drink of the free world, I had a serious problem.

I would enter the room and the hostess would come up to me and inquire if I wanted a drink. I always replied, "Yes, please, I'd like a glass of water."

I remember the look of horror in her eyes. "I beg your pardon. I thought you said you wanted a glass of water."

"Yeah, but no ice. I can't stand ice with my water."

Word leaked out fast at the party that the guy in the blue blazer with the pink shirt and the yellow polka-dotted tie had asked for a glass of water. Believe me, cocktail-partying in those days was not much fun.

Then came Perrier, a mineral water in green bottles that spelled status over all its pot-bellied rivals. The man holding the glass of Perrier in his hand was the one who had the key to the washroom.

As a Perrier drinker from the start, I never doubted that one spring in the south of France supplied the water for the millions and millions of six-packs exported every year. My image of Perrier was that of an entire town working day and night holding bottle necks to the one spigot in the center of the town square, while their children blew in the bubbles.

I didn't do too well after the fall of Perrier. When I went to a party and someone asked me what I wanted, I replied, "Poland water." It just wasn't the same thing. Even Diet Dr Pepper doesn't have the éclat of Perrier.

My wife was afraid that I'd start drinking liquor again, and she kept telling me that I was not at fault for what had happened to Perrier water. She said, "You can't be responsible for all the benzene in the world."

I just answered, "I'd rather drink Perrier with benzene in it than some Colorado sparkling water with no taste at all."

At the last party I went to before the return of Perrier, I was very uptight. I asked the hostess, Joan Braden, "I don't suppose that you have anything in a green bottle from a small town in France?"

"We're not serving Perrier, if that is what you mean," she told me. "How about some San Pellegrino instead?"

"I don't drink domestic water," I said angrily. "The better houses in this town still serve Perrier under the counter."

In tears, she whispered, "You can go to jail for that."

"People are willing to risk it to show that they give a damn about their entertaining. I think I better leave."

"Wait. We'll find some. Promise me you won't tell anyone that we served it."

"Perrier drinkers can be trusted. That's why we always get invited back to people's homes."

SLIGHTLY NERVOUS

THERE ARE A few people, not many, who are slightly nervous about a unified Germany. These folks suffer from déjà vu and, while the world has no reason to shiver, we should address their fears.

Feldman, my watch repairman, is certain he knows how the trouble is going to start. He thinks it will be something like this:

It's eight years from today, and Germany is united. Schultz, a former East German bricklayer and now a prosperous orthodontist, is building a new house at Schnitzel Gardens, which is east of Leipzig.

Schultz's architect, Mendelsohn, comes to visit him with the plans. "Schultz, I can get the house on your land, but I don't have room for a garage."

"I have to have a garage," Schultz insists. "My new Mercedes-Benz is being delivered in six weeks."

Mendelsohn says, "Look for yourself. Where are we going to build a garage?"

Schultz studies the plans. "How about here?"

"But that's Poland!"

"It was Germany before it was Poland. The people of Poland stole it from us after World War Two. We must be allowed to build German garages on German soil."

Mendelsohn explains, "If we built your garage in Poland, we would be violating the Treaty of Perrier, which states that Germany cannot covet any territory that belonged to somebody else in the year 1990."

Schultz says, "A bunch of old men who sold us out signed that treaty. We have a new Germany now, and that Germany permits us to build on any part of the fatherland that we want to."

Mendelsohn tells him, "I'm not suggesting that you are wrong. Admittedly, there are a lot of German-speaking Poles living on the land where we want to build our garage. At the same time, I don't think that Berlin will give us a permit to construct a garage so close to Cracow."

Schultz slams down his fist. "It is not Polish soil, it is German soil. To teach them a lesson I should put the whole house in Poland, and the garage in Germany."

"They could try to stop you."

"Then Germany must rebuild its air force and its Panzer divisions and begin a crash submarine program. I will not park my car in the driveway to satisfy the scavengers of World War Two."

"If you feel that strongly about it, Schultz," Mendelsohn says, "I'll build the garage in Poland while no one is looking."

"I *want* everyone to be looking. This is my house, this is my garage, this is my land, this is my Europe. *Heil* real estate!"

Mendelsohn responds, "*Heil* real estate. Now can we talk about the cost of the land we're going to take from Poland?"

"Why should we pay for what was originally ours?" Schultz asks him.

Mendelsohn agrees. "Good point. Schultz, you told me last time to get some estimates for the cost of building a hunting lodge in Czechoslovakia. I have two estimates. One if Czechoslovakia remains independent, and another if it is annexed to us."

"Just give me the annexation figure. Why would Czechoslovakia stay independent when all our German citizens still live there?"

PARDON MY SANCTIONS

THERE IS NO doubt that life is unfair. For many of us life couldn't be more unfair than when the NCAA declared sanctions against Rimshot Tech's basketball team. Rimshot Tech, located in the heart of Maryland's low-ball country, had one of the most outstanding records of any school in the Hurricane Zelda Conference. There was even serious talk of the school's going to New Orleans for the Jambalaya Playoffs.

Brad Taicher, who rides shotgun in our car pool to Rimshot games, said, "You'd think that the NCAA Committee on Sports Infractions would have something better to do than look for recruiting violations in a university's athletic program."

Chili Kohlmeyer asked, "What's wrong with giving an incoming freshman a small BMW if he needs transportation to and from practice at night?"

I was in the backseat of the car. "Here's what I think: If the alumni didn't give them six-hundred-dollar weekly handouts, the players would go to school in another state. All our alumni do when they subsidize a good player is guarantee that he won't leave his mommy and daddy and go far from home."

Danny Hawke, who was taking it harder than the rest of us, said, "They announced that Rimshot couldn't appear on television for two years, since the school had provided parents of

169

players with free housing at Trump Tower. An NCAA action like that only makes it tough on kids who are looking for a good education."

Brad added, "They want to put Coach Savory on ice because a couple of players shaved points in their last game."

"It's the NCAA's word against the coach's," Chili told us. "He didn't see anything, he didn't hear anything, and he says that he was making popcorn with a meter maid on that particular evening."

I was really mad. "How can anyone have a good basketball team if they're going to make a federal case out of every tiny infraction? I haven't heard of *one* kid who was ever corrupted in sports because the school gave him a brand-new Harley-Davidson motorcycle."

Brad tried to sound upbeat. "I like the way the president of Rimshot is handling this. At the press conference this morning, he announced that the school really got a raw deal. He vowed that he would stand by his team no matter what penalties were meted out by sanctimonious members of the NCAA. In order to make up for the loss of athletic scholarship funds that Rimshot Tech had to return, the president said that he was going to give the team the money originally set aside for a new science library. Now there's a man who knows his priorities."

Brad continued, "What bothers me is that with all the heat, many high school recruits may bypass Rimshot and go to another college which hasn't been caught yet by the NCAA."

"No way," I yelled. "There isn't a university with the reputation of Rimshot when it comes to basketball perks. We can match any school's recruiting program, and still have cash in the bank for someone who runs out of laundry money."

Danny chimed in, "The thing I hate about college sports investigators is that they don't give a hoot about the fans. To the schools we're nothing but warm bodies that fill up seats and buy franks and draft beer. Yet we're the ones who support the teams and make sure that the school turns out winners.

170

Basketball and football are the key to a university's reputation in the community. The NCAA never cares about the pain they are causing the fans when they rap a school's knuckles."

Brad announced, "Let the word go forth to the NCAA that, while we admire their efforts to keep sports from corrupting the students, no school of higher learning can maintain its scholastic reputation if viewers aren't able to see how well the basketball team is doing on television."

TO SMOKE OR NOT TO . . .

I KNOW THAT you were expecting an extra dividend from the new smoking bans that have gone into effect—but it is not to be. According to *The Washington Post*, the reduction in smoking will cause havoc with Social Security and health care programs.

In the good old days, smokers could be counted on to die far before their time, and therefore they did not use up their Social Security benefits or health plan credits. Nonsmokers, on the other hand, live too long, and to this day they are a tremendous drain on the country's finances. We're talking about hundreds of billions of dollars. So every time we turn a smoker into a nonsmoker we're destroying the entire pension system of the United States.

This discovery has caused many actuarial economists to reexamine Health and Human Services Secretary Louis Sullivan's severe anti-tobacco campaign.

Professor Scarcely Breething is one of them.

"An end to smoking is not a means to an end," he told me. "Nor is it an end to a means. What it does tell us is that unless a certain number of people die prematurely from smoking, we cannot afford to provide medical care to the nonsmoking survivors."

I said, "It seems a pity to root for smokers to expire early just so the rest of us can enjoy our September years."

Breething responded, "We're not asking for that at all. We're simply saying that the government should not be part of the campaign to prevent people from smoking, as it is a conflict of interest. Those who smoke should be encouraged to do so. That way, when they go to heaven their Medicare benefits will be doled out to the senior citizens who led clean lives. Economists want to alert the American people to the fact that it is the smoker, not the nonsmoker, who is saving mankind."

"What about secondary smoke—when the smoker causes a nonsmoker grievous harm by puffing into his face?"

Breething admitted, "No one likes it, but it is still better for the secondary smokers to do their thing than for the Social Security system to go broke."

I told him, "What you seem to be saying is against everything the medical profession has taught us. You indicate that we should encourage the nation's smokers so that we can get their Social Security benefits. Would you take the warning off cigarette packs and advertising messages as well?"

Breething answered, "Most certainly. I'd also reinstate smoking on domestic airliners and in public buildings. The anti-tobacco campaign has cost us a great deal in Medicare benefits already, and we have to put a stop to the HHS bad-mouthing of the weed."

"If smokers know that they are going to die, won't they give up the habit on their own?"

"They know it right now and it hasn't stopped them. What we economists don't like is the government telling nicotine lovers that Mother Nature has it in for them."

"Would you say that Darwin was counting on people to smoke?"

"He always maintained that the survival of the fittest depends on who sits in the nonsmoking part of the restaurant."

TO HAVE AND FORGET

IT USED TO be that this nation's heroes said things like, "I regret that I only have one life to give to my country," or "We have just begun to fight," or "Give me liberty or give me death," or "Remember the *Maine.*"

Nowadays all our heroes can come up with is, "I don't remember."

Here, purportedly, is an outtake from the deposition of Ronald Reagan, which was given for Admiral John Poindexter's trial:

"Mr. President, could you please tell us exactly what you knew and when you knew it with regard to the Iran-contra affair?"

"I ... I ... I don't remember knowing anything about the Iran-contra thing—this is the first I've heard of it."

"Well, let me try your memory on something else. Do you recall working for Warner Brothers as an actor before you went into politics?"

"Of course. I came from radio station WHO in Des Moines, where I was a sportscaster, and I covered the Northwestern football games. Northwestern beat Michigan twenty-four to twelve when Myron Hoffsteder fumbled on the three yard line. After that, I went to southern California with the Chicago Cubs for spring training, and did a screen test for Bill Meiklejohn at Warner Brothers. I was hired, luckily, because the cab fare came to ten dollars and thirty-three cents."

"Okay, Mr. President, can we get back to the illegal sale of arms to Iran and the laundering of money for the Nicaraguan rebels?"

"That was a long time ago. I wouldn't know anything about that. A president can't remember everything he did."

"But you do recall *Knute Rockne*."

"It was my favorite movie. I remember going to the commissary one day with Pat O'Brien. It was one-twenty P.M. and Pat had a bacon, lettuce and tomato sandwich on toasted rye and a glass of buttermilk, and I had cream cheese and smoked salmon on pumpernickel, with a bag of potato chips and iced tea. We sat at this back table against the wall, which had a picture of Bette Davis and Humphrey Bogart. She was in a domino-print dress and he wore a striped suit with no tie. Pat said to me, 'Don't you love the movie business?' "

"Mr. President, did you know that Lieutenant Colonel North was going to lie to Congress?"

"How could I know that, when I didn't know anything? North, South, East, West—when you've seen one National Security aide you've seen them all."

"Then you maintain that you don't know who Colonel North is?"

"I can't recall the gentleman—I tried not to remember names when I was in the White House."

"Can you remember *Bedtime for Bonzo*?"

"Who can forget *Bedtime for Bonzo*? I didn't like the chimp very much because he used to bite me on the knuckles and he tried to steal the picture from me. He smelled a lot and ate only green bananas, which in those days cost eight cents each. I used to buy them for him at the Fairfax farmers' market—bananas were always in row D, aisle six."

"You seem to have a good memory, Mr. President, except for the Iran-contra affair."

"I'm racking my brain to help you, but it's all a blank. I'm sure Iran had something to do with something, but I don't know what."

"Maybe you lost your memory when you were informed that you had violated the law."

"Right. That's why I'm calling my new book *Where Is the Rest of Me?*"

THE OTHER WOMAN

IF THE DONALD TRUMP divorce fracas has done anything, it has once again put the spotlight on what is known in social circles as The Other Woman. Fortunately, under the Freedom of Information Act, the nation's tabloids must give as much space to The Other Woman as they do to the wife.

Sometimes the press is not as fair toward The Other Woman as it is to the spouse.

My friend Debbie, who has been The Other Woman several times, believes that the system is unjust.

"Most women in this country have been The Other Woman at some time or another, and they should be the last ones to throw stones at another person's girlfriend."

"But," I protested, "we perceive The Other Woman as a home wrecker."

"Other Women don't break up homes. Those homes either have been broken up already or are about to be. All The Other Woman does is act as a support system when it happens. The wife likes to blame us for destroying the marriage, because it makes her look good. That won't fly, because I don't know of one Other Woman who can break up a home if nobody wants her to."

I said, "I believe that one of the reasons The Other Woman is distrusted is that in the majority of cases she looks better than the wife. What I am really saying is that The Other Woman pays more attention to her wardrobe and makeup than a lady who cleans the dog dish every morning."

Debbie did not argue with me. "Maybe it's true, but then again The Other Woman has to work twice as hard to hold onto what little security she has. We don't own any casinos in Las Vegas, nor are Other Women given prenuptial contracts. All we have are our looks. Once we lose our paramour's undivided attention, it's Katy-out-the-door."

I told Debbie, "The problem is that many women feel threatened by The Other Woman, particularly when she shows up on the front page of the New York *Daily News*."

Debbie responded, "I suppose they are, but let's be honest. In the pursuit of men, most females who now criticize have played the role of The Other Woman and relished stealing from their competition. What's the big deal if she happens to be a good friend of Donald Trump's?"

"Because in Western culture, The Other Woman has no credentials. She is a huntress without a license, so to speak. I personally have nothing against The Other Woman. I believe that when it comes to a happy marriage, a person should live and let live."

Debbie was determined to make her point. "Do you realize how many women eventually become the wives of the men they have been sneaking around with?"

"One hundred and four?" I guessed.

"Millions," cried Debbie. "As soon as they are married they are awash with respectability, and everyone, but everyone, forgets that they were once The Other Woman. The only people we consider scarlet women are those who didn't make it to the altar."

"It's true," I agreed. "There are many Other Women I have known who now wear rings on their fingers and are pillars of their communities."

"Someday, when all the accountants get finished with the case, Donald Trump's girlfriend, if she becomes Mrs. Trump, will be a woman of respect and reverence. She will also live happily ever after—unless another Other Woman steals Trump away from her."

I remarked, "It sounds as if it takes a lot of energy to get your man."

Debbie said, "Being The Other Woman means never having to say you're tired."

TIE A GREEN RIBBON

I WALKED OUT OF the house one Sunday morning and found Jill Stevens tying a green ribbon to her old oak tree.

"What's up?"

"It's for George. I want him to know that there is always a warm welcome for him when he comes back."

"Comes back from where?"

"From playing golf. He left at seven o'clock this morning, and I don't know if I'll ever see him again." She burst into tears.

"You'll see him again," I assured her. "He has to come home after it gets dark. Did he leave a note when he went out?"

"Yes. It was stuck to the mirror and it said: 'I'm off to kick some ass with a little white ball, and find the bluebird of happiness.'"

"Well, at least he didn't sound depressed. Have you told the children?"

"I explained to them that their daddy is on a very important mission to Central America to save the country, and that's why he couldn't spend Sunday with them."

"Did they buy it?"

"You have to be kidding. They may be lazy, but they're not dumb. I've been thinking that since he won't come to us, maybe we should go to him."

"You mean, show up on the fairway?"

"Not necessarily. It could be near a water hole or in a sand trap."

"I don't think that's a good idea. If every fatherless family showed up to see a loved one on the golf course, there would be no place for the golfers to play. In my opinion you're better off keeping the vigil here."

"I worry about him," Jill confided. "He's been complaining about his game lately. He mentioned that he's overshooting the hole."

"All golfers say things like that. Just be grateful if he returns home. Many duffers are too ashamed to face their families after playing eighteen holes."

"He claims that he's doing it for us."

"I believe he's telling the truth. Most golfers maintain that they play the game to protect their loved ones from Castro's Cuba. I know George, and I am sure that, at this moment, he is dedicating every chip shot to you."

"I sent him a note from the children, but it was returned with an 'Addressee Unknown' stamp on it. I wonder if he'll find me as attractive as he did when he left."

"Sure he will. You're a beautiful woman. Remember this: Golf doesn't change a man's attitude toward his wife. He'll always remain the same person, unless he crashes into somebody else's golf cart."

"I was thinking of taking up the sport myself," Jill said.

"Don't. George has enough trouble with his putting without worrying about yours."

"Do you think he'll get the significance of the green ribbon on the old oak tree?" Jill asked.

"He would be a very, very insensitive golfer if he didn't."

HEY, BABY!

SOME PEOPLE WHO believe that everyone should have babies tend to throw out the bathwater as soon as the baby is born.

"It's a boy! What a wonderful thing, a beautiful baby boy."

"Who takes care of him?"

"Don't worry. He belongs to all of us."

"The baby is one year old. He needs some milk."

"That's not my department. I was only concerned with making sure he was born."

"The boy is six years old. He's awfully thin and not getting much nourishment. Would you send someone over with food?"

"How did you get this number? Let me tell you something. I don't have any use for welfare cheats. If he's able-bodied, he can go out and get a job at McDonald's."

"He's nine now and he seems slightly backward in school. The doctor said it was lack of a balanced diet after he was born. Do you have any idea how that happened?"

"There is just so much I can do. Once a baby has his own latchkey, it's everybody for himself."

"I'm calling to tell you that there was an altercation at school. The child you sponsored picked up a knife and tried to stab his teacher. He needs some immediate psychiatric treatment before he goes off the deep end forever."

"I can't afford psychiatric treatment. The trouble with kids today is that they are coddled by society. Give him a taste of hard-knocks school and he'll straighten out."

"The boy has just turned sixteen and he's joined a gang. The police believe he is into dope. If you give us two thousand dollars, we can get him out of the neighborhood."

"That's ridiculous. Why should I bail out this child?"

"We assumed that since you campaigned so hard for his birth, you might help him in his teenage years."

"You had no right to think any such thing. He was a problem kid to start with. I saw it on his face in the hospital."

"He's twenty now. You probably read about him in the newspapers. The doctor who interviewed him said that he didn't have a chance. From the day he was born the boy felt that no one cared about him, and all he was trying to do was get even."

"You're not going to blame *me* for what that boy did. I haven't seen him since he was in the nursery."

"You fought so hard for him to see the light of day."

"I fight to bring a lot of children into the world—I couldn't take care of all of them even if I wanted to. That's the government's job."

"He got fifteen years in prison. He still has no idea why he did it."

"What am I supposed to do?"

"Not too much. But it would be nice if you had a plan for a few of these children."

"I think you've got the wrong number. I'm with the Right to Life, not the Right to Live."

BASEBALL CARDS

I never saw a Mapplethorpe,
I hope I never see one;
But I can tell you this right now,
I'd rather live in Cincinnati than be one.

THE RUMOR THAT an exhibit of nude baseball player cards was coming to Cincinnati hit the town like a tornado. After the Mapplethorpe photography show, people were quaking with fear.

Where the rumor started no one knows, but by the time it reached downtown, people were telling each other, "They're going to show Pete Rose in the buff."

Cincinnati has a law specifically forbidding the display of baseball nudity on the grounds that it is offensive and generates controversy. This includes not only the Cincinnati Reds but visiting teams as well. It specifically forbids trading of all cards with players who are not in full uniform. That is why the news of a nude baseball player card show caused so much alarm.

Authorities have warned that if any nude baseball cards are hung in a public place, the police will take videotapes of them, which will then be used in court. The sheriff and the mayor have said that they will not stand by and see first and second basemen exposed to the elements. They have promised arrests and jail terms, whether the players are posing in left field or at home plate.

A law enforcement officer has said that Cincinnati is the baseball card capital of the world. "Anybody who would show a naked shortstop deserves to have the book thrown at him."

On the other side are those who maintain that displaying nude players on cards is a form of free expression, and preventing the public from seeing them is censorship. They feel that the city fathers want to do away not only with nudity on baseball cards but with nudity on Nintendo games as well.

This is the first time the baseball card issue has become a constitutional one. The people who want to ban them swear that the cards are pornographic, pure and simple, and that the community has a duty to stop them from being exhibited. The other viewpoint is that it doesn't matter if they are baseball players or weightlifters, they have as much right to be displayed in a museum as members of Jesse Helms's family.

What makes it so sad is that no one actually has seen a nude player on a baseball card. At first it was believed that the entire New York Yankees team had posed without clothes. Then that rumor changed to the Los Angeles Dodgers. But there is still a question of whether the pictures exist at all.

This has not stopped Cincinnati citizens from lining up in front of the baseball card museum to get a look at the exhibit. Police estimate that at least 56,900 people have been waiting— not counting 4,000 undercover agents from the prosecutor's office.

"We have a right to see Dave Winfield without his clothes on," a female art lover declared, "before they take him away."

182

Her companion said, "I drove all the way from Louisville, Kentucky, to get a peek at Yogi Berra in his birthday suit."

It's been so long since the whispers about the baseball cards were first heard that many art patrons are befuddled. That's why the rumor of them has split Cincinnati wide open.

You can't tell other folks what they can or cannot see without their getting mad at you.

You may be curious about where I stand on all this. Personally, I don't like pictures of nudes. I prefer people with their clothes on. That's why I read the Victoria's Secret catalogue from cover to cover.

EARTH DAY RECYCLED

THE GRIZZLED OLD MAN was sitting on the park bench, eating a recycled cheese sandwich, when a group of youngsters stopped by.

"How old are you, Gramps?" one of them asked.

"Pretty old," the man replied.

"Are you old enough to remember Earth Day?"

"Yup, it was April 22, 1970, but it seems like yesterday. It's hard to describe it if you weren't there. Fumes were coming out of the tailpipes of cars, black smoke was billowing from factory chimneys, and we soon discovered we had something called acid rain that killed all the fish in the freshwater lakes."

"Aw," said one of the kids. "No one would be stupid enough to kill all the fish."

"It was worse than that. People threw anything they wanted into the rivers, and they flushed garbage and other stuff into the ocean. I saw it myself. We couldn't even go swimming in the ocean because it wasn't safe."

"Wow," yelled one little boy. "I'm glad that I wasn't alive then."

"Developers built houses over nuclear waste sites, and legitimate companies hired gangsters to dump poisonous waste material from one end of the country to the other. Nobody in the government would take responsibility for it. In those days the average citizen didn't do too well against the lobbyists when they appealed their case to Washington."

"Not like today, huh, Gramps?" one of the kids said, laughing.

"That's right. Today the government really worries about its dumps. Before Earth Day people sprayed insecticide on everything. That's because no one knew it was bad for kids."

"Have they stopped spraying?"

"No," Gramps told him, "but they now give you time to cover your car with plastic and crawl into your house. I guess the biggest thing that concerned us in those days was pesticides running off into the drinking water. The chemical companies claimed that we had nothing to be afraid of, and to prove it, the president of one company drank a glass of water on TV."

"Those must have been exciting times, Gramps."

"We were pretty wild back then. We used to throw our bottles into the street and burn our trash in the backyard, and even toss Styrofoam plates and cups into the ocean."

"We still do that," another boy said.

"Well, you can't expect the population to change its habits in just twenty years. Our one objective on Earth Day was to prevent the next generation from inheriting a cesspool. Two decades ago we declared, 'Enough is enough. We have to make the highway smell like the sea breeze and the sea breeze smell like the highway.' Of course, everyone was for it even after they found out how much it would cost."

"So what did you do when you found out how much money was involved, Gramps?"

"We sang a lot—mostly, 'This land was made for you and me.' "

"Are you sure you're telling us the truth, Gramps?"

"What part of it, son?"

"The part where people didn't care what they discarded or where they tossed it."

"I swear to you it was that way. I know it's hard for you kids to imagine how different it was, compared with how spick-and-span everything is today. It was so bad then that you couldn't see the forests for the rain."

Dirty Pool

It was a sorry day in Texas when Ann Richards won the Democratic nomination for governor over Jim Mattox, in what has been described as one of the dirtiest campaigns in the history of the state. It was sad because the dirty tricks used in the fight backfired on the political system as we know it.

When all the results were in, Political Mudslingers of America—the organization of dirty pol managers—called an emergency meeting to find out where they had gone wrong.

"This is the lowest day in the history of political campaigning," One-Eyed Robemutter declared. "It may mean that fighting in the gutter doesn't work, and we could all be out of work for the 1992 elections."

Shorty Benzedrine said, "Let's not panic. Just because our vicious, below-the-belt personal attacks on Ann Richards didn't catch on doesn't mean we should discard them as a fair campaign tactic. Don't forget she's a woman, and occasionally, dirty tricks can backfire when you're trying to defeat one of them for public office. Going on national television and accusing your opponent of using dope is still a good political move, and should not be eliminated just because of one primary in Texas."

Alonzo Mobley stood up, "As you know, I was one of the first people in this organization to sling mud. It was working well up until the Richards contest. My analysis is not that we threw too much mud at her but that we didn't throw enough. There were many more things she could have been accused of doing.

"For example, people are pretty nervous about hepatitis these days. I urged Mattox's people to make a commercial showing her at a blood bank with a voice-over saying, 'How many people will Ann Richards infect?' But they felt that it was *too* dirty, and they preferred to stick with the dope campaign."

"With all due respect," said Michael Minimal, "I believe that we're breast-beating too much over this. The public expects us to take the low road. The trick is to be nasty and untruthful at the same time."

Roger Dodger asked, "Does that mean we can continue to show a man on death row endorsing our opponent for giving him weekend leave?"

"Yes, but we have to be careful about how we show the opposing candidate pushing an old lady in a wheelchair down the stairs. Ann Richards's victory was an accident. The clean-election people are using it as an example of what can happen to candidates who resort to dirty tricks. We have to prove to the politicos that we can still win elections with a mad-dog attack approach. Our living depends on bad taste and no scruples."

Rapido Doyle said, "Everything was going so well. I thought that after 1988 the appetite for dirty campaigns would be insatiable. I'm not sure I want to stay in politics if I have to maintain an ethical standard."

One-Eyed Robemutter tried to sound upbeat. "Forget Ann Richards and go for the big one in 'ninety-two. Willie Horton is still alive and well for another presidential campaign. We're hired mudslingers, the best in the business, and the politicians are going to need us as soon as their ratings in the polls drop. Our message to them is: One Ann Richards victory does not mean you can't continue to use inexcusable, unpardonable and unforgivable TV commercials to win elections."

Shorty Benzedrine suggested, "How about us having a film festival to show all the dirty commercials we made in the last four years? This would give the candidates in 'ninety-two an opportunity to see how hitting below the belt can benefit them."

One-Eyed Robemutter said, "Good idea, Shorty. If we're going to sling mud we may as well relax and enjoy it."

A GOOD LITTLE BOY

MIKE MILKEN EDGED his way up to Santa Claus and climbed onto his lap.

"Have you been a good boy?" Santa Claus asked.

"It depends on who you talk to. The prosecutor said that I was a bad boy, and my lawyer maintained that I was as good as gold."

"Who do you expect me to believe?"

Milken replied, "It doesn't make any difference. If I snitch on my friends, the judge will cut my time."

"Well, then, I think you should snitch. They would do the same to you. What do you want for Christmas?"

"I'd like you to sell kids securities instead of toys. You could have them gift-wrapped and called Junk Bonds 'Я' Us."

"That sounds very wild. I don't think that kids want Christmas junk bonds."

"They would if they knew that they pay sixteen-percent interest."

"Are these bonds one of the reasons the prosecutor called you a bad boy?"

"No, he was talking about the ones I sold on the Fourth of July. The Fourth of July bonds are still a very good investment, if all the S&Ls that bought them ever rise from the ashes."

"Michael, I'm not sure that I want to pass along a recommendation for securities from someone who has been convicted of fraud and perjury."

"Okay, if that's the way you feel, we'll pay eighteen percent."

Santa said, "I'm just uncomfortable with the idea of children investing in Christmas junk bonds."

"That's because you've been so busy listening to other people's stories that you don't have time to play the market."

"Michael, everyone is getting impatient. Why don't you pull my beard once and get the hell out of here?"

"All right, what about a merger?"

"Who am I going to merge with?"

"The Easter Bunny. Between the two of you, we could drive Walt Disney's stock into the ground."

"Michael, you're getting heavy. I don't usually hold business conversations with people sitting on my lap. The boys and girls waiting in line have thoughts of sugar plums in their heads—they don't yearn for junk bonds and leveraged buyouts. Their dreams are all about Nintendo games and Barbie dolls."

"I could provide all the capital they need to take over the Lionel train company."

"Michael, I have nothing against someone who is motivated by greed, but you cannot persuade children that money is everything. They don't learn that until they grow up and watch Donald Trump on television."

"You say that now, but what happens to you when Matsushita buys this department store and sends in a Japanese Santa Claus from Tokyo?"

"Is there anything else you're here for, Michael?"

"I was hoping that you might put in a few good words for me with the court."

"What for?"

"After the judge handed down my sentence, my lawyers told me, 'The only one who can save us now is Santa Claus.' "

House for Sale

Real estate is not the fun game it used to be. In the eighties everyone talked about making a killing with their houses, and there was hardly a man or woman alive who didn't own a house that had sextupled in value. Now all the great homes that were built with borrowed money are going begging in a market that most S&Ls believed would last forever.

Everyone has a real estate story. My cousin Flo's tale more or less sums up what people are experiencing now that the boom times are over. She called me a few months ago to tell me she was about to sell her house and move to a leisure garden apartment in New Jersey.

"How much are you asking?" I wanted to know.

"Well, I paid $45,000 for it, so I've priced it at $210,000."

"Could you tell me how you arrived at that figure?"

"The real estate person said that I should be able to get $150,000. My son thought that $200,000 was about right, and I added an extra ten thousand as icing on the cake."

"It sounds good to me. I wish you luck."

Flo telephoned a month later and told me, "Nobody wants to buy my house. The market is dead. What shall I do?"

"How about lowering the price?"

"If I do that I'll lose money on it. I am not going to let some bargain-chiseler steal it from me."

"I agree. If you lower the price it will only be a sign of weakness."

The following month she was on the phone again. "I've decided to advertise it for $200,000. I'll eat the $10,000 loss because sometimes in business you have to take it on the chin to survive."

"I believe that you have done a very wise thing. You are now competitive with all the other $45,000 houses in the neighborhood. Let me know if you sell it. I'll have an announcement placed in *The Wall Street Journal*."

Flo called again after three weeks. "It isn't moving. Bloomfield, New Jersey, is in a real estate wasteland—it's worse than Chernobyl."

"There's only one course of action, Flo, and that is to lower the asking price even further."

"Are you suggesting that I sell my $45,000 house for $160,000?"

"I'm just advising you to do what the big guys on Wall Street would do in your place. They would take their losses and get out of Bloomfield as fast as they could."

"If I follow your advice I'll lose $50,000. Life can't be that unfair."

"Then keep the house and hope that the price will rise."

"No. I'll sell it for $160,000, which means I'm going to be the laughingstock of the Garden State Parkway."

"If you don't sell it, you could always give it back to the savings and loan people and let them deal with it. How big a mortgage did you get on it?"

"It was $140,000 two years ago."

"Well, call them up and inform them that you would like to refinance the house."

"I can't. They are no longer in business. It seems that they kept making million-dollar loans to people who were buying $45,000 houses."

READ MY LIPS

"OKAY, MR. PRESIDENT, let's try again. Say, 'Read my lips. There *will* be new taxes.' "

"Why do people have to read my lips all the time?"

"Because that's what you told the voters to do during the election campaign when you promised them no new taxes. Now that you're changing your position, we feel that it is important for the public to know that your lips won't be saying what they did in the past."

"Heck, everyone knows I didn't mean no new taxes when I said it. That doesn't make any sense."

"You were the one who raised the lip factor. The American people have been reading yours since you came into office. When they find out that you're willing to change your stand, your credibility is going to go down the drain. That's why we're making this TV special from the Oval Office. We want the country to realize that even the president can speak out of both sides of his mouth."

"Well, what am I supposed to say?"

"I'd like you to announce that, while you maintain your pledge on no new taxes, you might be prepared to go along with desperate Democratic measures for tax enhancers and surtaxes which could help the economy."

"You expect me to say all that?"

"Yes, but I want you to move your lips when you do it. We'll run subtitles for the viewers who cannot read what you're saying."

"Shouldn't I mention that I am keeping my options open, so that the voters don't think I caved in?"

"That's a good idea. We'll shoot you doing it from a wide-mouth-angle lens."

"I wish I hadn't told everyone to read my lips. I feel so stupid."

"It wasn't your fault, Mr. President. How could you have known interest rates would be higher, tax revenues would be lower, and the S&Ls would break the banks in Texas?"

"I'm so ashamed to go back on my promise. Couldn't you film me without showing my mouth?"

"For the whole press conference!?"

"You're right. If they couldn't read my lips they would think I was holding back on them. I'll say that I was misled by someone in the White House who told me that there'd be no more taxes."

"Who?"

"How about Poindexter?"

"Mr. President, if I were you I'd bite the bullet and just talk about new taxes for now. Tell them that everything is on the table except your lips."

"Good thinking. It makes sense and it will help people forget the one-trillion-four-hundred-billion-dollar budget they are going to have to pay for as soon as possible."

"Okay, can we take it from the top?"

"Right. My fellow Americans, when I came into office some time ago, I formed certain words with my mouth, which many of you apparently misread. You thought I said, 'No more new taxes.' In reality, I uttered, 'No more flag-burning.' I never said, 'No more new taxes,' because I believe in new taxes, as does my wife, Barbara. New taxes are what made this country great, and they are something we should all be proud of."

"You're biting your tongue, Mr. President."

"Why can't I say, 'If you don't believe me, read my Su-nunus?' "

HERE'S THE SPEAKER

ONE OF THE myths of higher education is that students care who their graduation speaker is going to be. We saw the Barbara Bush brouhaha at Wellesley. Graduates and faculty members ferociously debated the merits of having Mrs. Bush deliver a message of significance that would remain with the class of 1990 for the rest of their lives.

It is a myth because, according to the recent census figures, ninety-nine percent of all students graduating in a given year will not recall what the speaker said. Twenty minutes after the ceremony is over they won't even remember who he or she was.

I speak with some authority on this. Over the years I have addressed many graduating classes, and I found the only measure of a successful speech was to talk fast and leave out as much substance as I possibly could.

This has been my experience: I have noticed that as soon as I start to speak, the students look at their watches. Although this is disconcerting, it is not disruptive. The disruption comes from those *without* watches who keep asking the others what time it is.

In the midst of making some of my most significant points,

foaming champagne bottles always appear and are passed up and down the rows. Swigging champagne from the bottle during a commencement speaker's talk has now become the most sacred of all graduation rituals.

The way many students kill time during a speech is to pull the tassel on the cap of the person seated in front. If the person whose tassel is being pulled likes the person who is pulling, there is a great deal of giggling. But if he or she doesn't like the tassel-tugger, then loud, harsh words are exchanged.

One of the reasons students don't pay too much attention to the speaker is that they are using the time to locate their parents and relatives sitting in the bleachers. If it's a large ceremony, this requires a tremendous amount of scouting. Sometimes the relatives are helpful because they start yelling at the graduate, which, by the way, doesn't do the speech any good at all.

Another factor making it difficult for the speaker to get a message across is that students are much more concerned about their appearance as they walk across the stage to receive their diplomas than they are with what the speaker is saying. The conferring of degrees takes place right after the commencement speech, so everyone is adjusting his or her gown. Some students will decide to take their bows with their gowns zipped up. Others will leave them open, as their first postgraduate act of defiance.

There are even students who will sleep during the talk, but I have discovered that it's nothing personal. The reason they can't stay awake is that they haven't had any sleep the night before. The mistake most speakers make is to keep staring at the student who is sleeping, and this can throw off a speaker's timing something awful.

Of course, in every graduating class there will be a few who bring their morning newspapers with them and then turn the pages while the speaker is talking. The only way I can deal with this is to say to myself, "Thank God they can read."

As a speaker, the most important lesson I have learned is this: No matter how pertinent my message, it was not appreciated, because the audience was unable to hear one word of it over the school's 1943 loudspeaker system.

WHEN YOU HEAR THE BEEP

NOT SINCE ALEXANDER GRAHAM BELL invented the whatchamacallit has the phone system gone through so many gyrations. The big breakthrough recently is that companies are installing direct dialing so that you are never able to speak to a live operator. Every employee has his or her own line and it's up to the caller to figure out how to get through.

The other day I needed to talk to Dumphries at my favorite utility company. This is how it went:

The recorded voice said, "You have reached the Darkness Unlimited Telephone Company. If you know the extension of the party you wish to speak to, you may key it in at any time. If you do not have that number, dial 233-5570 or 554-6784. If you wish to talk to the service department, ring 312-6789, or if you have questions regarding a bill, dial 908-7654 or 345-7890. If you prefer to speak to the advertising department or public relations, then ring 800-234-5670. If you get a busy signal, drop the 800 and add area code 999 instead. Any questions regarding the environment will be answered by calling our branch office

in Toronto. You can obtain this number by requesting information through our Atlanta substation at 900-345-789-0000."

I wasn't having much luck finding Dumphries, so I telephoned his wife at home. She gave me his direct line at work,
897-6550.

My problem was far from solved. When I dialed his extension
I got the recorded voice of Dumphries: "This is Harcourt
Dumphries. I am sorry I am not at my desk right now. If you
wish to leave a message, you may do so at the sound of the beep,
and I will get back to you. If you don't hear from me within
three days, call my secretary at 456-7800. If she's not there, you
can leave a message with the receptionist at 403-4557. You'll
know you have reached the correct number because she always
plays 'The Ride of the Valkyries' on her line when she asks you
to wait."

Dumphries did not get back to me, so I called him again. He
told me that he had received my call on his answering service
but he could not return it because the tape jammed up.

"What gives with the direct dialing?" I asked.

"The company installed it for ten thousand employees because it enabled Darkness to lay off two telephone operators
and save twelve hundred dollars a year."

"But it's so impersonal," I protested. "A caller feels at a terrible loss trying to get through to the person he wants to contact."

"That's because you don't pay enough attention when you
phone us. We give you the choice of every telephone number in
the system. Next month we're going to put out a company
phone book which you can buy for nine ninety-five. Direct
dialing is the wave of the future. The more live people a company eliminates from its telephone system payroll, the more
efficient that company will become."

"No doubt, but I'm old-fashioned and I feel a lot less helpless
when I hear a human voice at the other end of the line. Why

couldn't customers have a choice, the same as in restaurants? Instead of Smoking or Nonsmoking, we could choose Human Voice or Recorded Voice. It would be wonderful for your clients."

Dumphries said, "We are not going to placate customers who are against computer technology. Direct dialing has been a breakthrough comparable to man landing on the moon. Just because the public is confused doesn't mean that the system is unworkable. The money saved is channeled into research to find better ways of dialing people *without* having to go through the switchboard.

"We try very hard to make our recorded voices sound human. We auditioned two hundred applicants before we found a woman who could give us the perfect, 'All our lines are busy. Please do not hang up.' "

GIVE ME NAMES

"THERE'S SOMETHING MISSING from the S&L scandal," Tom Jolly told me.

"What's that?"

"There are no names. How can people scoop up five hundred billion dollars and we don't even know who they are?"

"What about Charles Keating? He's a name."

"He's not a household name like the guys in Watergate. At least with Watergate we knew who did it to us. I think the rule should be that if someone walks away with more than one hundred billion dollars, the public ought to be told who he is."

"You can't compare Watergate with the S&L scandal."

"Why not?" Tom asked.

"Because Watergate was a crime of passion. The S&L ripoff was a combination of ignorance and greed. That's why there are no S&L names. You don't think that Nixon, Haldeman, Ehrlichman or Colson would steal the savings deposits of widows and orphans, do you?"

"What about the five senators who made life easy for Charlie Keating when the feds were after him?"

"They're small potatoes and don't belong in the same league with the men and women who sank five hundred of the biggest S&Ls in the country. Your problem is that you are looking for someone to hate, because you and every other American are being stuck with the tab.

"It's true that a good deal of the five hundred billion dollars went to S&L executives for wine, women and lawyers. But you can't demand your pound of flesh just because somebody is driven by avarice and the will to win."

Tom said, "Irangate didn't involve as much money, but at least it had someone you could point a finger at with contempt. Take Ollie North, or General Secord, or Admiral Poindexter. Americans had a rooting interest in what happened to them. We know less about the S&Ls than Ronald Reagan remembers about Irangate."

"I'm sure that the administration is working on finding the wrongdoers right now," I assured him.

"Why weren't they working on it before the money was stolen?"

"Because at that time the savings and loans were deregulated. If you watch an industry that is deregulated, it could appear that it is being regulated. The government had assurances from the owners of the S&Ls that they would operate strictly within the law. Unfortunately, under deregulation

199

what is within the law to one banker is not necessarily within the law to another. What more can the Treasury be expected to do?"

"I want them to round up the usual suspects, march them into the courtroom and, at the end of the trial, sentence them to community service scrubbing the marble floors of the S&Ls they drove into the ground. I'd like to see their faces plastered on the front pages of the newspapers. I also want them to return all the money that they gave to their girlfriends before they went bankrupt. Then I think they should go to jail."

"You're asking a lot for the looting of a paltry half a trillion dollars," I said. "I have nothing against going public about those who filched the money, but the purpose of prison is to rehabilitate people. If they are sent to the slammer they won't be any the wiser about S&Ls than they are now."

"So what! If Leona Helmsley can go to jail, why can't the S&L guys?"

"We all wish we knew the answer to that question."

GOING, GOING, GONE

IT'S VERY POSSIBLE that someday you will run into people who'll ask, "Why didn't you buy van Gogh's *Portrait of Dr. Gachet* for $82 million, or Renoir's *At the Moulin de la Galette* for $78.1 million?"

You needn't be embarrassed by the question. Just use one of these replies:

"We don't have the wall space for the van Gogh because our children wouldn't let us take down their Mother's Day drawings."

"I intended to bid, but the Japanese had their hearts set on the pictures, and they have so little of anything as it is."

"Renoir's colors don't go with our drapes."

"Do you know what it costs to frame an impressionist painting these days?"

"We would have bought the *Moulin de la Galette* but it wouldn't fit into our Volkswagen."

"I have a friend, Bill Morice, who told me that I didn't have to go to the auction because he would take me to van Gogh's studio to meet him personally."

"My wife might have been persuaded to buy the Renoir, but she can't stand Mrs. Renoir."

"I'd rather have new patio furniture than an old French painting that has hung on God knows how many people's walls."

"I started to collect van Goghs the day he cut off his ear."

"We don't have eighty-two million for a picture but if we did, we'd buy a Mapplethorpe photo instead."

"The *Moulin de la Galette* isn't a bad painting, but unfortunately it has too many people in it for our taste."

"Years ago we had a choice of collecting either Rembrandts or baseball cards. Thank God we chose the baseball cards."

"Lucy Scott asked me not to bid on the Renoir so that she could have it. Then she stopped raising her hand when the bidding reached $330."

"We'll probably buy both works this summer when the Japanese businessman Ryoei Saito has his annual garage sale."

"My wife was about to purchase the *Dr. Gachet* when I pointed out to her that we would then be stuck with two van Goghs in the rec room."

"Because we are favored customers, we have reserved seats at Sotheby's for any softball game on their schedule."

"I hate the role money is playing in the art game. The halcyon days of paying a lousy five million for a White Rock calendar are over."

"I would have bought Renoir's *Moulin de la Galette*, but the artist refused to retouch it to make it more American."

"The reason we don't buy anything is that the auctioneer at Christie's never looks our way when we're bidding."

"He may have talent, but van Gogh is no friend of the farmer."

"Someday the Japanese are going to return to New York on their hands and knees and beg us to buy their paintings back."

"Picasso makes me smile, but Norman Rockwell makes me think."

"Ralph went to the auction with me but lost interest when he found out that van Gogh never painted any landscapes of the Augusta National Golf Club."

FOOD FOR THOUGHT

EVENTS IN THE Soviet Union had a tremendous impact on the Gorbachev–Bush arms talks held in Washington in May 1990. Here is how the exchanges between the two men went:

President Gorbachev opened the conversation with, "Mr. President, as you say in your country, I am willing to deal. For openers, I will give up three thousand five hundred forty intercontinental ballistic missiles."

"Good, and what do you want in exchange?"

"Three thousand five hundred forty 7-Elevens."

"I don't understand," Bush said.

"My people no longer demonstrate for missiles, but they are dying for convenience stores."

Bush told Gorbachev, "It isn't my decision. I'll have to go to Congress with that."

"Don't take too much time. I could be out on my ear. Now Mr. President, what do you want from us?"

"We are asking you to give up all your strategic bombers and blow up every nuclear warhead in your arsenal," Bush replied.

Gorbachev countered, "It's possible, but we cannot do that unless you give us something in exchange."

"Such as?"

"We want your entire Frank Perdue chicken production for the next five years."

"Are you mad?" sputtered Bush. "This country needs all the poultry it can get. The Defense Department would never let me give away our chickens to a nation that still maintains the largest standing army in the world."

"Mr. President, you are aware of what is going on in the USSR. The people are very upset at the food shortages. We've had riots in Armenia, Lithuania and Latvia. Estonia doesn't love me either. I must have something to offer the citizens of my country, and I am willing to abandon every weapon to do it."

"Mr. Gorbachev. Arms reduction isn't as simple as it used to be. The only way you can prove to us that you are sincere about *perestroika* is to invest in American junk bonds."

"Mr. President, we will bury every cruise missile we have if you promise to build thirty-four hundred Safeway stores in Siberia—but they must come with food in them."

"You drive a hard bargain, Mr. Gorbachev."

"It's to your advantage to see that the Soviet people are happy.

You made a good start with McDonald's in Moscow, but that doesn't mean you won the hearts and minds of the Soviet consumer's stomach."

"What would it take for you to give up USSR conventional forces in Europe?"

"Ten thousand Dairy Queens, and every Dunkin' Donuts east of the Mississippi. It's the only way I can calm down the opposition in the Ukraine."

"Mr. Gorbachev, I wasn't prepared for these demands. We're willing to give up certain things like fixed-wing bombers and aircraft carriers, but when you demand Dairy Queens, you're asking for the moon. The next thing I know, you'll be wanting International House of Pancakes franchises."

"I was about to bring that up."

"Then what it boils down to is, you are demanding nothing but consumer goods and, in exchange, all you are offering is to destroy heavy war equipment. Why?"

"We have a new saying in the Soviet Union: 'Better fed than Red.' "

I DON'T REMEMBER

MEMORY IS SOMETHING we are all losing. Everyone I know complains about how much he or she is forgetting. Why can't we remember all the things we used to? This is the question scientists are asking of white rats all over America.

Dr. Colin Forbershare has been doing extensive research on the subject, although he cannot recall for how long.

He told me, "The brain is nothing more than a large vacuum cleaner. It sweeps up information as it goes along. At some time the bag gets full, and then you have trouble dredging up the one fact that you want to remember."

I said, "The brain can't just be a vacuum cleaner. That would make everything too simple."

Dr. Forbershare agreed. "You're probably right. I guess I'll have to get rid of my rats, which means thirty years of research down the drain. How about this instead? Let's say that memory is the in and out baskets of your mind. The facts go into the in basket for retention, and are pulled from the out basket for action. People's memories fail when their in baskets spill over into their out baskets."

"Does our drinking water have anything to do with the loss of memory?"

"Water could have a lot to do with it. However, it's hard to generalize, because some people are affected by the drinking water and others are not. In Washington, everyone drinks the same water from the faucet, but the only ones who experience memory loss are those who are asked to testify in front of congressional committees."

"One of my biggest problems," I confessed, "is that I can never remember anybody's name, even in my own family."

"That's not uncommon. None of the white rats I am working with can remember names either. Most of them don't even know mine."

He continued: "Let me explain how the memory of names works. Right in the middle of the head, just underneath the hairline, is the location of a person's Rolodex. It keeps track of every name heard by that person since birth. In the beginning, it's easy because we record only first names, like Shirley, Ollie, Tiger, Fatty or Stinky. As time passes, more and more names are added. When a person reaches forty, the Rolodex is full.

After that, whenever you meet someone new you have to drop a name already recorded. In order to accommodate the new name, you often wind up forgetting your boss's wife's name."

"I am guilty of that," I admitted.

"Memory does funny things. The mind prefers to remember the names of strangers and forget the name of a person's first-born child," Dr. Forbershare told me.

"What about overload?" I asked. "Everyone says the information glut is so great that the brain cannot absorb all the facts that are thrust at us every day."

"I don't discount overload. I have known rats who have been bombarded with so much data that they can't even remember Mickey Mouse's birthday. We are all just warehousing information. Scientists prefer to think of the human mind as an Apple computer: everything a person sees and hears and even smells goes into the machine.

"But the more information a person puts into the computer, the slower his or her printer works. Some fact that you were unable to recall at a particular moment may come back two weeks later—usually at three o'clock in the morning, when you're in bed."

Forbershare concluded, "What's interesting about the subject of memory loss is that no one talks about it unless another person brings it up. How do we know if we are losing our memory? Let's say you meet your next-door neighbor at the supermarket. He is a man with whom you have shared barbecues, car pools and touch-football games. You say, 'Hi, Fred.' He looks astonished and tells you, 'My name is Sidney.' Then you start telling him the same story you told him two days ago. At this point you begin to suspect that the old memory bag has a hole in it."

MR. MAYOR

DURING THE DRUG TRIAL of Washington mayor Marion Barry, the defense's strategy was to convince a jury that the reason the mayor had been charged with perjury and possession of drugs was his race. This was not the case. Most people tend to get nervous when their mayor is tooting suspicious substances.

The truth of the matter is that mayors have to make more split decisions than any other elected officials. They also need to make them with a clear head. Dope can slow you down.

Come with me to a mayor's mansion in Gotham City, USA.

Mayor Dubarry is reading the morning newspaper with a straw.

The phone rings, he answers it, and a voice says, "Mr. Mayor, we have a warehouse fire on Cunard and First. What do you want us to do?"

"Dispatch four thousand snowplows—and if that doesn't work, use your backup garbage trucks."

"We don't have four thousand snowplows, sir."

"Then order them from the Sharper Image catalogue," Mayor Dubarry says, and hangs up. He appears very restless and calls in his secretary.

"Do I have any grand jury hearings today? I feel like committing perjury."

"No, sir. They're coming up next week."

"That's a pity. Maybe I'll lie to the press."

"You always feel better when you do, Mr. Mayor."

The phone rings again. "Mr. Mayor, this is the chief of police. There's a madman on top of the library, and he's screaming that he won't come down until you pay for the last marijuana delivery he made to you in the Virgin Islands."

"Shoot him."

"You really want us to shoot him?"

"What choice do I have? I'm the mayor."

He hangs up and turns to his secretary. "Do you remember where I put the Percodan pills?"

"I thought you put them in the out box with the uppers."

"I better have a few while I design the plans for the new hospital."

"Mr. Mayor, you know that Margaret Thatcher is coming this morning for a visit."

"I wonder if she snorts."

"I don't think so. By the way, the State Department protocol people have requested that you do not giggle when you give her the key to the city."

"They've got a nerve telling me what to do," the mayor says. "Do I tell Margaret Thatcher how to run the Eiffel Tower?"

"Are you finished cooking with this white powder?"

"Of course I'm finished. I can take it or leave it."

"Then I'll put it away."

"No, leave it."

"Mr. Mayor, there is a subway derailment and all traffic in the city is stopped. The man responsible was on drugs."

"How sad. Let's give him another chance."

"Sir, do you think you should be sitting on the floor in the lotus position when Prime Minister Thatcher comes into the room?"

"She rules India, she should be used to it."

THE PARTY IS OVER

AFTER COLLEGE IS out and family ties have been renewed, there comes a time when the parent-child bond has been tested and all hell breaks loose. Then everyone decides that the idea of having the loved one home for the summer was a terrible mistake.

Most experts give the honeymoon three weeks, from the moment the student is picked up at the airport to the hour the father yells at his child, "When are you going to get a job?"

You can hear the confrontations all over my neighborhood. The other day I passed John and Lynn Minna's house and heard the agonized voice of a wounded mother.

"I can do without boarders who sleep until two o'clock in the afternoon."

"I read all night," came a coed's voice.

"I don't need people in my house who read all night."

"I have nothing to do all day long, why should I get up early?"

"You could work and earn some money for college."

"The only jobs available in the classifieds are for Midas Muffler mechanics."

"What's wrong with that?"

"I'm studying political science. It would only confuse me."

John Minna yelled, "You could help your mother clean up the house."

209

The girl shouted back, "You're only saying that because I'm a woman."

John said, "That's not true. I told your brother the same thing."

"He knew you didn't mean it."

Then I heard Lynn Minna's voice. "We don't have fights here when you're in school. Just because you have two years of college doesn't mean you can run roughshod over everybody."

The daughter answered, "You wanted me to come home. I would have gone to Iris Goldstein's in Potomac if I knew it was going to be like this."

John's voice: "Why didn't you?"

Daughter: "Because she isn't there. She had a fight with her parents."

Lynn: "This is my house, and I'm going to set down the rules."

Daughter: "You're doing to me exactly what Joan Crawford did to her daughter in *Mommie Dearest*."

John: "All the neighbors will hear us."

Daughter: "I hope so, because then they will know how you treat college students."

John: "Go to your room."

Daughter: "Does everyone around here talk in clichés?"

John: "How much more time do we have until she goes back?"

Lynn: "Two months, fourteen days, twelve hours and three minutes."

John: "I don't think we can last. Maybe we should go to Europe."

Daughter: "I'm not going to stay here alone."

Lynn: "How would you know?"

I decided that it was time to break it up, so I went to their front door and knocked. Lynn let me in and ushered me into the living room, where John and his daughter were sitting.

Lynn said, "You know our daughter, Muffie. We're so proud of her. She's captain of the volleyball team and a joy to have at home."

BON APPÉTIT!

To some people it's a problem—to most people it isn't. Food allotments for poor families are being cut all over this country, and expectant mothers and small children face serious cutoffs, and malnutrition.

Nobody wants babies to starve and women to go hungry, but in a country as poor as the United States, what other choices do we have?

Totie Button, a rich government consultant to the poor, told me, "We're facing a crisis. When we promised to provide nutritional subsidies to one-third of all the babies in the United States, we had no idea what the bill would be. We can't give away food willy-nilly to anyone who asks for it while so many savings and loans institutions are starving to death. That would be fiscal suicide."

"How did the poor women and children get into so much trouble?"

"It was just a question of the federal government wrongly estimating what food prices would be this year. There's been a cost increase in orange juice, cereal and infant formula.

All the money that Congress voted for the program has been used up."

"Why doesn't Congress vote more money?"

"Because nutrition for the poor is not an issue that attracts votes. Someone has to tell poor people what Mother Hubbard said when she went to the cupboard and found it bare: 'So much for tough love.' "

He continued, "There are solutions to the problem, but mothers are going to have to take the bit between their teeth. They must explain to their children that the reason they are getting only half a glass of milk a day is because of Gramm–Rudman. They will have to appeal to a child's love of country when the infant formula runs out. Needy people can't just keep consuming food while the deficit is where it is at the moment. There are a lot of things Washington has to spend money on—and food for the poor is at the bottom of the barrel."

"Impoverished people don't talk enough about food to their children," I said.

"I don't want you to think that I am unsympathetic about this, but every mother in the country has to choose between feeding her young and watching another Stealth bomber roll off the assembly line."

"If I were a mother, I'd want the Stealth bomber," I told him.

"Due to the unforeseen food price hikes, we've had to cut a lot of folks out of the program. In one way it's a good thing, because if a child has never had a nutritious meal he won't miss it. I didn't drink orange juice when I was a kid, and I'm no worse off for it. By removing pregnant women and nursing mothers from the rolls, we can give the money to those who are suffering from clinical malnutrition.

"I'm glad that we have this crisis, as it will send a message to all those mothers who are trying to get a free lunch. There are lots of welfare women who can afford to pay for their own dairy products, but who would rather play golf instead."

Button said, "The story of those of us who are fighting to

keep the food budget in perspective has been ignored by the media. Just because we are involved in the cutbacks doesn't mean we are responsible for the rise in the price of cream cheese. Maybe when the cost of food goes down, we can address ourselves to poor people's stomachs. Until then our women and children owe it to their country to tighten their belts and say to themselves, 'Missing one or two meals isn't going to kill me.' "

NASTY, NASTY, NASTY

I HAPPEN TO be one of the two million one hundred thirty-five persons who bought the recording *As Nasty As They Wanna Be* by a rap group called 2 Live Crew. I didn't want to buy the tape after it was banned in Florida and became a cause célèbre throughout the country, but what choice did I have?

I stood in a long line in front of the music shop holding my $9.95. The lady in front of me was as excited as I was.

"I never heard a rap tape before," she confessed.

"Neither have I," I admitted. "I understand that this one is really disgusting."

The lady said, "My grandson tells me that there are a lot worse tapes for sale. Why do you think they picked on *As Nasty As They Wanna Be*?"

"The sheriff of Broward County probably has a son who plays it all day long, and he couldn't take it anymore."

The man standing behind me joined in the conversation. "Why would they censor music?"

"It's not the music—it's the lyrics," I explained. "These are supposed to be the filthiest words ever put to music. They are just awful."

The lady said, "I wonder if they'll let me buy two."

The man sounded puzzled. "What can lyrics in a song do to provoke your prurient interests?"

I said, "This is a free country, but that doesn't mean you can cry 'Fire' in a crowded record shop."

"I'm glad they never censored *The Sound of Music*. That was my favorite," the lady told us.

"Are you really going to play *As Nasty As They Wanna Be* at home?" I asked her.

"I doubt it. I'll probably just stick it in my purse to use as a weapon in case someone attacks me."

"Why are you buying it?" the man asked me.

"Someday I hope to be block warden in my neighborhood, and I need to know what is good for the public and what isn't. It's my understanding that this tape might drive some people to commit unforgivable acts of violence."

"You mean the words could do that?"

"No, the music. The beat will drive them mad."

"Do you think they'll pull other records off the shelves?" the man asked.

"I should hope so," I said. "Censoring rap music could be the biggest gut issue of the next election campaign. Candidates are going to be falling all over themselves demanding the death penalty for those who play that kind of music."

Four hours later we reached the counter, and the clerk behind it handed me the tape in a brown paper bag.

I took it home, locked all the doors, pulled down the shades and placed the cassette in my player. When it began it was a jumble of sounds. I couldn't understand a word. I put it into another tape machine to check it, and once again it was unintelligible.

In a fury, I returned to the music store and told them, "I can't understand one dirty lyric on this tape."

The salesman said, "We never promised you 'My Wild Irish Rose.' "

APRÈS GOLF

FOR REASONS THAT escape me, the obsession of our time is golf. Not since bowling has any sport become such a craze.

It's not that people play it, but it has become their main topic of conversation when they are off the links. Golf is now *the* road to business success and is considered the only ladder to upward mobility.

If I sound bitter, I have reason to be. I spent a lot of money for dinner the other night, and the only subject my guests talked about was the difficulty of hitting a little white ball with a seven iron.

"Do we have to talk golf?" I asked.

They all gasped.

Dinah said, "Is there anything else to talk about?"

I replied, "What difference does it make if you hit the ball in the rough, the sand or the water? When the game is over, it's over, over there."

David expounded, "Golf is over only for those who were never there. Golfers remember every stroke of every game they ever played. That's because we have invested our lives in the sport."

I protested, "But do you really care if Dinah shanked her drive or not?"

"Not really," Richard said. "But if I don't listen to her story, she won't listen to mine."

"I'm very good on details," Dinah told us.

"The trouble with golf is that it has become more than a game," I argued. "Most of our important decisions are now being made on the fairways of this land. People are being given responsibility for nuclear reactors not on the basis of their ability but on the basis of their golf scores. A guy who shoots a seventy-six is considered a better architect than one who shoots a one-oh-three. A brain surgeon who scores an eighty-nine is held in higher esteem than one who can shoot only one-twenty."

"What's wrong with that?" Richard asked. "Americans look up to those players with low scores. I was on the course the other day with a terrific golfer. He birdied half his holes. Well, I did what anybody who plays golf would do under the circumstances. I gave my insurance business to him instead of Ida Kessel, who never leaves her office for lunch."

"People who don't play golf shouldn't pass judgments on those who do," Dinah said. "We who play at country clubs have paid our dues."

"All right. But if golf is such a healthy activity, why do you need golf carts to get around the course?"

"Because with a cart you can get back to the club faster and tell everyone about your game," David explained.

"He's making that up," Dinah said. "Golf is a sport on wheels, and the less time you spend walking, the more time you have to study the lay of the ball. I don't believe there would be this surge of interest in the game if there weren't public transportation from hole to hole."

"I got a fifteen-foot putt today," Richard told the group.

David sounded excited. "Let's hear all about it, and don't leave out any of the details."

"I don't want to hear about it," I protested.

"Don't be too sure," Dinah said. "Richard's stories are always much better than his golf."

THE GOLDEN PARACHUTE

THE DREAM OF every good executive is to have a golden parachute, so that if his company is ever sold or merged, he can bail out for a soft landing.

The finest golden-parachute company is located in Wilmington, Delaware. A visit there gave me an insight into the American business safety-net system.

Norman Bradford, the manager of the plant, took me on a tour. "There was a time when most upper-level executives were satisfied to just work for their salaries and pensions," he told me. "But ever since the hot trading of the eighties, everyone wants a golden parachute to protect Number One. We're backed up on orders."

I walked through the brightly lit, immaculately clean room where people in white smocks were bent over sewing machines.

Norman stopped at one and showed me a sample. "This is a parachute for the CEO of a book publishing house. He heard

217

that he was being raided by a razor blade company, so he ordered the parachute before the raider made a bid."

"Is he worried?"

"He couldn't care less because no matter who buys his publishing house, this parachute will guarantee him thirty million dollars."

"What about the shareholders? Do they know he has a golden parachute?"

"I doubt it. There was a time when CEOs worried about the shareholders, but it was a thankless effort, so they decided to look out for themselves. That's why they come here."

"How much does a golden parachute cost?"

"They can run anywhere from a million dollars for one year to a hundred million dollars for a lifetime. When a raider is after another company, he will pay for a top-of-the-line parachute so that the executive won't fight the buyout. Over here we have a golden parachute for the president of an investment banking company. The company lost eight hundred million dollars last year, but when the firm goes bankrupt the president won't even wind up with a sprained wrist."

"It's remarkable what silk and strings will do for someone who has run his company into the ground."

Norman said, "I wish you had put it some other way. With our golden parachutes we are making it possible for the average executive to have a little security in an age when sharks are eating dolphins, and Wall Street yuppies are tearing the heads off chickens. Without parachutes, the American landscape would be littered with the bodies of executives who lost their life's savings in junk bonds."

"I'm not saying that you don't provide a service," I told Norman. "But it seems to me that many executives are more interested in getting fitted for a golden parachute than they are in running their companies."

"Perhaps, but that isn't our worry. We don't ask what the condition of their business is. We might assume that anyone ordering a golden parachute is not as secure about his business as he would like to be. At the same time, we believe that such a parachute is as important to the financial health of this country as a sushi bar is to Rockefeller Center."

"There's a glass-enclosed booth over there with a gorgeous parachute inside. Who is that for?"

Norman whispered, "That's for *our* chairman of the board."

"He's having one made for himself?"

"Of course. The RJR Nabisco people have been sniffing around for the past week, and our chairman isn't taking any chances."

HUBBLE TROUBLE

WHEN THE $1.5 BILLION Hubble telescope went awry, the powers at NASA immediately called the telescope repairman.

Naturally, they got a recording. "This is Ernie, the telescope repairman. I am not in right now. At the sound of the beep leave your name and information about your telescope, and I'll get back to you as soon as I can."

Several days later the Hubble manager was still waiting to hear from Ernie. They called him at home.

"I was going to get to you today," Ernie said. "What's the problem?"

The manager answered, "The mirrors on the telescope seem to be showing a spherical aberration."

Ernie said, "Do you have a service contract?"

"No, I don't," replied the manager. "The telescope was under warranty for the first four million miles."

"That's only if the telescope falls into a black hole," Ernie explained. "You're going to have to pay for the repairs yourself."

"All right, but when can you get up there and work on it?"

"I don't have any telescope mirrors in stock. I'll have to get them from Spokane. The way they're shipping these days, it's going to take fourteen weeks."

"We can't wait fourteen weeks. The publicity is killing us."

Ernie said, "Let me ask you a question. Who put in the mirror in the first place?"

"John Scarsi of Telescopes 'Я' Us," the manager answered.

"I thought as much," Ernie replied. "He sells every piece of cut-rate space hardware in the book. Ever since NASA has been trying to save money, nothing works. You would have been much better off going to Sears, Roebuck."

"We don't need a lecture," the manager said. "All we want is the mirror fixed so we can get some photos on the Ted Koppel show."

"I can probably put a temporary mirror in the telescope, but I can't guarantee what kind of picture you're going to get."

"That would be better than nothing. When can you do it?"

"Tomorrow morning. I have to fix a flawed radio-signal antenna on the space station, so I'll be in the neighborhood."

The next day, when the manager didn't hear from Ernie, he called him. "You promised to fix our mirror today."

Ernie said, "I forgot when I talked to you that I had a golf game. I'll get on it tomorrow."

"A promise is a promise," the manager shouted angrily. "I have a good mind to find another space telescope repairman."

"Good luck. The way NASA is putting their things together you'd be lucky to find one who isn't tied up until 1995."

The manager asked, "Suppose you can't repair it in the sky? Can you lend us a mirror until you fix this one?"

"I can rent you one for fifty million dollars a month."

"That's outrageous."

"Don't get mad at me. You want to see the Milky Way, I don't," Ernie told him.

"Do I have your word you'll take a look at it tomorrow?" the manager demanded.

"Of course you do," Ernie said. "A licensed repairman never lies."

FIGHT DIRTY

IT ISN'T EASY being a Soviet politician anymore. In the old days you worked your way up through the Communist Party, got elected to office, and before you knew it you were in fat city in Lenin Square.

But now that a multiparty system seems to be replacing communism, those who devoted themselves to the hammer and sickle are faced with opposition from the likes of Boris Yeltsin and his left-wing counterrevolutionary friends.

To prepare for the future, the Communist Party has hired an American political consultant to advise it on how to win a democratic election in the Soviet Union.

The party diehards gathered at the dacha of First Communist Secretary Vladimir Bulkasky for a weekend retreat. The U.S. consultant, Richard Thompson, addressed the group. "I've taken a survey of Soviet voters, and eighty-five percent say they do not understand the difference between the radicals, the progressives and the conservatives. Your job is to help them stay confused."

"Which ones are we?" Chicken Kiev wanted to know.

"You are the party of the Supreme Little Guy," replied Thompson. "You have to get your story over to the voter that the opposition is a bunch of nerds without any respect for God and Gorbachev."

"God and Gorbachev?" Rude Shlepper said. "The Communist Party doesn't believe in God."

Thompson explained, "Not until now. You have to steal God as a symbol before one of the other parties in the Soviet Union does. Now among the most important things a political party does is perform dirty tricks. This is where you can learn from American politics. You must accuse the other side of things they wouldn't dream of doing. Who is your most famous prisoner?"

"Kalangin the Degenerate. He was arrested for opening his own discount shopping mall in Yalta last year and putting the Steelworkers' Cooperative Bazaar out of business."

"Good. Now your Communist Party candidate must announce that the opposition candidate gave Kalangin the Degenerate a weekend furlough at which time he raped three women and opened two more malls and a five-star laundromat."

"Is it true?" Chicken Kiev asked.

Thompson admitted, "It doesn't matter if it's true or not. In America, politicians deny everything, at least until the election is over."

Boris Borscht said, "With the help of the KGB, our politics used to be so much cleaner."

"The reason for that," Thompson explained, "is that you had only one party. Now that you have several, you can no longer be Mr. Good Comrade."

"It's true," agreed Ivan. "We were the good guys. That was the main advantage of having only one party. You didn't have to resort to dirty tricks to win. People voted for you either because they believed in what you stood for or because they were afraid of being sent to Siberia. Now we have to get our hands dirty and cheat and lie and steal, which no Communist likes to do."

Thompson went on, "Now this is going to be the hard part. In a multiparty system of government, you must raise money. If you don't have a war chest, you're dead Reds."

"How do we raise money?" Boris asked.

"You tell everyone that if they donate to the Communist Party PAC they will receive favors that no other government official will give them, including complete deregulation of the savings and loan industry."

"That's bribery," protested Chicken Kiev.

Thompson replied, "No, it isn't. In a democratic society we have many private special-interest groups, and if they couldn't give money to their political parties, all the crooks would take over."

MOVING THE LINE

MY WIFE IS A strong women's rights advocate. She will fight for any kind of equal opportunity, except when it comes to large public restrooms.

The other evening we went to see a Broadway hit show. After the first act, she excused herself to wash her hands.

When she failed to return to her seat twenty minutes later, I decided to look for her. She was in line on Fifty-second Street, slowly wending her way toward the washroom.

"What do you think?" I asked her.

"I'm not going to make the second act."

"Why?"

"Because I never make the second act when I go to the washroom. I don't even know how *The Phantom of the Opera* ends."

"You're a pessimist," I told her. "As I see it, you have only another hundred yards to the restroom door. All you need are a few breaks, and you'll be home free."

"Why do they build a theater for two thousand people and a women's restroom for two?" she wanted to know.

"I think it's because theater owners have to put their money where it will help the show—in the scenery. As far as they are concerned, washrooms are a waste of space. The owners would rather have the square footage for standing room only."

My wife said, "If I don't make it, brief me about the second act on the way home."

"You'll make it. Remember when you were waiting at *A Chorus Line*? Despite your doubts, you got back for the final curtain."

"That's because I went to the restroom at the beginning of the first act. I missed the opening and all the scenes that followed."

"Look, you just moved up three places. This could be your night."

She said, "Why don't you find someone to sit with in the second act? Then my seat won't be wasted."

"Nosirree. I came with you, and I won't let anyone take your place. I can't understand why women don't raise more hell about the restroom facilities of our theaters and sports arenas. They will protest every indignity heaped on their sex except what architects do to cut down on their washroom rights. If you don't raise your voices, you're going to be standing in line for the rest of your lives."

"It's undignified to make a fuss over those rights," she explained. "We do have pride."

"Maybe so—but that doesn't mean you're going to see the big finish of this performance."

"What do you suggest women do?"

"Take over the men's john, for starters, and lock them out. If males can't get back for the second act, they will be the ones to let management know about it."

My wife was in tears. "The last time I saw an entire show was when I was six years old."

"I hear music. I think I'd better go back to my seat."

"Au revoir," she said.

I told her, "It isn't your fault that the theater owners won't build decent facilities for their customers."

The lady behind my wife asked me, "Are you in line?"

I told her I wasn't.

"Good," she said. "That means I can still catch the midnight local to Stamford."

BIG NEWS

TOBEY HAD BEEN backpacking and his only connection with the outside world was a small portable radio which he tuned in for the news. The reception was not as good as he hoped it would be.

"I hear Roseanne Barr was appointed to the Supreme Court," he said to me.

"Roseanne wasn't appointed to the Supreme Court. David Souter was nominated for the Court."

"Who is David Souter?"

"Nobody has the foggiest notion," I answered. "He never left any footprints. The only thing we know about him is that he lives alone in the woods and is a solitary thinker."

"Well," Tobey said, "what was Roseanne Barr appointed to?"

"She wasn't appointed to anything. She sang 'The Star-Spangled Banner' at a San Diego Padres game."

"Why would that be news?"

"After she sang it she grabbed the lower part of her body and spit on the ground."

"Was that because she hadn't been appointed to the Supreme Court?"

"No one is quite sure why she did it. The crowd got upset, but we're not sure whether it was for her holding her groin, her spitting on the ground, or the way she sang the national anthem."

Tobey asked, "Why didn't George Steinbrenner sing 'The Star-Spangled Banncr' instead?"

"Because George Steinbrenner has been banned from baseball."

"What for?"

"For hiring a thug to get bad information on the Supreme Court nine so he could fire them. The baseball commissioner said George was giving the Court a bad name."

"I heard that on my radio. Is it true Neil Bush is going to take over Steinbrenner's job?"

"No, Steinbrenner's son is going to take over the job. Neil Bush is going to take over all the S&Ls in Colorado."

"Why?"

"Because his father said he didn't do anything wrong."

"I failed to hear that on my portable. How much money do the taxpayers owe for the S&L bailouts?"

I said, "One hundred billion dollars more than they did before you went backpacking."

"I don't have the money," Tobey announced.

"You can borrow it from an S&L."

"I heard that," Tobey admitted. "What I missed was the news that Iraq had won the Goodwill Games in Seattle."

"Iraq didn't win the Goodwill Games in Seattle. It invaded Kuwait."

"That's dumb," Tobey said. "Was it because Bush had appointed Jane Pauley to the Supreme Court?"

I could see that Tobey had spent too much time in the mountains. "Let's get it straight once and for all: George Steinbrenner turned down the offer of Supreme Court justice because he wanted to spend more time developing Roseanne Barr's musical career. Neil Bush has become Donald Trump's financial advisor, and Pete Rose has agreed to be mayor of Washington as part of his community service."

"I missed all that on my radio," Tobey declared. "Is there anything else I should know?"

"President Bush is going to ask for a constitutional amendment making it a federal crime to sing 'The Star-Spangled Banner' off-key and scratch yourself at the same time."

IT'S YOUR RAISE

RAISING THE PRICE of oil and gasoline in the United States is a serious business. While the price is based in part on supply and demand, other factors are also involved.

One of the largest price-fixers is Nathan Cheesebelt, who works in the boiler room of the Spitball Oil Company.

The only reason Cheesebelt agreed to see me was that his mother told him he had to.

He was at his desk facing a large blackboard, with a telephone against each ear, and shouting at the people in the room. "We just got word that there is going to be a full moon tomorrow. Let's raise super leaded to two dollars and ninety cents a gallon."

Someone wrote "$2.90" on the blackboard and everyone cheered.

Then Cheesebelt turned to me. "What do you want?"

"I was wondering if you could tell me how you arrive at your prices?"

"We do it by crisis. For a long time the price of oil was down, down, down. We could get more for Evian water than we could for gasoline. The oil companies were starving to death and no one cared. Then came Iraq and we started to live again. The threat of a shortage gave us an excuse to send the price soaring."

"There is a rumor that some companies are gouging to take advantage of the Middle East conflagration. Any truth to that?"

"Lies, all lies. We're only charging a minimum price to make up for all the years we had to eat dog food." The phone rang and Cheesebelt picked it up. "Right." Then he yelled at the woman standing at the blackboard: "The New York Yankees just lost a double-header—move everything at the pump up another ninety-five cents."

"Do you always raise the price of gasoline when the Yankees lose?"

"In an oil crisis you raise it every chance you get. We went up forty-five cents yesterday because the air-conditioning unit in the basement broke down."

"Do you have carte blanche to increase prices as high as you want to?"

"Of course, but we don't do it willy-nilly. For example, there was a traffic jam this morning on the Capital Beltway when a tractor-trailer flipped over. We didn't increase the prices over that."

"Why not?" I asked.

"Because we had already raised them after a three-car collision that completely stopped everything on the Triborough Bridge."

"At the very time you are raising prices because of events here, you are also hiking them according to what's going on in the Middle East."

"It's all part of the same package," Cheesebelt told me. "Once you have an excuse to push up gas prices, you use it. Nobody was sorry for us when we made more on the diet cola we sold in our machines than we did on gasoline at the pump. Now the oil can is on the other foot, and people are going to be coming to us with tin cups and fistfuls of dollars begging us to fill their tanks."

"The beauty of the oil business," I said, "is that one day you're up and the next day you're down."

"In a crisis all we do is provide a product."

The phone rang again.

Cheesebelt shouted, "What did you say? . . . Mayor Barry is going to make a videotape for MTV? Right . . ." He yelled up to the person at the blackboard: "Raise everything on the board another dollar."

FASTEN SEAT BELTS

I TOOK my friend Pierce to the airport the other day. He was flying coach from Boston to Los Angeles. The gentleman behind the counter said, "That will be seven hundred dollars."

Pierce exclaimed, "Seven hundred dollars! I'm not flying by Concorde."

The man replied, "That is our special summer rate for tourist class."

"It's outrageous," Pierce blurted. "How can you charge someone seven hundred dollars for that flight?"

The man said, "You are our only paying flyer. Everyone else is either a free-mileage passenger or an employee of the airline heading back home."

Pierce asked, "Don't you have people who purchase their tickets anymore?"

"Hardly ever. It's refreshing to meet someone like you who isn't looking for a free lunch."

"Since I'm the only paying passenger on the flight, couldn't I be upgraded from tourist to first class?"

"I hardly think so. Most of our upgrades are people who have sixty thousand miles in credit and have slept in a Hilton Hotel for three nights. They naturally get priority over someone like yourself who is paying cash for his seat."

"How does an airline earn money when it gives away all its flights?"

"We make our profit on cheap maintenance. What we lose on our fares we save in our hangars."

I said to Pierce, "It looks as if you don't have any choice."

Pierce spoke up, "Wait a minute. How long will it take before I fly for free?"

The clerk looked in his book. "I would say two more flights should do it, provided you eat at a Red Lobster restaurant and see *Dick Tracy* sixteen times. We have tie-ins with everyone for our 'Come Fly with Me' August free-fall program."

"Okay," said Pierce. "Give me a ticket."

As the man wrote it out, he murmured, "We would prefer if you didn't mention to the other passengers that you paid for your seat."

Pierce turned red. "Why not?"

"Because they'll think you're a snob. Most of our free-flyers are very proud, and they won't sit next to people who bought their tickets."

"You just made me pay seven hundred dollars for a trip to L.A., and now you tell me I can't talk about it?"

"It's not an FAA regulation, but it has been our experience that people who have purchased their tickets at full price are considered dumb, and no one has respect for them."

Pierce said, "I don't see any humor in this. If you really cared about paying passengers you would give us the red carpet so everyone in the airport knows who we are."

"We don't want to start a precedent. If we give paying passengers the royal treatment, then our employees will demand the same thing, and we can't offend them, because they take up a lot of free seats on our planes. You ought to feel lucky I sold you a ticket. I have someone who won a trip on *Wheel of Fortune* waiting on standby for your seat."

"Why did you take me over him?" Pierce wanted to know.

"Because the FAA insists we set a number of seats aside just in case some sucker wants to pay."

HOTLINE

IT WAS SURPRISING that no one had thought of it before. The idea was to establish a hotline for people who are threatening to kill themselves, not for major reasons but for minor ones.

Zimsky, who founded the hotline, explained: "More and more people keep threatening to do away with themselves over matters that really aren't that important. Our hotline exists to talk them out of it. Here is a call. Listen on the earphone."

A hysterical woman's voice said, "If my meatloaf doesn't come out, I'm going to kill myself."

Zimsky replied, "You shouldn't kill yourself over a meatloaf."

The lady shot back, "That's easy enough for you to say. But I'm taking this to a potluck dinner, and if it turns out lousy, everyone will know I made it. I'd rather go out the window than have a meatloaf that doesn't work."

"You make a good case for doing yourself in, but have you thought what something like this will do to your family?"

"It doesn't matter. They never did like meatloaf."

Zimsky went on, "You're assuming that the meatloaf is not going to work. Suppose it is the hit of the party, and everybody says this is the most delicious dish they've ever had. Wouldn't it be terrible if you weren't around to hear them?"

The lady admitted, "I never thought of that. I have changed my mind. I want to live, so every meatloaf I make will be better than the last one."

She hung up, and Zimsky turned to me. "That's more or less a typical call. The lady wanted to kill herself because she was certain that people would laugh at her meatloaf. But she was willing to be talked out of it."

The phone rang again. It was a young girl who said, "I'm going to die if I don't lose five pounds before I go back to school."

Zimsky told her, "You're going to feel fat and unwanted, but you are not going to die."

"Oh, yes I am. Just before I left school in the spring I heard two boys refer to me as 'Butterball.' This summer I vowed to take off ten pounds, but I've put on eight. I don't deserve to live."

"Ordinarily," Zimsky answered, "that would be true. But these are not ordinary times. People who never put on weight before are putting it on for no reason. You are not alone. You should not harm yourself because you want to eliminate weight from your body."

"What should I do if I don't want to die?" the girl asked.

Zimsky replied, "Cut out bread and desserts."

After the girl had hung up I said to Zimsky, "You're a good counselor."

"There are far more people threatening to take gas over trivial matters than consequential ones," he responded.

Once again the phone rang. It was a man's voice. "I'm going to jump off the roof if my wife tells me one more time what my mother said to her at my brother Charley's birthday party."

Zimsky said, "It was that bad?"

"You'd think so if you had heard it as many times as I have. Apparently my mother told my wife that she doesn't dress me well, and every time my mother sees me I look down on my luck."

"That does sound heavy. But failing to meet dress codes should not be a cause for suicide."

"I am not concerned about the clothes. But I don't want to live in a world where I have to hear my wife tell me the story one more time."

"Nobody does," said Zimsky.

WHERE AM I?

I APPRECIATE THE anchormen of the network news shows going to the scene of the "big story." Nothing cheers me up as much as seeing Dan Rather, Tom Brokaw, Peter Jennings or Sam Donaldson in the hot desert sands of the Middle East giving a firsthand report of what is happening on the front lines.

If I have any problem with the coverage, it is that occasionally the anchormen land in the wrong desert. Then, because they don't want to admit they've made a mistake, we're all stuck with their reporting on an area where nothing is going on.

The rule of thumb for network anchormen is that the news is not where the news is, but where they are. You don't spend thousands of dollars shipping in crews of technicians to a foreign setting only to acknowledge that the anchorman is in the wrong place at the wrong time.

Let's say the anchorman, Horace Trotter, has been given a tip that the big news on the Mideast will break in Tangier. New York makes the decision to send the entire evening news crew to Morocco, and announces it will be broadcasting live from there until the Iraq crisis is over.

When he arrives in Tangier, Horace discovers all the action is coming out of Saudi Arabia. He is not deterred. He interviews a camel driver whose nephew has just slipped through the embargo and delivered a case of maple syrup to Baghdad. The camel driver tells Horace that his nephew was held hostage but managed to escape by giving his captors three legs of lamb and a microwave oven.

After this lead story, the program moves on to the U.S. embassy, where Horace interviews the commander of the U.S. Marine Corps guard detail, a master sergeant, who gives a briefing on the military situation in the region.

Horace then shifts to the university to explain why Morocco plays a key role in the Iraq war. He brings on a professor from Western Illinois University who specializes in Bedouin camel racing. The professor feels that since Morocco supports the moderate Arab states, Iraq will have to give in.

The picture shifts back to New York, and Flora Delta, Horace's assistant anchor, reports on a heart transplant operation between a Yankees owner and a player on the team, and on a crack bust in Washington in which no video pictures were taken. Then she throws it to Horace for his final commentary.

"It's hot in Tangier," Horace says as he takes off his tie on camera. "It's hot because the sun is hot, and that makes people hot. I've been hot ever since I arrived here, and yet it was the king of Morocco who told me during an exclusive interview in his air-conditioned palace, 'If you can't stand the heat, get out of the desert.'

"Nobody knows what is going to happen in this climate, but we know this much—the key to everything lies somewhere out there in the sand. Americans have not been asked to land in Tangier, but I have been assured by U.S. military authorities that if they wanted to, they could. Tonight at midnight we're going to talk to an Algerian communist and a Yemeni capitalist, who will discuss ways out of the mess the area has gotten itself into.

"On behalf of everyone at QBC, this is Horace Trotter bringing you the news when it happens, at the moment it happens. And if we're in Tangier, you better believe that's where it's happening."

PEEPING KLAUS

ONE OF THE reasons things are not going as well as expected in Eastern Europe is that so many jobs are being eliminated by the new regimes.

I met an East German immigrant in the Boston air terminal recently and we started talking about the old country.

"What did you do in East Germany?" I asked him.

"I watched people," he said.

"What do you mean, you watched people?"

"I got up in the morning, dressed, and climbed a ladder behind the Berlin Wall and watched West Germans."

"What for?"

"Anything. For example, if a West German woman went into a laundromat, I wrote it down in my book. I even watched the driver when he delivered a Domino's pizza. No one escaped my sharp, piercing eyes."

"What were the West Germans doing while you were watching them?"

"They were watching me. There were times when things were very quiet and we did nothing but stare at each other for hours on end."

"Besides peering at West Germans in the streets, did you also watch them in their apartments?"

"No, we had special people to do that. You had to know someone in the secret police to qualify as an apartment watcher, because obviously there were more exciting things going on in someone's flat than outside in the street. To tell you the truth, I was hoping to be promoted to apartments when the roof fell in on watching West Berlin."

"During all your years as a street spy, was there any particular incident that stands out?"

"I once saw an American student come up to the Wall, pull his pants down and turn his backside toward East Germany, while photographers took pictures of him."

"What did you do?"

"I made a note of it in my book."

"After looking at Berlin through binoculars for so many years, did you ever have the desire to go over the Wall yourself?"

"Never. If I had gone to West Berlin, then I would have had to get a job watching East Berlin, and that would have been really depressing. I was one of the few East Germans who liked where he lived."

"Then what are you doing in the United States?"

"I lost my job. They called me in and said, 'Klaus, you don't have to watch West Germans anymore.'

" 'Why not?' I asked them.

" 'Because we are no longer interested in what they do. They can toss Frisbees into the center of Odenstrasse and we couldn't care less.'

"I told them, 'Right now is the honeymoon, but someday when we get mad at West Germany again, you are going to need professional watchers, and they will all be retired.' "

"Are you optimistic about getting a people-watching job in the United States?" I asked him.

"Yes. I hear that the Justice Department is looking for some-one to keep an eye on Leona Helmsley."

YOU ARE WHAT YOU EAT

THE BEST NEWS of the year came when scientists announced that body fat could be produced by genes. This was counter to all the conventional wisdom that overweight people are no good.

I received the news while eating a dandelion salad sandwich and drinking a diet cola at the lunch counter.

J. David Emge was the one who gave me the information. "The latest research says that if you get fat you have no one but your grandparents to blame," he said. "It's all in your body make-up. One person can eat an apple pie and not put on weight. Others can put four poppy seeds in their mouths and balloon. It's not food but your chromosomes that makes all the decisions."

"I knew that science would finally find a cure for large suit sizes."

Emge was pleased that he could bring me such glad tidings. "Sometime back in antiquity, possibly even before man invented French-fried potatoes, it was decreed that people like yourself would have a slightly pudgy, though not unattractive, girth. Our mistake was to believe that being heavy was a character flaw, when in fact it was Darwin's choice all along."

"How did this happen?"

"Stunkard at the University of Pennsylvania worked with twins. He found that environment and diet had little impact compared with that of their genes. He concluded that since genes are so important, those lacking in willpower are blaming themselves needlessly for not being able to see their toes when they bend over."

"How does Stunkard feel about buttered garlic bread?"

"I'm sure he's not against it. It's quite possible a person's genes tell him when he should or should not eat bread. Bouchard of Laval University in Quebec worked with twins as well and came to the same conclusion."

"Which is?"

"When you're fat, relax and enjoy it."

"Overeaters owe a lot to Stunkard and Bouchard," I said. "I wonder what it would mean to them if I ate this piece of chocolate layer cake instead of these string beans with lemon juice on them."

"They'd probably have a hard time telling you what it meant, unless you had a twin brother in a diner across town."

"I think it would be wonderful if everyone in the world had genes that could burn up all their calories instead of turning them into fat."

"It will be done," Emge said. "That's why we have genetic engineering. In the meantime I'd say that since it isn't your fault when you gain weight, you might as well eat what you want."

"That seems to be the best solution," I agreed. "If my genes are programmed for bread pudding, it makes no sense to feed them raw carrots."

Emge nodded. "The importance of this study is that it changes the way people look at each other. Maybe they'll stop being critical of others now that they know it's not their hips but their heredity that makes it so difficult to fit into a new bathing suit."

THE NEWS ACCORDING TO HONEY MAID

I TURNED ON the network news the other evening, and lo and behold, the announcer said, "*World News Tonight* is brought to you by Honey Maid Grahams." The first thought to go through my head was, Why in the world is Honey Maid Grahams bringing me the evening news?

Fortunately, the producer for the network lives down the street. After the show I stopped by his house to try to get an answer. "How come your network is now giving us the news via the courtesy of graham crackers?"

"Would you rather we present it through Chicken of the Sea?" he asked.

"That's not the point. My question to you is, What does it mean when the news is brought to me by Honey Maid Grahams? Did Honey Maid gather the news, and did they decide what goes on the air?"

He smiled as if he was talking to the village idiot. "Honey Maid had nothing to do with gathering the news. The network did that. But somebody had to pay for it, and that's where the graham crackers come in. The Honey Maid people agreed to pay a bonus, and we guaranteed that we would tell all you viewers that they brought the news to you. When we want to attract sponsors, the network will always walk the extra mile."

"That's fine and dandy," I said, "but if you announce at the beginning of the program that a graham cracker company is bringing us the news, how do we know we're getting all of it?"

"I'm not sure what you're driving at," he answered.

"Well, suppose some big scandal on graham crackers broke that day. Would the network sit on it because Honey Maid Grahams was sponsoring the news?"

"Absolutely not. We have an understanding that if anything happens in the graham cracker industry, we play it just like we would the Perrier accident—straight down the line."

"Why does Honey Maid Grahams think that sponsoring the evening news will help sell more crackers?"

"Because their surveys indicate that people who watch the news are very nervous and will consume an entire box without even knowing it. You have drought, pestilence, war and dope trials on TV every night. The only thing that makes any sense for people watching the news is the commercials."

"I don't have a problem with who sponsors the news. What bothers me is that company gets credit for *bringing* it to me. I am sure that Honey Maid Grahams had nothing to do with Mr. Gorbachev defending his economic reforms, or Margaret

Thatcher lecturing President Mitterrand at Ten Downing Street, or Neil Bush explaining his role in the S&L scandal. You don't serve up news like that with graham crackers."

My producer buddy said, "These are not easy times for the networks. The price of news collecting is going up, and the number of minutes advertisers are buying is going down. We welcome the fact that Honey Maid Grahams will share our costs for covering major catastrophes."

I asked him, "As part of the deal, does everyone at the network have to eat graham crackers?"

He flushed. "There's no tie-in with Honey Maid. The network staff is free to eat Oreos, ginger snaps or Fig Newtons. I don't know of one news reporter who eats graham crackers because Honey Maid is paying his or her salary."

"What about the people on the business side of the network?"

"They'll drink Quaker Oil if it will help sell the show."

TV BITES FROM HITLER

SUPPOSE THERE HAD been television at the beginning of World War II. Would the Nazis have appeared different to us?

"Tommy, this is Joan. I'm standing in front of Hitler's bunker in Berlin, hoping to get a few words from him on why his army walked into the Sudetenland."

"Joanie, can we count on Hitler for the evening news?"

"Not so far. All the Germans are offering us is Joseph Goebbels, but everyone here says that the guy is lacking in credibility."

"Joanie, I don't want Goebbels. He bombed out on the *Today* show last week, and he doesn't answer questions—he makes speeches."

"Albert Speer is in Makeup if you want him."

"I want Hitler. Adolf Hitler with a big A. The guy was on Ted Koppel last night. He owes us."

"Tommy, I heard that Hitler is willing to do it but members of his kitchen cabinet have promised him to CBS. They said that they would give us Hermann Göring, wearing all his medals. I didn't say no, because Göring hasn't been on television in a week. Tommy, while I was standing here, Heinrich Himmler of the notorious SS went by and indicated that he might do a one-on-one with Hugh Downs on *20/20*. Are we interested?"

"I want Hitler, not Himmler, Joanie. Adolf was on Connie Chung last week telling his side of the war. Why can't we get him for five minutes?"

"Hitler doesn't do five minutes. He's asked for two full hours to explain why he plans to goose-step into Austria."

"We're giving him the opportunity of his life. What other mad, bloodthirsty dictator has a chance to make his case on prime time to the American people?"

"It's a good point, but Hitler is mad at U.S. television ever since Dan Rather stuck a microphone up his nose and called him a psychopathic screwball."

"Dan Rather doesn't work for us. We're almost at war, and we're going to have egg on our faces if we are the only network not to have interviewed the Führer. Don't you see, Joanie? No one knows what evil is until they see the little Austrian rat on television. Tell Hitler we'll let him tell his side of the story about why he intends to go into Poland—with no editing on our part."

"I'll try, Tommy, but won't we catch hell with the American public for that?"

"Probably, but we'll also get the ratings."

"Tommy, if we can get Hitler, don't you think that we're obliged to have Roosevelt on as well?"

"I know the Nazis, and they won't go for it. As a matter of fact, Roosevelt is asking for equal time on German TV to balance the airtime Hitler got in the States."

"That will make good television. By the way, Tommy, there's a guy in the German SS named Adolf Eichmann who wants to go on *Good Morning America* and say that he is only following orders."

"Everyone in the SS claims to have an alibi. There is only one person to speak for Germany, and that's the big H himself. You tell him that if he doesn't go on tonight at seven o'clock, he'll never be invited on with Tom Brokaw again."

"I'll try, but it's hard for an American to get through to Hitler's inner sanctum ever since Jesse Jackson came over and started passing himself off as a journalist."

Tommy said, "You can do it, Joanie."

Joanie responded, "While I've got you on the line, the Italian Ministry of Propaganda is offering an interview with Benito Mussolini. They're talking about his being Person of the Week."

"Refer him to Geraldo Rivera. He specializes in windbags on the right. Tell Hitler that if he goes on our show, we'll pay his way over on Pan Am, put him up for three days at the Waldorf-Astoria, and get him two tickets to the Max Schmeling–Joe Louis fight."

THE FORTIETH ANNIVERSARY

I WENT BACK TO Paris to celebrate the fortieth anniversary of the running of the Six-Minute Louvre. Yes, I know it's hard to believe that forty years ago a young American student named Peter Stone broke the Six-Minute Louvre, and brought glory and honor to American tourists everywhere.

For those of you who weren't around, this is the story:

It is common knowledge that there are only three things worth seeing in the Louvre. They are the Venus de Milo, the Winged Victory and the Mona Lisa. The rest of the stuff is all junk. For years tourists went to see those three works and then rushed out to continue their shopping in Paris.

Before World War II, the record for going through the Louvre was seven minutes and thirty seconds, held by a man known as the Swedish Cannonball. After the war, an Englishman, paced by his Welsh wife, did it in seven minutes flat, and pretty soon everyone started talking about a Six-Minute Louvre.

Thus it was in 1950 that the young Peter Stone went in on a Sunday (a day when you didn't have to pay) and, while thousands cheered, ran around the Venus de Milo, up past the Winged Victory, down to the Mona Lisa. You always have to say something when you look at the Mona Lisa. Peter's famous remark was, "I know the guy who has the original," and then he drove away in a waiting taxi. Peter did it in five minutes and fifty-six seconds, a record no tourist has ever been able to beat.

As I stood in the courtyard of the palace, looking around me at the seasoned veterans who had come back, I recalled the fifties and thought, When it came to sightseeing, we were the best and the brightest.

Our group gathered outside the Louvre to try to relive the memories. Many of us had brought our children to share the moment. I told my son, "I. M. Pei's glass pyramid has made it impossible to get near the record. Look at us—we've been standing in line for an hour."

"Give me a pair of Reeboks or Nikes and I could do it," my son said.

"The kind of shoes you wear doesn't help, when there are now escalators all over the museum. The French always had a fear that an American would beat the Six-Minute Louvre, and they did everything to confuse us. That's why they would point you in the direction of the Mona Lisa, and you'd wind up in the *salle* displaying twenty-two armless and headless Roman statues from Sicily. The reason Peter broke the record was that he refused to take any directions from the museum guards."

A man with a cane came up to me and stuck out his hand. "My name's Gerry Tornplast. I was on Thomas Cook Tour Number Two-thirty on September thirteenth when it all happened. My God, I was proud that morning. The French didn't think we could do it, but we proved that when the dollar is strong and the franc is weak, an American can achieve anything."

My son asked, "Wasn't there something else you wanted to see in the Louvre?"

"There was nothing. You have to remember, son, in those days the American tourist was strapped for time and there were just so many hours in the day until we trotted off to see the Folies-Bergère."

I continued, "I brought you here today so that you would be

aware of your heritage. Once upon a time there were thousands of American tourists who never failed to visit the Louvre for a very short time. Now they are all gone, but the halls still echo with Peter Stone's voice, as he broke into the sunlight, proclaiming, 'There isn't a museum in the world that can keep me inside for very long.' "

BAGHDAD *ÜBER ALLES*

THE SECRET IS OUT. Germany was the most reluctant of dragons to give support to the Western allies in the Persian Gulf war.

I asked a German acquaintance, Otto Kraus, why Germany was refusing to help the United States in its battle with Iraq.

With tears in his eyes, Otto replied, "We don't have any money."

"Come off it, Otto. What do you mean, Germany doesn't have any money?"

He explained, "Iraq won't pay us for all the poison gas equipment and the biological weapons we sent them. They won't even pay for the nuclear machinery that we delivered. We're stuck with so many bills Germany can't afford to get into a quarrel with Iraq at this time."

"Why not?"

"Because Saddam Hussein has been one of our best customers. We are unable to sell him anything now. However, once the embargo is lifted, we want Iraq to remember us with kindness."

"That's fair, and yet don't you feel an obligation to the UN countries who are spitting mad that Iraq annexed Kuwait?"

"We don't like it, but you must remember that Germany annexed a lot of territory at the beginning of World War Two, so we're not in a position to criticize anybody else. It is unreasonable that we should be singled out because we won't send troops to Saudi Arabia."

"Does this have anything to do with your constitution?"

"No, it's because it's too hot there. German troops hate the heat—that's why we never did well in North Africa."

"Otto, you owe it to the United States. We helped rebuild your nation out of the rubble. We initiated the Berlin airlift to protect you from the Russians. We bought every camera Germany could make. Now that the chips are down, your people should reciprocate and come to our aid."

"Of course we should, but that means sending troops to the desert. Are you sure you want us to do that?"

"I'm very sure. After all, the oil in Kuwait is your oil as well as ours."

"Nobody knows this, but we are in fact assisting the United States in the Middle East."

"How?"

"We are supplying stereo equipment to U.S. PXs. This is top-of-the-line stuff you don't even find in Crazy Eddie's."

"I hate to tell you, Otto, but Germany is considered the Cowardly Lion of the Western world."

"It doesn't matter what the world thinks, as long as we can get Iraq to pay its bills."

"Once you had a reputation for being a bully—now everyone says that you are a wimp."

"What business is it of yours what we do?" Otto wanted to know.

I replied, "I have a vested interest in everything Germany does. I own a Mercedes-Benz."

Otto defended himself. "All we have been doing in the Middle East is following orders."

"Whose orders?"

"The German Central Bank's."

THE MARLBORO MAN IN MOSCOW

THERE ARE OTHER things going on in the world besides the Middle East crisis. One is that Philip Morris and RJR Nabisco have just signed a contract to sell 34 billion cigarettes to the Soviet Union.

I asked Boris Gum, a Russian trade official stationed in Washington, if the importation of that much tobacco would cause a coughing problem in the Soviet Union.

"Smoking has never been a health issue in the USSR," he replied. "Finding the cigarettes has been the difficulty. We don't have any consumer goods in our country right now, so people smoke a lot to forget that this is the first day of the rest of their lives. Russian citizens would kill for cigarettes sooner than for raspberries," he assured me.

"But with thirty-four billion cigarettes, the United States could bury you!"

"Why do Americans care, as long as they make money on it?"

"In the past we didn't care, but now we need every Soviet citizen we can get, to beat the hell out of the Iraqis."

Boris said, "Don't worry about our health. Your cigarettes are too mild to hurt our people. The major difference between our countries is that Russian cigarettes taste like blowtorches and yours taste like rice pudding."

"Are you going to put warnings on the U.S. cigarettes before you sell them?" I asked Boris.

"The Soviet Union does not believe that government should interfere in the private lives of its citizens," he said.

"What about people who object to other Russians' smoking? Will their rights be respected?"

"We plan to divide the Soviet Union up into smoking and nonsmoking sections. The smokers will live in Siberia, the nonsmokers in the Ukraine."

"How did the tobacco deal happen?" I wanted to know.

Boris told me, "The Soviets have always admired America's ability to blow smoke. We dreamed of manufacturing our own cigarette which would match the firepower of a Camel or a Virginia Slim. Unfortunately, our nicotine scientists could never come up with anything as good. So when the American cigarette companies offered to sell us cigarettes, we threw out the food budget for the next five years to buy all the butts in Philip Morris."

"I guess now the Russians have it made."

"Not exactly," Boris said. "We're still lacking."

"In what?" I asked.

"Matches. The U.S. deal didn't include matches."

"Why not?"

"The Americans were afraid that we'd set fire to Lithuania. It doesn't matter, because this agreement will make it possible for the U.S. and the Soviet Union to become brothers again. It's a religious experience."

"How?"

"Every time a Soviet citizen lights up he says, 'Thank God for the Marlboro Man.' "

ARMS AND THE MAN

I WENT OUT to Big Al's Weapons Bazaar in Alexandria, Virginia, and found the warehouse was stacked with crates addressed to Baghdad.

"You seem overloaded," I remarked.

"Ever since the U.S. embargo of Iraq, I've been stuck with all this stuff. Our government doesn't give a damn about what happens to its businessmen."

"Was Iraq a good customer?"

"The best. They bought everything in my catalogue and paid cash on the barrel."

"Does it bother you that so many of the weapons you sent to Iraq might now be used against us?"

"Listen, we were encouraged by the State Department to sell to the Iraqis so that they would beat the hell out of the Iranians. Everybody—the French, the British, the Russians, the Germans—was after Iraq's account. I underbid them, and by beefing up Iraq, I helped the U.S. trade balance. If it hadn't been for me, China would have stolen all the business."

"Are you saying that the United States urged you to sell to Iraq?"

"The Commerce Department doesn't regard arms as weapons of war, but rather as export products that can benefit the U.S. economy. The Soviet Union was discounting their ammunition until we had a pre-Christmas sale."

"Did you send any chemical weapons to Iraq?"

"None that I know of. At the same time, you never ask a country why it wants airtight shells. It's rare for a nation that's up to no good to buy all its equipment in the same place. It may purchase computers in Japan, casings in Sweden, delivery systems in France and chemicals in Germany. I sold them masks and protective suits to repel the gas. No one can be criticized for selling a country like Iraq defensive weapons."

"I guess the good news for the rest of us is that there's not much more you can do for Iraq as long as the embargo is on," I told Al.

"I'm going to testify before Congress about how badly the government treats its arms merchants. We have a political action committee too."

"There are some who say that the munitions people are part of the problem. If you hadn't sold all the equipment to the Iraqis, they might not be in a position to threaten the entire Western world."

"Arms merchants don't start wars. All we do is make sure that both sides involved are properly equipped."

"What are you going to do with all this stuff that you can't deliver to Iraq?"

"Sell it to Iran."

"But Iran has declared a holy war against us and may help Iraq!"

"Nobody's perfect. If I don't get rid of all this equipment I'm going to take a terrible bath, and President Bush will have no one but himself to blame."

"Where did you originally get the supplies for Iraq?"

"From U.S. government stockpiles. You see, the Pentagon has two departments—one that buys weapons and one that sells them. The latter gives dealers far more respect, because if the arms merchants don't buy surplus equipment, the Pentagon will sit on a lot of stuff that everyone is dying for."

CREDIT CARD

Recently one of my credit cards was stolen. The problem was, I was unaware of the theft, and therefore the criminal had use of the card for about thirty days.

I got wind that something was wrong when the charges started to come in.

"Did you have a nice time in Puerto Rico?" my accountant wanted to know.

"Not really," I told him. "Mainly because I haven't been there in over ten years."

"Well, you got a credit card bill for three thousand dollars for a stay there, and it looks as if you had a wonderful shopping spree. I wish you would tell your wife to buy quarts instead of gallons of Joy perfume."

"That wasn't my wife," I protested. "She hates Joy. It's obvious that someone else is using my card."

My accountant said, "There's no need to be hasty. I heard a story where a woman's credit card was stolen and her husband decided not to report it because the thief was spending only about half of what his wife usually did."

I told him, "You're not taking this seriously. This person must be brought to justice."

"You don't have to pay the charges once you report the loss," he assured me.

"I'm not worried about that. I'm concerned that he's going to hurt my reputation as a big spender. Suppose he buys his socks at People's Drug Store? How is that going to make me look when the story gets into the newspaper?"

"You're overly concerned. These guys spend big, and they spend fast, before there is any chance of getting caught. I have your bill here in front of me. Your friend bought a beautiful cashmere jacket at Barney's for fourteen hundred dollars."

"Single- or double-breasted?"

"Single."

"That's good," I said. "I hate double-breasted."

My accountant continued, "He had dinner for two at the Ugly Seaport for a hundred twenty-nine dollars."

"That's a tourist trap," I yelled. "The man has no taste."

"Maybe his girlfriend insisted on going there."

"How do you know he has a girlfriend?" I asked.

"He ran up a tab for two hundred fifty dollars at Victoria's Secret."

"I wonder if he took her with him to Puerto Rico?"

My accountant said, "Don't be too hard on him. The man rented a Chevy from Hertz, when he could have driven a Jaguar. He was probably trying to save you money."

"I don't want him to save me money when he's taking a girl out," I protested. "It makes me look cheap with Master-Card."

"The worst mistake someone can make is to feel sorry for the person who stole his credit card," my accountant warned.

"How long do you think this joker can keep this up?" I asked.

"Not much longer, now that we have reported him."

"Will they be rough when they arrest him?" I wanted to know.

"Beats me. Why do you care?"

"I don't want anything to happen to my cashmere jacket."

BUSH GOES VOODOO

WASHINGTON HAD A terrible time with the budget. The only thing the White House and the conservative Republicans agreed on was that the other side was to blame for the mess. The Democrats had no choice but to watch the spectacle in horror.

Now that a compromise has been reached, some questions can be answered.

"Why was the president so insistent on a cut in the capital gains tax as part of his budget reform?" I asked Frederic Decker, a deep thinker on the Hill.

Fred said, "Mr. Bush is always looking for new ways to help the rich."

"Why was Mr. Bush so sure that a tax cut would stimulate the economy and encourage people to invest in the nation's business?"

"The president assumed that the investments people would make would all be in successful things, like Silverado Savings and Loan Association."

I then talked to a White House spokesman. "Mr. Bush blames Congress for all the troubles he has been having with the budget. How can he be certain that the opposition is at fault?"

255

"If you are a president, you automatically know who is responsible for your woes," the spokesman said. "Bush and his administration have been honest and forthcoming in trying to present a budget that will strengthen the country and the economy. But with so many Benedict Arnold Republicans the president has no choice but to take his case to the public."

"How does Mr. Bush intend to do that?" I asked.

"He will carry his message to every state in the union, as well as parts of the District of Columbia."

"Does he mean that?"

"Not really. He'll go to a few big fund-raisers and then send Dan Quayle to all the others, if he can ever find him."

"What good will it do if the vice-president does take Bush's message to all the states?"

"We don't know about him, but it will give Marilyn Quayle a rest. In order to get the budget he wants, President Bush has to use all the hyperbole he can muster. There is nothing that pleases him more than to stick his finger in Newt Gingrich's eye."

I had another question for Frederic Decker. "Do you believe that the president frightens the Democrats?"

"They're scared silly. When he threatened them with excommunication because they wouldn't give the country a cut in the capital gains tax, they all hid under their desks."

I spoke to a Democratic congressman. "The president doesn't believe in new taxes. He believes that the lower the taxes the better the economy will survive. We're in a recession and the deficit is the worst it's ever been. Could it be that the president is practicing voodoo economics?"

The congressman said, "Who knows? But one thing we're sure of, Mr. Bush believes that you'll never stop white-collar crime in this country until you give the people in the highest income brackets a break."

THE LAST MILE

ONE OF THE most fascinating cases of the decade was heard recently by the Supreme Court.

This is true—I did not make it up: A murderer on death row named Michael Owen Perry killed his mother, his father, two cousins and a nephew, and was sentenced to die in the electric chair. He happens to be a certified schizophrenic, and by law he cannot be executed if he is insane.

The prosecution took the case to the Supreme Court, requesting permission to force the defendant to take antipsychotic drugs so that he would be sane long enough to sit in the electric chair. The convicted murderer's lawyers are fighting this, maintaining that the state cannot give their client drugs to make him healthy just so they can kill him.

The Supreme Court is not the only place where people are taking sides on the case. At Duke Zeibert's restaurant in Washington, many learned lawyers debated the appeal while their clocks were ticking away at the office.

Tenderfoot said, "The electric chair takes precedence over a person's mental state of health. The guy should take his drugs like a man, so that he can walk the last mile with a smile on his face and a shine on his shoes."

Grimsley, a great defense lawyer, raised his fork in anger.

257

"The state has no right to force any person in this country to be sane if it's going to kill him. According to the newscasts, Perry thinks he's God. Is there any politician in the state of Louisiana who wants to kill God?"

Blowman, a former prosecutor, refused to buy this. "We only know that Perry says he's crazy. That's pretty weak evidence. I believe that we should kill him, and then do an autopsy to decide whether he was schizophrenic or not."

Grimsley asked, "Don't you think that would be a little late?"

Blowman retorted, "The state shouldn't worry about what it takes for someone to be capitally punished. A crime has been committed, and justice will be served if we do the only sensible thing, and that is to shave his head and strap him into the chair. If he's nuts, he won't know what hits him, and if he isn't, he can fake it."

Ludlow, a practicing psychiatrist, spoke. "The prosecutors insist that if you force antipsychotic drugs down a death row inmate's throat he will get better. That doesn't necessarily follow. My fear is that after medicating him the state will certify that the defendant is sane, when in fact there has been no improvement at all."

Blowman blew. "Who is to say who is sane and who isn't? The man murdered people. It doesn't matter if he doesn't know what day it is. The rest of us do. So I say, Get the priest and let the games begin."

A woman CPA said, "I can't understand why a state would go to so much trouble to electrocute someone who is around the bend."

"The prosecutors have to do it because it's an election year," Grimsley said.

Ludlow added, "If you ask me, they should give the antipsychotic drugs to the government for bringing the case to the Supreme Court."

"Is it possible that they were angered because the murderer claims he is the Deity?"

"Maybe, but if the Supreme Court decides he *is* God, they will have a real hot potato on their hands."

EXCUSE ME

WHEN MEMBERS OF official Washington get into trouble, they usually go to see Alan Kent, who runs a shop behind the Capitol called The House of a Thousand Alibis. Kent produces strong statements that they can use to defend themselves.

Kent, wearing a green eyeshade and an apron, was putting the finishing touches to a congressman's press release concerning some charges of ethical hanky-panky.

He held it up to the light and read out loud, " 'I did nothing wrong, and even if I did, everybody else does the same thing.' How do you like it?"

"It's very good because it's creative," I told him.

Kent showed me another one, which said: "This is nothing more than a vicious political attack by the opposition to get even for what we did to General Custer."

I nodded. "There are Democrats out there who will buy it."

Kent told me, "When someone is accused of screwing up, it's best to go on the offensive. I wrote this the other day on the bus: 'It would be easy to resign. However, such action would be tantamount to admitting that I didn't know it was illegal to take money from a savings and loan and bet it on the horses.' "

"Sheer poetry. That's all the convincing I would need," I admitted.

"I only take clients who will read exactly what I write for them. Let's say a congressman has a friend who is very rich and makes a lot of investments. The partner asks the legislator to intervene for him on certain bills before Congress, which might or might not benefit the both of them. I have to create a few lines that will take the sting out of it."

"In this case, what would they be?"

" 'Anyone who thinks I would go into the tank for a two-hundred-fifty-thousand-dollar condo with a pool and golf privileges doesn't know me.' "

"That's it?"

Kent smiled. "Short and sweet. One of the best ways to fight fire with fire is to attack the press for printing things about the congressman that are not true. When someone is in trouble, I first write an official statement on his behalf declaring that the press is waging a vendetta against the congressman, and that everything written about his situation is garbage."

"Do you have anything that says your client wants his day in court?"

"I have it in any one of a hundred flavors. I also have one that says, 'I don't care if they attack me—but when they attack my dog, they have gone too far.' "

"Suppose the congressman doesn't have a dog?"

"Who's to know?"

"How many excuses for ethical misconduct do you offer?" I asked.

"Enough to fill all the filing cabinets against the wall. But our specialty is to custom-tailor statements for every situation. For example, we might have one congressman protest that he was 'railroaded' by the media, and another declare that he was 'a victim of mob hysteria.' "

"Are most of the people who come here innocent of any wrongdoing?"

"We never ask them. Our only business is to put words into their mouths."

I looked around the room and suddenly I saw something that knocked me for a loop. It was in neon, and all it said was NO QUID PRO QUO.

"Who did you make that for?" I asked Kent.

He pursed his lips and said, "I can't tell you."

THE RICH AND PUT-UPON

THE QUESTION THAT the White House has posed to the American public is, Can a country that has everything ignore the problems of the rich?

There are heartless congressmen and senators who not only have closed their eyes to the "rich problem," but are even talking about taxing wealthy people's incomes and cutting back on their capital gains.

They are opposed by warmhearted people, like the president, who say that a country that doesn't take care of its wealthy has no right to call itself a civilized society.

Angelo Montana, an estate planner who is a volunteer dishwasher in a Palm Beach tax shelter, said, "If we don't help the rich now, we'll pay for it one day, when all those top-income-bracket people turn their polo mallets against us."

"Why is Bush so concerned about the rich?" I asked him.

"Because they are the most ignored segment of the population. We need the rich. If you cut the income tax for the poor it doesn't mean anything, because they don't have any money to start with. But if you give a tax break to the rich, they'll go out and spend their money like drunken sailors."

"Then what you're saying is that rich people are much better consumers than poor folks."

"Take the capital gains tax. Bush wanted to cut the capital gains tax on investment. Do you know why?"

"He has friends who asked him to."

"No, because it would have encouraged the rich to invest in this country and make more money to avoid a recession."

"What does he want the rich to invest their money in?"

"It doesn't matter, as long as the IRS doesn't get its greedy hands on it. The president promised that he would not tax anyone in order to cut the deficit. To prove that he was serious, he gave the rich the first break. By doing this he sent a message to the middle class that he means business."

"Is this the first time anyone has struck a blow for the rich?" I wanted to know.

"No, but it's the first time a president has drawn a line in the sand. Congress wants to compromise on the budget, but Mr. Bush has told them, 'I don't care what you do, as long as you leave Rodeo Drive alone.' "

"Is the president doing this because there are more rich people or fewer rich people than ever before?"

"There are a lot more rich Americans than in the past. All you have to do is go to any private golf club in this country—it will break your heart."

"Are the rich organizing themselves to fight against increased taxes?"

"They would, but most of them are too busy moving to their winter homes. If it weren't for people like myself, willing to do their dishes for them, they would be lost souls."

"What message are the wealthy sending Washington?"

"The same one that Bush is sending—*No new taxes*. The rich are sick and tired of being treated like middle-class citizens. If the government can't find enough money to pay for the deficit, then they should forget it and go on to something else. There is nothing more unfair than putting a surcharge on the American Dream."

DON'T USE MY NAME

WE HAVE A rule in our family that if anyone gets a speeding ticket while he or she is a designated driver, the name of the person is not to be given out to the press.

Such an incident happened the other day, when someone driving several happy people home from a party was stopped by the police for doing fifty miles an hour in a twenty-five-mph zone. The reason we don't reveal the name, unless the family member wants us to, is that he or she could be harassed by the media.

Therefore it came as a surprise to me when a British tabloid, *The Daily Dirt*, identified the driver, and also ran a picture under the headline "Designated Driver with Party Girls in Backseat Wins Indianapolis 500."

I was disappointed, though not concerned, that the Brits had violated the American rule on confidentiality. But I figured, Who reads the London yellow press, anyway?

Apparently I was overconfident, because three days later in

the local supermarket I saw a copy of the *National Pinocchio* (a newspaper devoted to lies and innuendos). Blazoned across the front page was the headline "Police Say Designated Driver Depressed When He Received Speeding Ticket." Underneath was a color photo of the family member involved.

I called the editor of the *Pinocchio* and said, "Have you people gone crazy? Why did you print the name and picture of the driver, knowing that it could destroy his life forever?"

He replied, "The British papers used it, so we had no choice. Why should people in Britain know something we don't?"

It hurt, but I realized that nothing can be done to control trash. Then the other morning I went out to pick up my *New York Times*. Lo and behold, on the front page, right above a story on the Kurds, began a long feature not only revealing the name of the driver but devoting a page to a profile on him. It wasn't very flattering.

I telephoned the circulation manager for my area and told her, "I can't believe a paper of your distinction would stoop so low as to violate the rule of protecting the name of a speeding designated driver."

The circulation manager said, "We didn't print anything new. All we did was report the same terrible details that appeared in the *National Pinocchio*. As a paper of distinction, we feel that we cannot allow the *National Pinocchio* to be the only one to record all the news that's fit to print. We had to weigh the public's right to know against the circulation war we are now engaged in with the *Daily News*, the *New York Post* and *Newsday*."

I hung up in disgust. That night I got home and turned on the *NBC Nightly News*. The lead item was the network's decision to announce the name of the designated driver. The NBC vice-president in charge of revealing names appeared on camera and explained that NBC News could not stand by while there was one unnamed victim in this country.

Once *The New York Times* broke the silence, he said, the

NBC executives had no choice but to follow suit, not only because they had a duty to tell the truth but also because they needed a big boost in their ratings.

THE HOME STRETCH

DURING THE LAST WEEK before the election, it was tough for political managers to know how to coach the incumbents, particularly regarding budget legislation.

"Okay, Senator, let's go over it again. If they ask you, you tell them that you don't agree with the budget bill, but you had to vote for it because it's the best deal you could get from the cutthroat Democrats. Then you should add, 'It's good to get away from Washington and talk to real people.' "

"Right, Harvey. How do I feel about the president?"

"Sick. You can't support the president on the budget because he went back on his promise not to raise taxes, even though he is the leader of the party of no new taxes."

"I can remember that, Harvey. Why did I vote for the budget in the first place?"

"Because it's the only one we could live with under the circumstances, and something that the liberals will have to take responsibility for when they lead us into a recession."

"Let me ask you this, Harvey. Was the bill too tough on the rich, not tough enough, or just right?"

"Too tough. The Democrats are always trying to sock it to

the rich because they have more money than anyone else. But you have to say in your speeches that once they tax the rich, the opposition will want to tax the middle class and then the poor, and then the football fans. Your campaign must portray the rich as being just like everyone else."

"Is it too late to put that on bumper stickers?"

Harvey said, "Our polls indicate that no one likes the budget and the voter is blaming Congress for the mess we're in. We have got to put the blame on the ones who are really at fault."

"Who is that, Harvey?"

"The abortionists are responsible for the budget mess."

"The abortionists!"

"Why not? Better them than us."

"The voters should respect me for that."

"Senator, I want you to tell the people how much belt-tightening we have to do to get our house in order. This means finding capital-gains tax breaks for the guy in the street who wants to invest in America."

"Does that get votes?"

"No, but it gets contributions from those who would like the capital-gains tax breaks."

"Why can't I say that the president wants the same things as I do?"

"You can, but I wish you wouldn't. Bush's popularity is sinking in the polls. There is no reason for you to bail him out at this stage."

"Harvey, am I for or against the excise taxes on smoking which I voted in favor of?"

"Tell the electorate that on odd days you will be for them and on even days you will be against them. The smokers have vowed to defeat those who voted for the tax. They could be a problem, particularly if they are also joined by senior citizens who have promised to bury those members of Congress who've taxed their alcohol.

"Senator, we're in the home stretch and the people are fed up with everything. Our job is to make sure they understand that although you voted for all the budget reforms, you don't believe in them any more than President Bush does when he's speaking at a Republican fund-raiser."

PREVENTIVE RECESSION

I READ A story on the front page of *The New York Times* that made me whoop. Apparently, healthy companies are laying off employees to *prevent* a recession. This raises a question: Will firing people cause the very recession you're trying to prevent?

Take the case of the Extra Creamie Yogurt Company. The powers that be at Extra Creamie met to discuss how to avoid a predicted drop in sales.

"Gentlemen, we must try and steer clear of this business downturn. As a stopgap measure I propose that we terminate a thousand employees. This will give us some leverage if the good times don't roll by."

"An excellent idea. We've been overstaffed for years, and it's about time we took the bull by the horns and chopped off some heads below the knees."

"Objection. If we get rid of a thousand people we would be contributing to the disaster we want to prevent."

"That's ridiculous. All we're trying to do is protect our bottom line. I say we lay off fifteen hundred workers every

Thursday. In that way we'll scare those who are left behind, and they will produce twice as much yogurt as they did before."

"Gentlemen, let us suppose that every company fires a percentage of its staff. The purchasing power of the whole country could be put on hold and people will have a serious cash-flow problem—so serious that no one will ever buy a cup of Extra Creamie Yogurt again."

"You can't have a recession *that* serious. Consumers have killed to buy our yogurt."

"These are tougher times. It appears that the United States has talked itself into a recession and everyone is pushing the panic button. The newspapers scream recession—the TV stations feature stories on it. Economists are starting to ask each other, 'Which came first, the chicken, the egg or the recession?'"

"I have been in stormy seas before. They can get very ugly if you don't reduce the size of the payroll. Our actions today will long be remembered by our stockholders when they talk about the great plop of 1990."

"What is a recession? It's nothing more than a lack of customers in a store. It's empty seats at McDonald's. It's a showroom full of new, unsold cars. It has nothing to do with yogurt."

"Gentlemen, I say we keep all our help and fight the recession from within."

"No way. Lop off their heads. Someone read the list of the condemned."

"George Carricola."

"That's me. You can't fire me—I'm management."

"Companies always save money during a preventive recession by dumping managers."

"I demand an appeal."

"George, you can use a pistol or the gas oven—whichever you feel more comfortable with. In the meantime please accept this quart of Extra Creamie Yogurt as your severance pay. Preventive recession is a dirty business, but somebody has to do it."

POWER BREAKFAST

YOU HEAR A great deal about "power breakfasts," but most people don't know exactly what they are. The power breakfast is *the* essential meal now consumed by the business community. Without the wheeling and dealing that takes place over orange juice and scrambled eggs, all commerce in this nation would grind to a halt.

One of the most powerful places to hold such a breakfast is the Regency Hotel on Park Avenue in New York City. You must have at least $30 million in your personal banking account before they will pour you a cup of coffee. Not long ago, I was sitting at a table there and had an opportunity to observe a power breakfast in play.

Four men at the next table were all buttering their toast at the same time.

One man said to the others, "I will offer three slips of pink paper in exchange for two sheets of yellow paper."

"Are you crazy, Pete?" one of the other men shouted. "This deal is worth six slips of pink paper and four blue flimsies."

Pete replied, "It might have been worth that a month ago, but the price of pink paper has gone up and the price of yellow paper has hit a new low. But since the deal is so important to me, I will throw in a dozen pads of chartreuse unlined paper."

Another man joined in the conversation. "I can't accept that without talking to my lawyer." He stood up, walked over to the next table and spoke to a man writing figures on a legal pad. The man returned to his table and announced, "We don't want any chartreuse unlined paper. We got stuck with a bunch on our last transaction with Drexel Burnham, and we still haven't been able to offload it. We would really like a straightforward deal—purple memo-sized order blanks with pale green delivery receipts."

Everyone took a break while the waiter refilled the coffee cups. Then Pete said, "Gentlemen, I thought that when we met this morning we had all come intending to negotiate in good faith. It's obvious that you are using this breakfast to gain the upper hand. I can go to any hotel dining room in New York and be offered twice as much yellow paper as I can get here. But I chose instead to hold the negotiations at the Regency because I prefer their croissants. At the same time, I am not going to compromise my principles, even if I have to pay for the breakfast."

The man who had consulted with his lawyer intervened. "Don't get all upset. We have to take care of our own interests at power breakfasts. Colored paper isn't what it used to be. Look at Donald Trump's paper; look at Mike Milken's paper; look at HUD's paper. The reason you are stuck with pink paper is that nobody is crazy enough to give you yellow paper for it."

Pete said, "Would you be surprised if I told you that I am withdrawing my offer? I wouldn't give you any pink paper if you got down on your hands and knees and begged me."

"Nothing would surprise me," one of the men said. "Every time you try to exchange some colored paper, you back out at the last minute when nobody will pay your price. If you don't trade us your pink paper, you are not going to have any yellow to pay off your notes to Chase. We're your last hope."

Pete answered, "Okay, you've got me in a box. I'll give six pink sheets of paper for five yellow, and that's my final offer."

"How do we know that the paper is any good?" one of the other men inquired.

"Ask the waiter," Pete told him.

"Is his paper any good?" the man asked.

"It's okay," the waiter replied, "but the raisin muffins are better."

EXIT-POLLING

THE BEAUTY OF being a political pundit in Washington is that you can predict what the voter is going to do in an election—then, when he doesn't do it, you can explain why he was wrong.

On Election Day, I was out exit-polling in the neighborhood when I saw a voter come out of our local school. He was holding a ballot slip which he had made into a paper airplane. He was trying to get it to fly.

"What are you doing?" I asked.

He said, "I'm sending a message to Washington. Contrary to predictions, I'm not mad as hell and I am still willing to take it some more."

"Good for you," I told him. "Does this mean that you have not turned your back on the incumbent?"

"Yes and no. I decided to give him another chance, but not a standing ovation. If he screws up one more time he's out."

"All the conventional wisdom indicated that voters like you wanted to throw the rascals down the stairs."

He said, "We did feel that way, but then we saw the incumbents' TV commercials. We were impressed with their sincerity and their desire to serve this country to the best of their ability. We were also persuaded that their opponents were thieves, oddballs and soft on crime."

"How did you find that out?" I asked.

"By watching the same incumbents' commercials. Who are you?" he suddenly wanted to know.

"I'm an exit-poller," I said. "I'm one of the people who takes the political pulse of the American electorate every other November. Frankly, you have surprised and disappointed me. In my column I predicted that you were so fed up with Washington you were going to overthrow the government by force."

"I hate partisan bickering. You're lucky that I even came out to vote. I left the house in the middle of *People's Court* to be here. You pundits think that just because congressmen and senators act like a bunch of jokers, the man in the street is going to exchange them for another bunch of jokers. Voting is like going to the dentist—you try not to think about it, and all you want to do is get it over with."

"Would you like to tell me who you voted for?"

"What's-his-name."

"You don't know his name?!"

"He's the one who keeps kissing babies, even though he looks as if he doesn't mean it."

"Why him over the other candidate?"

"The opposition kissed off the country as if he didn't mean it."

"Do you see your vote as a warning to the politicians in Washington that if they don't straighten up and fly right, you will give them their walking papers in 1992?"

"Maybe. Why do you ask?"

"Because I'm putting that in my column next week and I would hate to be wrong again."

"I'd love to get this paper ballot to fly," he said.

"What do you dislike most about voting?"

"The exit-pollers. They're really a pain in the butt. By the time you get finished talking with them, the parking meter has run out and you wind up with a ticket."

"Exit-polling is essential to an American election. Without it we pundits would never know why Catholics who make more than eighty thousand dollars a year and live in a detached house with one dog and two children voted against Proposition 144, which gave gas stations the right to sell knitted sweaters on Sundays."

INSIDE THE BELTWAY

PRESIDENT BUSH SPENT a long hard week just before the elections campaigning for Republican candidates. Afterward, in his helicopter, he spoke with the White House chief of staff, John Sununu.

"Where are we, John?" the president asked, peering out of the window.

Sununu said, "We're inside the Beltway, Mr. President."

"Oh my God. How did we get there?"

"The White House is inside the Beltway, sir. We're going home."

"But there are terrible people inside the Beltway—liberals, abortionists and pundits. I don't want to be anyplace where the citizens do nothing but tax and spend, tax and spend."

"You're right, Mr. President. But we can't get you home without crossing the Beltway markers. Why don't you close your eyes as we fly over the National Press Building?"

"Whose idea was it to take this chopper inside the Beltway?"

"Nobody's. The White House is down there. If you want to sleep in your own bed tonight, you must stop worrying about all those folks who are trying to ram an equal rights bill down your throat."

"Everybody knows that I hate Washington, and I would prefer to spend my time with real Americans in Iowa."

"I understand, sir, but the campaign is over now and it doesn't matter if you run the country from the Okefenokee Swamp. We have to go inside the Beltway because that's where the Rose Garden is."

"I don't understand why you are so insistent."

"Because I need clean socks and fresh underwear, Mr. President. No matter what you think of South Dakota, the only place where you are going to get someone to do your laundry right is here in Washington."

"What's that building down there that's all lit up?"

"That's the Capitol, sir."

"Is that within the Beltway too?"

"Yes, and it's filled with Democrats."

"Maybe if we located it beyond the Beltway, we could get our own people inside."

"I don't think we have the votes to do it. I believe that we should land on the White House lawn and forget that we are part of a highway system we never made. The Beltway belongs to all Americans, whether they are rich or well-to-do."

"I wonder if Barbara knows that she's living inside the Beltway?"

"Not only does she know it, so does the dog, Millie."

"How can the dog know?"

"Barbara had to buy her a D.C. dogtag."

"What I like about living in Maine is that there are no belt-ways."

"Or left-wingers—or a do-nothing Congress to screw up your programs."

"If it weren't for the Beltway, I could drive my golf cart all the way to Camp David."

"We're going down, Mr. President."

"In the helicopter?"

"No, sir. In the polls."

GROUP THERAPY

OUR REAL ESTATE group therapy class meets on Thursdays at Rebecca Milikowsky's house. We discuss how terrible the market is, and share with each other the pain of living in a world where a house is no longer a ticket to instant wealth.

Janet Blankenship was the first to speak at one class recently. "I spent all Saturday night baking brownies, and on Sunday I put them out on the dining room table with hot apple cider. Everybody who showed up ate the brownies, but not one person bit on the house."

Ray Slattery said, "People don't buy homes in exchange for brownies, the way they did a couple of years ago. It's a buyer's market. Even chocolate eclairs don't do it anymore."

Jodie Torkelson joined in. "We took out an advertisement in *The Washington Post*, and the only response we got was from *The Washington Times* saying that they would run it in bold type for half the price."

"The funniest thing happened to us," said Herman Methfessel. "A woman came to the house and hammered a 'For Sale' sign into the lawn. When I yelled that the house was not for sale, she shouted back, 'You never know until the fat lady sings.' I asked, 'What the hell does that mean?' And she said, 'Beats me—they taught us to say that in real estate school.'"

The conversation got a little dicey when Lila Crimson informed us that she and her husband, Matt, had split and there were very bitter feelings involved. "If he had let me sell the house six months earlier we could have gotten five hundred thousand for the place. What a dummkopf! The reason I left him was, he never knew when to buy or when to sell or when to put out the garbage."

"Perhaps he didn't know that real estate prices would plummet."

Lila blurted out, "His girlfriend should have told him."

I tried to be helpful. "People who break up shouldn't get angry with each other because the price of their house isn't what it used to be."

Lila asked, "Why is it that your home is worth a fortune when you're living together, and it's not worth a Russian ruble when you're splitting up?"

"That's a good question," I said.

David Jaffe said to me, "You lied last year when you told everyone that your home was worth four million dollars."

I responded, "I didn't lie. Every toolshed in the neighborhood was worth four million dollars."

Rebecca Milikowsky spoke up. "People should exaggerate as much as they can about real estate prices because it helps the entire community."

"I heard that Robbie and Tommy Gresinger couldn't sell their place, so they turned it into a bed-and-breakfast business."

"They sound desperate."

"They told me that the bed-and-breakfast arrangement will guarantee them one meal a day, which is the minimum that doctors say you need during a housing slump."

Herman Methfessel said, "I think that the lesson from this meeting is, Don't sell your house for what it's worth—sell it for whatever someone is prepared to pay."

"But," protested Ray Slattery, "then you take all the greed out of real estate, and greed is what the business is all about."

DOWNTURN

HERE ARE SOME of the questions I am asked as I travel around the country, and some of my answers:

Can the president declare that the country is in a recession?

No. Under the Constitution, only Congress can do that.

What can the president declare?

He can declare an economic downturn.

Can the president place blame for the economic downturn on the Democrats?

Yes. Under the law he has ninety days to do this. If he doesn't, the country goes into a recession automatically.

At what stage of a recession may a president declare an economic downturn?

When all the economic indicators are falling and his popularity is dropping in the polls. Then, by decree, he must go on television and tell the American people that his administration had nothing to do with the slump, which was caused by fifty years of reckless Democratic spending and high taxes.

Can the president mention the word "unemployment" in his State of the Union address?

He can, but he would be crazy if he did. He'd be much better off referring to unemployment as an unexpected blip on the GNP screen which was triggered by a bad rice crop in Mongolia.

What does the president do when he declares an economic downturn?

He calls up all his economists and issues them gas masks.

Is he supposed to take any action to stimulate the economy?

That's what a president is for. He promises the country that the recession will disappear as soon as rich people get tax breaks and start buying houses in Palm Springs again.

What is the danger of having Congress be the only one to lawfully declare a recession?

The big danger is that whenever Congress votes an important measure such as a recession, it tacks on many pork-barrel amendments that have nothing to do with the crash. These include bailouts for S&L bankers, pollution relief for special-interest groups and appropriations for new military weapons that don't work. It is estimated that a congressional bill on a recession will cost this country $90 billion in legislation that Congress would ordinarily have no chance of getting passed.

Should the president consult with Congress on the economic downturn?

It helps, because if he stays mum about it, they will refuse to help him get out of his doldrums. When it comes to assigning blame, it is very difficult for the president and the Hill to have a meeting of the minds. This is because there is enough to go around for everybody.

Is the problem that the president wants to turn a corner in the economy, and the Democrats can't see the woods for the trees?

You said it, I didn't.

Isn't it strange that the president has mentioned nothing about Reagan's sticking all of us with a trillion-dollar catering bill?

By law President Bush is not permitted to criticize President Reagan for his voodoo economic policies.

When does a recession become a depression?

When you can no longer read Mr. Bush's lips.

ROULETTE

NOT ALL THE news out of the Soviet Union is bad. The word from Red Square is that the Russian people can now purchase guns as easily as Americans, and one hopes there will be as many shootouts there as there are here.

Fyodor Dostievsky, president of the National Russian Roulette Cooperative (the equivalent of our National Rifle Association), is touring the United States as a guest of the Ricochet Rifle Clubs of America.

I met him on a rifle range in Virginia. He told me, "Guns don't kill commies. People kill commies."

"Right you are," I said. "Is the USSR's great interest in guns due to *perestroika*?"

"It didn't hurt. Russians never dreamed that when democracy came Gorbachev would throw in guns as a bonus. We even had a shooting in front of Lenin's Tomb the other day."

"Did anyone get hurt?"

"Not really. Most Soviet gun owners still can't aim straight."

"Do you believe that this incident will bring about antigun legislation in the USSR?"

"It can't, because ownership of guns is part of the Soviet constitution."

"Who says so?" I asked.

"Karl Marx. It's in *Das Kapital*. The Politburo won't enact any law that prevents the secret police from bearing arms."

"Come to think of it, I remember reading that. Are you meeting with many gun lovers in this country?"

"All I can. National Rifle Association members believe that the only thing that can save our country is an armed population. The NRA has been very kind. Its people have offered us Charlton Heston to do our TV commercials."

"Is there any resistance to weapon ownership in the USSR?"

"There is some among the bourgeoisie wimps, who have no use for hunting and target practice. But we're fighting back. The NRA is teaching us how to give funds to Kremlin politicians so that the USSR will keep all its gun laws in place. I was amazed to see what the NRA is able to do with a U.S. congressman for a few thousand dollars."

"Russians can learn a lot from Americans about how to buy legislators," I said. "Do you plan to acquire any guns during your visit?"

"Yes. I want to take back as many as possible. The ethnic minorities are going to need guns if they ever hope to settle their language differences."

I said, "We have a saying in the United States: 'If it weren't for democracy you couldn't have guns. And if it weren't for guns you couldn't get rid of the opposition.'"

"That's exactly the way the National Russian Roulette Cooperative feels about it. We dream of someday producing enough automatic weapons to protect every man, woman and child in the Soviet Union. At the same time we have to have tougher laws for our criminals."

"Fyodor, people purchase guns out of fear, and Russians are as frightened as anybody. That's why your drive for members will not fail."

"It's true. For sixty years we lived in fear of the secret police and the Politburo. Now we are afraid of our economic system. Soviets must have guns under their pillows to ensure that they get something to eat."

"Can you do it?"

"Why not? At least it's a shot in the dark."

PRAISE THE LORD

"SUPPOSE SOMEONE GAVE a war and nobody came?" George Canterbury asked me in a bar the other day.

"That's a hypothetical question," I told him. "I never answer hypothetical questions when I'm getting drunk."

"Nevertheless, the situation is reaching a point that fighting for God and country has less meaning than a Giants–Raiders football game. In the past our boys marched off with a band playing 'I'm a Yankee Doodle Dandy' and the crowds shouting 'Give 'em hell!' It's so different now."

"Maybe it's because no one can make the big money on a war the way they used to," I suggested.

He said, "Everyone would like to give Saddam Hussein a bloody nose, but we are all afraid that we could get one too. Going to war is a questionable business, and all the great minds in the country are split on what to do about it. Are you for war?"

"Nosirree. I want to kick Saddam's butt out of Kuwait, but I'm not certain that he's worth losing one Milli Vanilli record over."

"If you had to answer a *Newsweek* poll tomorrow, where would you stand on hostilities?"

"Somewhere between 'undecided' and 'don't know.' Why are all the pollsters trying to find out who wants to go to war and who doesn't?"

"It helps the leaders in Washington make a decision." Canterbury continued, "The problem with the Iraqi situation is that in order to avoid a war, we have to convince Hussein we mean to fight one."

"Teddy Roosevelt always said to carry a big stick if you're going to use sanctions against another country."

Canterbury yelled, "Praise the Lord and pass the UN resolutions—and we'll all be free."

"Even the former Joint Chiefs of Staff are against war. That leaves only George Bush and Dan Quayle for it."

Canterbury told me, "They'll gain more support when the public gets tired of seeing Saddam Hussein on the Ted Koppel show. I'll ask you a question that I'll bet you a drink you can't answer: Why is this hostility different from all other hostilities?"

"Why?"

"There are no women for the American GIs to date. For the first time in history it's possible to have a war without the soldiers making babies."

"How can you have a babyless war?" I asked. "It goes against all the rules of fraternization."

"It's hard to believe, but the native women in this conflict are locked up, and the GIs have nothing to do but make mud pies in the sand."

"Without women there is no peace dividend," I protested.

Canterbury said, "When we chose to fight in Saudi Arabia we did it to protect the oil, not for war brides. Now our boys can come home with a clear conscience."

"Maybe," I said, "but it's going to make a lousy movie."

GIFT-PASSING

KLEPTO WAS SITTING on his front stoop. "I'm waiting for the mailman," he told me.

"You must be expecting an important letter."

"I'm actually on the lookout for Christmas packages. The more I get, the happier I'll be."

"Most of us feel that way," I said.

"The gifts are not for myself—they are for other people."

I looked confused.

Klepto explained, "As you know, we're having a conservative holiday and are being frugal. So Ruth and I came up with this idea. Instead of buying any new gifts, we'll just pass along the ones that are sent to us, minus the card, of course."

"But if you give away everything you receive, you won't have anything for Christmas."

"It doesn't matter. Most of the presents we get aren't

anything to write home about. Look at this ratatouille popcorn in a barrel. Many folks couldn't do without it, but we can. Believe it or not, Ruth and I have spent eight or nine Christmases without ratatouille popcorn."

"What will you do with it?"

"I'll send it to my brother-in-law, Toady. He mailed us a pound of goat cheese last year which, I am certain, his boss gave him. We've been very lucky this December. The Rapps sent us a letter-opener, which we immediately passed on to the Ludwigs after they mailed us a Christmas washcloth."

"Who gets the washcloth?"

"We can't decide. We still haven't received a gift from the Lyons or the Porters."

"The system is great as long as you don't get the presents mixed up," I said.

"We did that last year. The Constantines gave us garden shears. By mistake we sent the shears back with our card attached. Damned if we didn't get a rave note from Fitzi Constantine saying that they were the most beautiful garden shears she had ever seen."

"That must have made you feel good," I told him.

"Sending other people's gifts for Christmas isn't as cheap as you might think. There is the cost of wrapping paper, ribbon and postage."

"Why can't you use the same wrapping paper that it came in?"

"That would be cheating," Klepto said.

"Suppose you pass along a gift to someone, and that person doesn't send you one?"

"You mean like you?"

"Okay, like me."

"I don't keep score. You can still hold onto the cactus plant from Mary Ellen Clarkin, with no questions asked."

"If I mail something to you, Klepto, can I designate the person I want you to send it to?"

"No, because you may not know what he or she likes. I believe when one is gift-passing, the most important thing is to do it with love."

"You certainly have taken the Grinch out of Christmas," I said.

"Someone has to support the economy."

THE SANTA CLAUS POLL

THE ABC, NBC and CBS polls on Santa Claus have just come out, and they indicate that his popularity has not diminished. Here are some of the findings:

Eighty-five percent of all the people polled thought that Santa Claus was doing a good job.

Ten percent disagreed.

Five percent had no opinion because they hadn't read the papers.

Q: *Do you believe Santa Claus could do a better job with the recession than, let's say, Alan Greenspan?*

The majority did not blame Santa Claus for the recession, but forty percent felt that if Santa Claus was in charge of the Federal Reserve Bank he'd make sure that the money got to where it was supposed to go.

Q: *Do you blame Christmas for the recession?*

Nearly one hundred percent of all retailers affected by the holiday season disaster said that they would have been better off without Christmas this year.

Q: In order to economize on the high costs, it has been suggested that Santa drop at least four reindeer from his sled. What do you think?

Forty-five percent felt that this might impede deliveries.

Forty percent said that it was okay to drop more.

Fifteen percent suggested that instead of cuts, Santa should charge a delivery fee for getting the package to the correct chimneys.

Q: Do you think Santa Claus should have a mandatory retirement age?

Fifty percent answered that Santa should quit at sixty-five to give a younger person from the Harvard Business School an opportunity to take the position.

Forty-five percent said that Santa should stay as long as he wants to.

Five percent felt that he is too fat and should start jogging daily if he wants to stay in the Christmas business.

Q: Do you approve or disapprove of Santa Claus's staff?

Thirty-five percent approved and forty-five percent disapproved. Some remarks were, "Every time Santa says 'Ho, ho, ho,' someone in the North Pole announces that he misspoke," and "Santa's elves never return telephone calls."

More people think of Santa Claus as having a good effect on children rather than a bad one.

When asked, "If you had the choice of having an Iraqi volleyball team, the KGB String Quartet or Santa Claus over to dinner, which one would you choose?" more than seventy-two percent chose the bearded guy in the red hat.

When faced with the question, "What do you like least about Santa?" the majority replied, "He didn't warn us about the savings and loan scandals." A further query about what Santa had to do with the scandals brought the response, "Every savings and loan manager who lost his bank said at the height of the boom, 'I am Santa Claus and I would like to help you.' "

Santa Claus was asked about the poll, and he said, "I don't

believe in surveys. If you do right by the people, they will follow you. I'm not saying that this is the greatest Christmas I've ever had, nor am I saying that it's the worst. But I know from my own experience that more people had a good time this year than had a bad time. The only trouble is that there was more talk about everyone having a bad time than a good time, and that's why most polls are for the birds."

SEND IN THE CLOWNS

THE NETWORK NEWS EXECUTIVES met to decide what politicians they would book for the upcoming season.

All the guests for the news shows had been used up the year before, and therefore the executives were faced with renewing them or putting them on waivers.

Blunt said, "Do we want to sign up Secretary of Defense Cheney for another twelve months?"

Blowtorch replied, "He's been on every program, including *People's Court*. Frankly, I think he's overexposed."

"Who else can we get to speak for Defense—Ollie North?" Notory yelled. "Let's renew Cheney until we find another spokesperson, preferably a tall blonde who looks like Jane Pauley."

"Okay, we stick with Cheney. What do we do about Secretary of State Baker's contract?" Blunt asked.

"If we keep Baker as a guest, why do we need Henry Kissinger? They both say the same things."

"Yeah, but with different accents."

"Why don't we hold onto Baker for television and save Kissinger for the radio?" Notory suggested.

"How about Baker for the Brinkley show and Kissinger for *Nightline*?"

Blunt said, "The last time we used Baker on the Brinkley show we got a three rating."

Blowtorch protested. "It's not the person, it's the job. Secretaries of state never get good ratings."

Notory said, "Are we renewing Sununu?"

"You better believe it. There is nobody with as much fire in his belly as Sununu. Barbara Walters would take him over Donald Trump and Marla Maples combined."

"I hate to think of what *Meet the Press* would be like without Sununu."

"Not to mention all of CNN."

"I know this is a silly question," Notory said, "but are we renewing Dan Quayle?"

"We have to lighten up Sam Donaldson somehow," Blunt replied. "Besides, our surveys indicate that the viewers like watching Quayle for the same reason they enjoy watching a train wreck."

Blowtorch interrupted, "Let's move along. How do we feel about signing up Secretary of the Treasury Brady as a guest?"

"Nobody knows who Brady is. You could put his picture on every milk carton in America and people still wouldn't have any idea why he was on television."

"If we don't take Brady we need one more person from the Bush administration to service *Face the Nation*."

"There is none," Blunt retorted. "We're going to have to sign Newt Gingrich again."

"If we use Gingrich, then we'll to have to invite House Speaker Tom Foley."

"I saw Foley talk about the budget on *McNeil/Lehrer*, and he took the show to the bottom of the sea."

"So where does that leave us?"

"We still have one more possibility. Are we going to use Jesse Jackson as a guest on the *Today* show or not?"

Blunt sighed, "What choice do we ever have?"

BYE, BYE

RIP VAN WATTLE woke up. He had fallen asleep during a Jerry Ford State of the Union speech in 1975 and opened his eyes just in time to see the Madonna video on Ted Koppel's show.

"I must have drunk too much Sleepy-Time tea," he said. "Did I miss anything?"

"Not much," I told him.

"Have we beat the hell out of the Russians yet?" he wanted to know.

"No," I said. "As a matter of fact, we're now sending them a billion dollars' worth of food because they are not doing too well."

"You have to be kidding," Rip yelled. "Why are we bailing out communists?"

"Because they have become our friends. They're pulling their troops out of Eastern Europe, and we're dismantling all our missiles in Western Europe. There is even a McDonald's in Moscow."

"Now I know you're joking. America would never permit a

McDonald's to open in Russia. They could steal our recipe for French fries."

"Rip, I don't know if anyone told you this before, but the Berlin Wall is down and there is only one Germany."

"Why would they do that in a cold war?"

"Because the Russians decided that the Wall was a German problem, not a Soviet one. Germany is one country, with one beer and one Volkswagen."

"I'm sorry that I woke up. What other things did I miss?"

"We're at war with Iraq because she invaded Kuwait."

"Does that mean we have to fight Syria?"

"No. Syria is on our side."

"How did Iraq get to be so powerful?"

"All the NATO powers armed her when she declared war on Iran."

"Does Margaret Thatcher know about this?"

"She lost her job because her party thought she was too tough."

"As a woman?"

"No, as a man."

"How much is a gallon of gas?"

"One dollar and sixty cents. It will probably go higher, unless we get a deal from Iraq."

"Is Jerry Ford still president?"

"No, he's playing golf. He was replaced by Jimmy Carter, who was replaced by Ronald Reagan, who spent a trillion dollars fixing up the country. You didn't have any of your money in a savings and loan institution, did you?"

"Just my life savings."

"You're lucky. Some people lost a lot more than that. Are you aware that George Bush is president of the United States?"

"No. Does it have anything to do with me?"

"Not much. Bush wants to fight in Iraq, give tax relief to the rich people at home and veto any civil rights bills. You don't fit into any of those categories, do you?"

"No, I don't. Well, I guess I'll go back to sleep."

"How are you going to do that?"

"I'll watch Dan Quayle talk to schoolchildren."

ONE JUNK CALL AWAY . . .

THE KEATING FIVE hearings are an education in how our senators serve their constituents. Some members of the Senate argue that there is nothing wrong with doing favors for people and/or accepting political contributions, as long as the two don't conflict.

The thrust of Senator Daniel Inouye's testimony was, That's how the game is played.

Maybe so. Recently, I had had it up to here with the junk phone calls that were polluting my home. So I decided to call Senator Twopockets to ask if he was planning any laws that might demand the death penalty for those who claimed to be taking a survey or those who were selling a piece of swampland in Florida.

I didn't get Senator Twopockets, but rather an assistant who dealt with nuisance calls, such as mine.

He was quite friendly. "The senator is aware of junk telephone calls," he said. "Did you know that he's holding a thousand-dollar-a-plate dinner to celebrate his wife's birthday in February?"

"No, I didn't. Why tell me?"

291

"It would be a great opportunity for you to meet the senator."

I said, "Do you think that Twopockets would speak to me about junk calls for a lousy thousand dollars?"

"Oh no, but an extra thousand entitles you to attend the VIP party in the presidential suite."

"What would it cost for him to hear my story and start some hearings on the junk calls that are driving everyone crazy?"

"We're having a January white sale on domestic legislation," the man said. "For ten thousand dollars the senator will personally indicate his interest in the matter, which should create a firestorm in the Senate."

"I don't suppose that the senator would do anything about junk calls if I didn't buy a plate for his wife's birthday."

"I'm sorry, I can't hear you."

"Look, I know that you need money, but when is a little guy ever going to have his story heard if the big guys are buying all the senator's time?"

"You sound like a chronic complainer."

"I'm not an agitator. All I am trying to do is get Senator Twopockets to find out if junk calls fall under the heading of 'invasion of privacy.' "

"The senator has already looked into it and is certain that no laws are being violated."

"How can he be so sure?"

"He read a report by the direct-marketing people who are responsible for making all the calls."

"Did direct marketing buy any tables for the senator's wife's birthday party?"

"Forty, but that's none of your business."

"Is there any chance that I can talk to the senator personally?"

"Are you trying to gain access to him without paying for it?"

"Doesn't Twopockets have a few free meetings with his constituents?"

"We'd love to be able to, but time is money, and we have an election coming up. The senator's advice is to do what everyone in this country does—consider a junk call as a message from a loved one that you never met."

"One more question. Where does the senator stand on Charles Keating?"

"The senator doesn't approve of everything he did, but he certainly has nothing against Keating's generosity."

NEW STUDIO HEAD

MR. HOYADO HODAI, representative of the Tokyo consortium that had just bought Beneficial Motion Pictures, arrived in Hollywood to inspect the property his people had purchased for $20 billion.

Thomas Killright, Beneficial's production head, escorted him to the studios in the longest limousine Tinseltown could provide.

Hodai said, "I want to see the studio's library, particularly the pictures you made concerning World War Two."

"No problem," answered Killright. "We'll show you everything we have."

Hodai sank into a first-row seat in the screening room. He was surrounded by Beneficial executives who didn't want to lose their jobs.

"You'll love this one," Killright said. "It's *Tora! Tora! Tora!* and it's about the Japanese attack on Pearl Harbor. The Americans got the hell beat out of them thanks to faultless Japanese planning and ingenuity and the element of surprise."

Hodai stared at the screen as the film unfolded.

"Why do you show so many Japanese planes being shot down?"

"I guess it was mainly to give the American audience a rooting interest in the film. You'll like this part where you people sink the battleship *Arizona*."

"I think you're using too much smoke. What else do you have to show me?"

"We have *Wake Island*, where your brave Japanese soldiers overcame hordes of ruthless, unshaven American Marines who committed every atrocity in the book to save the island."

"Why are the Marines calling the Japanese dirty ethnic names?"

"We made the picture before we knew you were going to buy the studio. Would you like to see *Bataan*, with Robert Taylor? It's the story of American soldiers who are beaten by superior Japanese freedom fighters in the Philippine jungles."

"I like it. Let's put it in color and release it again."

"That's exactly what I was planning to do," Killright said.

"I understand we own *Destination Tokyo*," Hodai said. "It is a submarine picture with Cary Grant in which the Americans attack Tokyo Bay and sink the entire Japanese fleet."

"We do," said Killright, "and I was always against the movie's being released."

"People won't buy our cars if they see Cary Grant sink our ships."

"We could cut the picture so Grant sinks only one North Korean fishing boat."

"You understand, we don't want to interfere in how you run the studio, but when you see an American submarine in Tokyo Bay you have our permission to cut out the violence."

"Mr. Hodai, we have one more picture to show you. It's *Sands of Iwo Jima* and it stars John Wayne. He kills more Japanese in this movie than were killed in World War Two."

"Then cancel Wayne's contract with the studio."

"We can't—he's dead."

Hodai handed Killright a hara-kiri dagger and said coldly, "That is your problem, not mine."

REST IN PEACE

THEY SAID GOOD-BYE to the Bank of New England this year.

When a bank dies there is no ceremony; no tears are shed and few mourn. It gets buried with only a small obituary in the local paper.

This is wrong. A bank is a loss to everyone when it dies, and the least it deserves is a eulogy, something like this:

Dearly Beloved,

We are gathered here today to bid farewell to the National Bank That Couldn't, which passed away in its sleep just days ago when it ran out of funds.

This is a sad moment for those of us who knew the Bank That Couldn't over the years and were befriended by it time and time again.

The Bank That Couldn't did not die because it couldn't get a money transfusion. It died of a broken heart, when the people it loaned money to told the bank to shove it. People say that the bank had only itself to blame for its demise. But it is cruel to speak this way about the dead. Sure, it made mistakes, but no more than Chase, Citibank or the Bank of New England. It invested its depositors' savings in the future at a time when there was no future.

I'm not here today to talk about the bad things that happened to the Bank That Couldn't. I'd like to say something good about it. This was a happy bank. Even when its loan officers made grievous errors you could still hear singing in the back rooms.

I remember one time walking into the bank and seeing Jed Tobin, the vice-president, sitting behind his desk, splitting his sides.

"What's the joke?" I asked.

"We were holding thirty million dollars in junk bonds and the department store chain defaulted on them."

"What's so funny about that?"

"The investment bankers who sold us those bonds offered to sell us more for another thirty million."

"I still don't see the humor."

"The bank's officers bought them."

There was never a dull moment at the Bank That Couldn't. This valiant institution invested not only in our little town but in Argentina as well. If you deposited more than $50,000 you got a calendar featuring Evita Perón. Everyone had faith in the bank because its marble floors were cleaned twice a week, and the bronze bars on the tellers' cages were polished every day. The bank even paid to put up a Christmas crèche on its roof.

When it was in serious financial trouble it did not cry and whimper—like a savings and loan. It went to its senators and said, "We will finance your campaign if you get us out of this jam." Few senators could say no.

Why, many of you are asking, did the Bank That Couldn't pass away? It died because it lost the will to live. It was driven to its death by heartless examiners and federal insurance accountants who cared more about the bank's books than they did about the people who owned its stock.

When it could not take the pain any longer, it pulled down the blinds, closed its eyes and stuck its head in a twenty-four-hour deposit box.

We will all miss the Bank That Couldn't.

Perhaps the money is gone, but as we all know, there is more to life than a bank with money.

Let us pray for the Bank That Couldn't and hope that it will find eternal peace in the big Chapter 11 in the sky.

LET'S KILL THE LAWYERS

WHEN SHAKESPEARE SAID, "Let's kill all the lawyers," he never thought they would do it to themselves. It used to be that during dark periods law firms fired associates and people who had climbed only halfway up the ladder. But lately the lawyers are firing their own partners.

How does a law office make the decision to force one of its own to walk the plank? Like this:

The Sudden Death Committee of Dubah, Doodah & Dipthong met secretly in one of the firm's paneled conference rooms to decide whose heads to chop off that week.

Grumbach said, "I say that in order to bring some financial order to the firm we push O'Toole out the window."

Sincere responded, "But O'Toole has been a law partner with DD&D for forty years. He was a founder of the firm."

"Exactly. For forty years he's worn the same tie to court. The man has no sense of fashion."

Bogley interrupted: "I have nothing against dumping O'Toole. He's always losing his men's room key. But I think if we're going for savings we ought to put the ax to Ladeeda. He entertains clients at the Downtown Topless Cafeteria."

Sincere added, "What I don't like about him is that he never once has put a quarter into the canister for his share of coffee. When I mentioned it one day, he told me to take it to the Supreme Court."

Comstock spoke up. "We can't fire people for personal reasons. It must be for the good of the firm. Zeigfried is my candidate. The man lost his last ambulance case to an insurance company, and he took it on contingency. It cost us twenty million dollars."

Bogley retorted, "Zeigfried may be lousy in court, but he's one helluva golfer. The partnership needs good golfers more than it needs competent litigators."

Grumbach came back, "Then it follows that if you are a lousy golfer, you should be fired before a good lawyer."

"Without question," Bogley said. "Most of our business is picked up on the golf course. Judges uphold lawyers who shoot under ninety."

Comstock said, "This is a sad day. Firing one of your partners is like kicking your brother down the stairs. It hurts all of us because it could be any one of us."

Bogley replied, "That's why we're all on the Sudden Death Committee—so it doesn't happen to us. And the responsibility is so great. It's no fun going to the office of a man you've worked with for twenty years and saying, 'You can have one cigarette before emptying the drawers in your desk.' "

Comstock was irritated. "Enough of the hearts and flowers.

The sooner we make our friends walk the plank, the less rent the rest of us will have to pay next year."

Bogley agreed. "We'll be doing the fired partners a favor. Most of them are burned out, anyway. Let's get the pink slips and hand them out."

"Why don't we make them into paper planes so we can toss them into their offices? There is no reason why people have to lose their sense of humor just because they're being dismissed," Comstock said.

"Are we canning Riverhaven or not?" Sincere asked.

"Why?" Bogley wanted to know.

"Because he has the best view from his office, and he promised me I could have it if anything ever happened to him."

WHITE COLLAR

THERE IS ALWAYS someone questioning the status quo. This week it was my friend Alonzo Powdama, who believes that it is a mistake to refer to many criminal activities as white-collar crimes.

"I suppose you'd say Michael Milken committed a white-collar crime?" he asked me.

"He must have," I said. "He did it in his office overlooking Beverly Hills."

"But it was the crime of the century. People lost millions of dollars investing in his junk bonds. Many were widows and orphans," Alonzo said.

"They were greedy widows and orphans. They were always going for a higher interest rate, and then when they lost their money they cried crocodile tears."

"Why isn't stealing other people's money through an investment bank, an S&L or a regular bank the same as holding them up on the street?" Alonzo wanted to know.

I replied, "The difference is in the quality of the criminal. Most stickup men are sloppy and do not observe the dress code. They carry weapons and resort to violence. White-collar robbers are pillars of the community. They hold up their victims with calculators and computers. You can't put white-collar and blue-collar criminals on the same volleyball court."

"What about this one?" Alonzo argued. "The defense companies, including some of the largest aviation manufacturers, have been caught cheating the government on their contracts. Some did such shoddy work that it could cost the lives of the pilots flying the planes. Is that a white-collar crime or first-degree murder?"

I replied, "We would have to designate it as white-collar. When you judge crimes committed by multibillion-dollar executives you can't treat them as thugs. These people are involved in short-changing the government, unlike the street criminal, who has no idea of right or wrong."

Alonzo was agitated. "I'm for abolishing the use of the term 'white-collar crime,' because if you embezzle someone's pension, which they worked for all their lives, it's rape."

"That's ridiculous. The reason the legal system uses 'white-collar crime' as a designation is that it helps the judge know where to send the wrongdoers. You can't send a white-collar criminal to a low-class prison."

"Why not?" Alonzo yelled.

"Because you want the punishment to fit the crime. You have to distinguish between the sleazeballs who sell dope on the street and MBAs who launder their money in skyscrapers forty stories above the ground. White-collar criminals are different from you and me, Alonzo, and must be shown respect."

"What makes them different?" he demanded.

"They have better lawyers. The worst thing you could do to prevent white-collar felonies is single out business criminals for serious punishment. If you take their tennis courts away from them at Allenwood, they'll go back to crime as soon as they come out."

Alonzo was not convinced. "What I don't like is that white-collar criminals get to plea-bargain. We had a bank in Washington where all the poor people put their savings. It turned out to be a phony bank and was not insured by the U.S. government. The individuals who started the bank stole the poor people blind. Why should that be termed a white-collar crime?"

"Because," I said, "except for people's life's savings being taken, no one really got hurt."

SUPER BOWL DIET

I HAVE RECEIVED many queries about whether I would print my Super Bowl Quick Weight-Loss Diet this year. As you recall, last year I lost four pounds in January, gained seven pounds in February, maintained the same weight as Tommy Lasorda in March, had a slight setback by putting on eight pounds in

April, and lost eleven pounds and my will to live in May and June.

The rest of the year was devoted to serious dieting on odd days and serious eating on even days. It balanced out to a net gain of fourteen pounds, which was two pounds less than Teddy Kennedy put on in 1989.

What are the secrets of my Super Bowl Quick Weight-Loss Diet, and why do so many people follow it?

Scientists now know from studying rats that most weight gain takes place in front of television sets during sports events. A rat watching an exciting football game will consume twice as many wheat kernels as one watching George Bush coming back from Camp David.

Therefore the trick is not to look at the Super Bowl in the kitchen. No one can be expected to watch a goal-line drive without consuming two large bowls of potato chips.

I permit rats on my diet to have food only at halftime. The combination of watching football and no food has caused most rats to lose two to three pounds in one afternoon.

One of the reasons it is difficult to get started on the Super Bowl Quick Weight-Loss Diet is that there are so many leftovers from the holidays that have to be consumed.

In my house, for example, there are still a ten-pound can of chocolate-coated popcorn, a three-pound box of Mrs. See's chocolates, buttered shortbread, and glazed fruit and stuffed dates from California. Happily, they are all permissible on my diet, provided that one doesn't add salt. It is essential to use up all leftovers in January so that you won't be tempted to eat them during the rest of the year.

The question of exercise is vital to my diet plan. Jumping up and down in your chair while watching your team score is the best kind of exercise you can do. In diet terms we call it "toning the body while watching the big one." Walking is as good as running, so if you walk at a fast pace from the living room to the kitchen to bring in the cheese dip, you will get as much exercise as someone who runs a twenty-six-mile marathon.

Changing chairs at halftime is also a good way of keeping that tummy in shape.

The most important thing about the Super Bowl Quick Weight-Loss Diet is that you must accept failure. You can't expect to win at every TV commercial. Sometimes when things are not going well, you're going to reach for the salted peanuts or shove a fistful of pretzels in your mouth. It doesn't mean you have no willpower, and even if it does, the Super Bowl Diet always forgives. It wants you to get off the floor and start over again.

I was on the Oprah Winfrey show not long ago, and people in the audience kept asking me how I had lost so much weight. I told them the truth: "By eating only one Super Bowl meal a day."

COUCH POTATOES

At the beginning of the Persian Gulf war we all sat quietly on our couches and left the fighting to the network anchormen. We also deferred to the military wisdom of the retired experts hired to guide us through the mine fields.

But as the days and nights wore on, Americans became battle-savvy and, like football fans, they all started developing their own opinions as to how the game should be fought. Suddenly, the generals' strategy was being questioned by the man in the street, and there were rumblings that those giving the briefings did not know what they were talking about.

I first sensed skepticism when my taxi driver said, "You know what we ought to be doing? We should find Hussein's bunker and drop a thousand-pound delayed bomb loaded with TNT down his chimney. It has thirty seconds to go off, and if Hussein doesn't give up Kuwait, we will drive a stake through his heart."

"That's a good idea," I told him.

"Then how come Tom Brokaw never thought of it?"

"He's been dealing with the Scud missile problem, and he can't think of everything."

"If you solve the Hussein question, you don't have a Scud problem."

"You sound as if you know a lot about the military situation. Were you in the service?" I asked.

"No, but my brother was a truck driver in Korea."

When I reached the office, I found Bob Goodier studying a map of Kuwait in *The Washington Post*. "This is where we make our next move," he yelled, bringing his thumb down on a spot in the desert.

"Have you checked it with Dan Rather?"

"What he doesn't know won't hurt him." Bob chuckled.

"But you can't call for a military operation without having approval of at least two of the four networks."

Goodier said, "This is no longer an anchorman's war. It's a couch potato's war and we call the shots."

"You really want to open up the front in Kuwait now?"

"What if Eisenhower had hesitated to invade on D Day?" he asked.

"He had no choice. George Will wasn't there to tell him what to do. Look, there's a danger in letting the couch potatoes run the war."

"Then why do they allow us to watch it on the tube? We cannot be expected to sit there and just suck our thumbs when there is so much bombing to be done."

"All we Americans want is to be a well-informed public. We can't call the shots too."

"It doesn't take a couch potato long to know how to shoot down an Iraqi fighter plane."

"Goodier, you have to leave the fighting to Peter Jennings."

"It's like watching football and not being able to tell the coach how to run the team."

"What do you think we should do?"

"I think we should drive a stake into Hussein's heart."

"That's strange."

"What's strange?"

"You're the second person today who suggested that."

I THINK THAT I SHALL NEVER SEE

SOMETHING THAT HASN'T been discussed with regard to the Kitty Kelley biography of Nancy Reagan is the effect that the book is having on the environment.

Irwin Goldberg, president of the Anti-Bestseller Wilderness Fund, is trying to draw attention to the damage Miss Kelley's book is doing to this nation's forests.

He told me, "Thousands of acres of trees have been chopped down to make pulp for Kitty Kelley's book. If people keep buying it at the present rate, they may have to start whacking away at the rain forests of Brazil. We're looking at an ecological disaster."

"It's funny, but I don't think of trees when I think of Kitty Kelley," I said.

"That's the trouble. People are under the impression that biographies grow in bookstores. They don't realize that everything about book publishing begins and ends with trees. Our organization wants the public to understand that every time they buy a book they are helping to create a vast wasteland."

"Then you're warning everyone that the Nancy Reagan biography is an environmental hazard?"

"We don't care how many times Frank Sinatra visited the second floor of the White House," Goldberg said. "Our only concern is how many tree stumps it took to describe those visits. The fierce urge by the public to read the worst about a First Lady is turning Canada into another Sahara Desert."

"Is that the message the Wilderness Fund is trying to send out?"

"Something like that. Books full of innuendo not only hurt people—they also hurt nature."

"What about the public's right to know?" I asked, playing the role of devil's advocate.

"If the citizens of this country realized what damage was done to produce enough paper for this book, they would waive their right to know. When it comes to deforestation of woods, as opposed to decapitation of personalities, there is only one choice to make."

"Mr. Goldberg, isn't it too late to rescue the forests, now that the book is on the bestseller lists?"

"We are still hopeful. Our only chance is that word of mouth will slow down the book's sales. Please understand that we are not passing judgment on whether the book is good or bad. All we're trying to do is save our wilderness from being lost to the sawmills just because Nancy didn't speak to her children. So far, they've cut down every tree in the state of Washington, and they are now buzz-sawing their way through Oregon. For what? So that thousands of nameless sources can get their revenge on the Reagans?"

I told Goldberg that Shakespeare once said, "Anybody can write a book, but only a bestseller can flatten a forest."

"We have studies to show that it is not books of poetry but biographies bursting with undocumented quotes that are lousing up planet Earth."

"I have one question to ask you."

"Shoot," Goldberg said.

"If a tree falls in the forest and no one hears it, can it still be used for a Kitty Kelley book?"

HAIL TO THE BUDGET!

YOU MIGHT HAVE missed it when President Bush's budget was unveiled. It was a mere $1.45 trillion. It didn't bother me, but when I told my friend, Gordon Manning, he expressed surprise. "Bush told us during the election campaign that it would be only $1.35 trillion."

"Presidents always fudge on budgets. They can never distinguish between a billion and a trillion."

Manning asked, "How do they come up with the figure in the first place?"

"They have trained chimpanzees who work with slide rules. At the beginning of the financial year each chimp in the Office of Management and Budget is allowed a trillion dollars to shape into anything he wants. Once you crunch numbers, it's every budget director for himself."

Manning was fascinated with the process. "Has anyone ever seen a trillion dollars?"

"Not too many people. We've seen military weapons that cost a trillion dollars, and HUD obligations and S&L debts. But not even the president's dog has seen a trillion dollars piled up in front of the White House."

"How does the president know that the $1.45 trillion is all there?"

"One of Dan Quayle's jobs is to count it and make sure that it checks out."

"The president is lucky to have a vice-president who can count."

"That's why Bush took Quayle on as VP. Dan can do wonders with a golf score."

Manning said, "The president is asking for $1.45 trillion. Where is he going to get the money?"

"Mostly from the boom times that should be with us at any moment," I told him.

"What boom times?"

"The ones that are just around the corner when the white clouds drive the dark clouds away. Some budget money will come from income tax, some from excise taxes, and a lot from borrowing. When it comes to borrowing money, the U.S. is number one."

Manning said, "How much in new taxes is needed for the $1.45 trillion to make sense?"

I got mad. "Wash out your mouth with soap and water. You don't ask for new taxes when you have a budget of a little over a trillion dollars. Anyone who talks taxes in the Bush administration is nothing but a Scud missile. As Bush has stated many times, 'My country right or wrong—but my country with no taxes.' "

"I would like to do something with the budget," Manning said.

"Such as?"

"I'd like to cut it, so that it would be easier for the White House to count it."

"It really doesn't matter. Unfortunately, no one cares what the president's budget is anymore. Once you break the trillion-dollar barrier it all becomes rather boring."

"If we agree to the president's budget, will our children have to pay for it?"

"No, *their* children will. But you don't have to worry about being stuck with the bill."

"Why not?"

"You have already paid for the thousand points of light."

Happy Valentine!

THE FIRST VALENTINE'S DAY CARD I ever handed out was to a nine-year-old girl named Fern Hoffman. I made it myself, with paper, glue and crayons. Nobody at school had ever heard of Hallmark, and the labor we put into the card was what made the love.

In those days, and I'm not pinpointing what days they were,

you didn't sign your cards. No one had any idea who gave them. It was the guessing that caused the blood to boil.

I understand that the present generation does not observe the anonymity ritual. As one eleven-year-old explained it to me the other day, "Cards cost so much that you want to make sure the person you're giving it to knows where it came from."

Back to Fern. The distribution of the Valentine cards in Mrs. Egorkin's class went as follows: We brought them in and put them on her desk. Most people carried several—a few came empty-handed. I always wondered if the ones who came empty-handed ever found anyone to rub suntan lotion on them when they grew up.

In our world, volume was everything. The more cards you received, the better your chance of success in real life. I believed this at the time, but I am not so sure now. The most popular boy in the class, Roy Bellman, averaged eleven cards per Valentine's Day and was our role model. When he grew up I heard that he had been married four times. One might wonder if too many Valentine cards in his youth caused his downfall.

So the cards were spread out on the desk and Mrs. Egorkin acted as mailperson, calling out each name with care. It should be remembered that in those days life was unfair—unlike today, when everyone in the class gets the same number of Valentines. Back then, you got what you deserved.

Some kids were handed two by Mrs. Egorkin, others twelve. The trick was to pretend that you didn't care whether you got any or not. I was good at this, and only those who saw me sitting in my seat tearing up little scraps of paper knew that I had more than a passing interest in this pagan ceremony.

Fern, as you might have guessed, received anywhere from ten to fifteen cards. I saw her get mine and waited expectantly for her to open it. She didn't. When you are as rich in cards as she was, you could take all afternoon opening them and never be finished. My only hope was that when she opened the card at home she'd see that it had my name all over it.

Then something weird happened. Mrs. Egorkin called my name. Someone had sent me a Valentine's Day card. It was hard to believe. I took it back to my seat and stared at it. I turned it over and over. It was addressed to me, but when you're nine years old a lot of mistakes can occur. I finally opened it and found lipstick smudged on it. Whoever sent this card was serious.

Fern never did open my card, but just as class let out, a girl named Audrey Zoeller came up to me and said, "Did you get my smudge?" I mumbled something about it being okay, but in my heart I thought, How can I respect anybody who would send me a Valentine card? Doesn't she have any taste in boys at all?

I don't know where Fern is today, or if she ever found out who sent her the great card. I would like to believe that she puts it on her mantel every Valentine's Day.

As for Audrey, I no longer hold it against her for sending me a card. The girl was too young to know what she was doing.

THE HARASSED MAN

"A FEDERAL JUDGE has ruled that a Reston woman was not being sexually harassed when her boss gave her cards and gifts, rubbed her back and hands, and regularly escorted her to the bathroom and her car." So reported Mark Potts in *The Washington Post*.

It was a landmark decision, since the judge said that the person who claimed she had been harassed was sending out mixed signals, and that the attention the plaintiff had received did not create an uncomfortable working environment. There was, the judge declared, no direct sexual harassment.

We've had a similar situation on our third floor, so we empathize with the woman in this case. Katrinka, who is involved with computers, seems to have a mad crush on Orloff, the librarian. She is serious about this, and she has told anyone who will listen, "I'll follow him to any Club Med he will lead me to."

Katrinka doesn't pinch Orloff in the library, but witnesses have seen her rub against his shoulders and place Snickers bars on his desk. On a few occasions, Orloff has broken into tears and cried, "Why are you doing this to me?"

Katrinka has replied, "You're all I've got."

Orloff consulted us about what he should do.

I told him, "You can't do anything unless she engages in sexual harassment."

Orloff asked, "What does that mean?"

"She has to make an indecent proposition that would sicken Jesse Helms."

"She never fails," Orloff said.

"Did you encourage her in any way?"

"No. On the contrary. I begged her to stop dancing on the library conference table."

"Do you have that on tape?"

"No, most of my work is with microfilm."

"I'll see how I can help." I went over to talk to Katrinka. I told her, "You have to stop sexually harassing Orloff."

"Why? I hope that someday he will be Mr. Katrinka. How do you think people get married if they don't buzz around the office with each other?"

"The office is not the place for women to sneak up on men and rub their necks."

Katrinka said, "It's not the end-all, but it's a start."

"You must stop," I insisted, "because Orloff doesn't like it."

Katrinka laughed. "Orloff doesn't know what he likes. Most of the marriages in this country were made in offices where women knew exactly what they wanted and men had no idea what they were looking for. Sexual harassment is in the eye of the person who drinks the most coffee at the vending machine."

"So you intend to pursue your campaign for Orloff?"

"Someday, when we're keeping house, he will realize that I am more than a potted plant."

"Let's switch it around. Suppose Orloff loved you and you couldn't stand him?"

"No problem. I'd sue him for molestation."

THE HEAD OF THE LINE

THE UNEMPLOYMENT LINE is the great leveler. You now meet people there that you used to run into at Nordstrom's.

My buddy Joe Doubleday was in row A when he recognized Sidney Tartar, the president of Megabear Manufacturers, standing behind him.

"Hi, Mr. Tartar," Doubleday said. "Long time no see."

Tartar asked, "Do I know you?"

"Joe Doubleday. I was in advertising. You laid me off six months ago."

"Oh, yes," responded Tartar. "I heard good things about you."

"Then why did you lay me off?"

"You were part of our economic safety net. We promised the bank we would let you go so that they'd ease up on our loans. It was nothing personal."

"That's what I told my wife," Doubleday said. "She never could understand why you didn't fire anybody on the fortieth floor. After all, they were responsible for the dumb decisions the company made."

"We never made dumb decisions. We were victims of bad luck."

"What about the Velcro beer bottles you tried to sell to the breweries? There was no market for them, and they didn't work."

"Nobody's perfect."

"Remember the fast-food chain specializing in calf's-liver sandwiches? Why wasn't anyone strung up for that?"

"We laid off five thousand high school kids. What more do you want?"

"You had a solid company before you started selling pothole insurance."

"Doubleday, just because we fired you doesn't mean that you're an expert on business practices."

"Mr. Tartar, as long as we're standing in line together, I'm going to take this opportunity to tell you what I think of the executives who are running businesses in America. A Japanese sumo wrestler could do a better job than any of them."

"Doubleday, if we weren't standing in the same unemployment line I would take severe disciplinary measures against you."

"Mr. Tartar, you drove your company into the garbage dump because you chose greed for your bottom line."

"My employees never understood me."

"What are you doing in this place? I thought people like you had golden parachutes."

"I lost mine in divorce court."

"It figures. You wreck the company and you can't even hold onto the money they gave you."

"Does everybody here have to take guff from everybody else?"

"No, the only ones who get it are those responsible for the rest of us being unemployed in the first place."

"Doubleday, I always worried about your problem. Megabear was one big happy family. Do you think I'll have any trouble getting my unemployment check?"

"I doubt it. In order to collect, you must prove that you are unable to handle another job—and you won't have any difficulty doing that."

A SHARE OF THE FUTURE

SOME OF YOU may have noticed that Wall Street seems to be marching to a different drummer. While the country's economic forecasts have been very gloomy, the stock market has been soaring—apparently unaware of any bad news from the nation's business community.

The question most people are asking is, "What does Wall Street know that we don't?" It's one that I took in my briefcase down to the Street the other day.

I sought out Florio, who has a seat on the Stock Exchange. He was on the floor of the Exchange waving his hands and nodding his head. I tugged on his shirt.

"Florio, what is going on with the market?"

"We're touting AT&T and shorting Chardonnay grapes."

"I don't want to buy anything. All I'm trying to find out is why the economy is drowning and you people are driving stocks up."

"We have to do what we have to do."

"Why?"

"The bulls are in charge, and if we don't follow them, we could wind up in the pits with the bears."

"Florio, don't you read the papers? General Motors dropped over a billion dollars, Ford lost its shirt, and Sears, Roebuck is laying off its labor force. It has to affect what you invest in."

"We don't pay any attention to the business news. It's too depressing. The only way for us to survive on Wall Street is to talk to each other."

"Who do you talk to?"

"Rembrecht. I roomed with him at Princeton. He knows a lot about the market because his grandmother was the first person in Trenton to buy IBM. I can learn more from Rembrecht than I can from *The Wall Street Journal.*"

"What is Rembrecht doing now?"

"He's looking for a job after being furloughed by Drexel Burnham."

"So most of your investment choices are recommended by a friend who is out of work."

"At least he is upbeat. A lot of the guys down here would rather sit on their money than invest it in stocks that are bound to go through the roof."

Two men grabbed Florio's legs and pummeled him in the stomach.

"What's going on?" I asked him.

"They want me to buy Eastern Airlines."

"If the airline ever comes back you'll be a hero."

"That's exactly what I was thinking." Florio took hold of each of the men's noses and twisted them, which made it a deal.

Florio told me, "The person to watch is Tenterhooks. He's been leading this market, and it will keep going up until he decides it's going to go down."

"I didn't know one man had that kind of power."

"People pay attention to Tenterhooks."

"Why is that?"

"He speaks in a very low voice and it's difficult to hear him."

A woman broker rushed up to Florio. "I have a hundred thousand shares of Federated Department Stores. Yes or no?"

"Why not? Who ever heard of anyone buying a bad junk bond from Bloomingdale's?"

DEATH IN THE AFTERNOON

THE QUESTION I am asked more than any other is, "Why don't we just blow away Saddam Hussein and be done with it?" I must admit that I think about it every waking moment, and watching Hussein go up in smoke is one of my fondest dreams.

Long ago and far away, when the Bay of Pigs missed being our finest hour, the CIA contracted with the Mafia to have Castro killed. The Mafia tried everything, including poisoning Castro's cigars, but they didn't succeed.

Today there are many in the United States who feel that just because the Brotherhood failed once doesn't mean we shouldn't give them a second chance.

I went to see my friend Lucky Rico to ask him if he thought that the Mob might be interested in doing one of its celebrated hit jobs on the infamous Saddam.

He said, "It's not easy. The main reason it's so difficult to kill Hussein is that every man in Iraq looks exactly like him. If you watch the evening news, the Iraqi males sport the same mustache and wear the same black beret. It's no accident. Saddam knows that if we tried to get him, we'd have to wipe out all the look-alikes in his country."

"I don't approve of assassination," I told Lucky. "At the same time, it seems a shame that Saddam is still breathing in and out after the grief he's caused. What would you do if you had the contract?"

"We're not certain that we want the job. The Mafia has always believed that dictators should be strung up by their own people—the way Mussolini was. On the other hand, if there was enough money involved, we might have a whack at it. I guess the easiest thing to do is get Hussein when he's having a shave in the barbershop. Then you don't have to worry about a moving target. If that didn't work, I'd plant cyanide in his mustache cup."

"And if those attempts failed?"

"As you know, Hussein is a very snappy dresser. I would intercept a package sent by his tailor from Italy, and sew a plastic explosive in the zipper of his trousers. Then when he unzipped them to go to bed—POOF—and the emperor would have no clothes."

"If you can do it, we'll pay for it," I said.

"Of course," he continued, "there's nothing wrong with taking Saddam out to a good Italian restaurant in Baghdad and holding his head under the minestrone for five minutes."

"I thought I saw that in *The Godfather.*"

"When we take a contract on someone we want the client to be happy."

"What about an accident? Could you arrange for Hussein to be kicked in the head by one of the camels he stole from the Kurds?"

"Yes, but Saddam is too wily to get close to a camel he doesn't know. It might be better to run over him in a Russian tank while he was giving one of his cousins a medal."

"Would you kiss Saddam before you eliminated him?"

"I'm not sure. Twenty-eight years ago my father kissed Castro, and it didn't do any good."

No Business Like . . .

THE LUFTHANSA VIP lounge at Frankfurt airport was jammed with passengers waiting for the Frankfurt–Baghdad flight to depart. Most of them were carrying attaché cases bursting with catalogues. They all seemed to know each other.

"Kraus, I haven't seen you since you were selling poison gas grenades to the Republican Guard."

Kraus had a big grin on his face. "I never thought that we'd be going back so soon, François. What have you got in your bag?"

"Heavy water. It appears that because of the coalition bombing, Iraq has a shortage, and we're the only people who can meet their specifications."

"Hey, McDonald. I didn't know that the Americans were interested in rearming Iraq."

"We're not officially, but no one said we couldn't sell M-I tanks to Jordan, which could then be transshipped to Baghdad via UPS."

A British salesman in a bowler hat said, "See here, old boy. The British were given rights to supply Iraq with tanks. After all, we are the exclusive tank dealers for the Middle East."

A Russian added, "Ah, but your Chieftain tanks proved to be lemons in the Gulf war. The Iraqis will need something like the T-72 if they are going to violate another UN resolution."

The American said, "We are not interested in the armored vehicles. We hope to sell the Iraqis some new long-range artillery so that they won't lose the next war overnight."

"Does the Pentagon know about this?"

"No, but the Department of Commerce does. The Iraqis may be down on their luck, but they are still a source of big bucks."

The French salesman told the group, "The money to be made in the arms business does not come from original sales, but from reorders. We would like to replenish the entire Iraqi missile stockpile with Exocets."

A Chinese businessman dressed in a Mao jacket took a long pipe out of his sample case. "Not after they see our new Silkworm missiles. The Iraqi generals are still mad at how poorly the Exocets performed."

The German salesman intervened. "Let's not fight among ourselves. There is enough business for everybody. Even if the Germans get a contract to build a nuclear factory, we're willing to let someone else supply the delivery systems."

"I think we deserve a break," the Russian said. "We should have priority for all fighter-plane sales, because we need hard currency to buy riot equipment to stop the traitors in Lithuania."

The Frenchman told him, "What makes you think that you are a favored nation? Our Mirage jets are superior to your MiGs."

"Then why didn't your Mirages fight well?"

"Because Saddam flew them all to Iran. He didn't want any of them to scratch their paint jobs."

The British salesman said, "Is anybody going to try to sell minesweepers to Iraq?"

There was silence in the room.

"Good, then we won't have to be the lowest bidder."

A woman's voice came over the loudspeaker. "Lufthansa Flight Two-four-four for Baghdad now leaving from Gate Twelve. Those who need assistance and all international arms merchants may board before women and children."

HE'S QUALIFIED

WHAT REALLY TICKS me off is when they say that Dan Quayle is not qualified to be president of the United States. Although fifty-seven percent of the American people are unsure that the vice-president should sit in the Oval Office, hardly any of them have met Mr. Quayle, or are aware of what a good guy he really is.

The person who knows Vice-President Quayle better than all of us is his caddy, and he sees the man much differently from how the rest of us do.

Wally Davis told me, "Dan is more qualified to be president than anyone who has played this course—past or present. He has a seven handicap. That's the lowest of any person who has ever served in the White House."

"I realize that his handicap is a big plus, but is there any other proof that he can handle the role of appointed leader of the free world?"

Wally said, "Well, he's very nice-looking. I don't think we've had a better-looking vice-president than Dan Quayle."

"What have looks got to do with the presidency?"

"He's going to bring those looks with him to Sixteen-hundred Pennsylvania Avenue. When they play 'Hail to the Chief,' everyone is going to say, 'What a nice-looking president we American people are blessed with.' "

"I hadn't thought of that."

"Dan is also a neat dresser. I don't think you'll find a man in Washington who can wear a blazer like he does. Our foreign enemies know that Dan is a clotheshorse, so they are not going to push him around."

"Everything you've said so far is positive, Wally. What else can you tell me about the vice-president to knock down the skeptics?"

"Dan speaks fluent English, which you hardly hear in the United States anymore. This will be especially helpful when he has to give the State of the Union address."

"What about his grasp of the grave issues that he must deal with in the Rose Garden?"

Wally replied, "Dan is aware that a president has to do more than just play golf and tennis. Therefore he intends to face up to his responsibility through either tough decisions or prayer, whichever comes first."

"It's a pity that more people can't see the man the way you do."

"Let me tell you something about Dan Quayle. A few weeks ago he flew down to Augusta, Georgia, to play eighteen holes with three defense company lobbyists. We were on the twelfth hole, about two hundred twenty yards from the cup. I handed Dan a two iron, and he shook his head and said, 'Gimme a five.' I protested that there was no way he could get on the green with a five. He just laughed in that engaging way of his and said, 'Allow me to be the one to decide what iron to use.' Now does that sound like someone who can't make a decision?"

I asked. "Did he make the shot?"

Wally went red. "What difference does it make? He proved that he was going to do it his way."

"Have you ever seen him angry or seen him lose his temper?"

"Only once, when a Secret Serviceman putted out while Dan was still stuck in a sand trap."

WAR MEANS VOTES

YOU CAN SAY what you like about members of Congress, but they are always aware of which way the wind is blowing.

Right now the wind is blowing toward George Bush, and the way he won the Persian Gulf war. The people in the most trouble are those members of Congress who voted against the president's use of armed force to teach Iraq a lesson.

So the naysayers have to play catch-up for their elections. They have ordered their political managers to change their image from doves to hawks overnight.

Freddie Havemeyer, who is in charge of Senator Hiram Whipple's campaign, was ushered into the senator's office.

Whipple said, "Were you able to kill the picture of me in an Arab headdress kissing Saddam Hussein? It was taken when I visited Iraq just before the war."

323

"No, sir. Your opposition is building its entire TV campaign around it. We have a difficult row to hoe. Here, try these on."

"What are they?"

"Eighty-second Airborne camouflage fatigues."

"With an ammunition belt!"

"That's just for credibility. Our staff has been working on some slogans. How do you like 'Today Baghdad, Tomorrow the World'?"

"That's strong," the senator said.

"We're way behind in the polls and we must destroy your wimp image. Now the next major concern is, How do we out-American-flag the other guy? We'd like you to wear this flag in your handkerchief pocket at all times."

"But it's bigger than a tablecloth."

"People have to see it, Senator. Okay, we've got you outfitted for the campaign pretty well. Let's discuss what you should say. Suppose they ask you why you voted against war powers for Bush."

"I'll say that I thought I was voting against farm subsidies for Russia."

"It's weak. The reason you voted against Bush is that his demand for using our armed forces wasn't tough enough. You wanted him to promise the country that he would nuke Basra."

"I did?"

"At this time it would be a mistake to attack Bush personally, so you should say that once the war started, you had no differences with the president. To prove it, you can hold up this picture of you and Bush shaking hands."

"That was taken in 1973."

"Nobody will know. Your job in this campaign is to attack Saddam Hussein for bringing so much misery to the world."

"What if they find out I gave him an autographed basketball from the Celtics when I went to Baghdad last year?"

"We're going to have to take a chance on that. Here's your standard speech for the campaign."

"Hey, this sounds just like the Gettysburg Address."
"What's the difference? If you've heard one war speech, you've heard them all."

CRUEL AND UNUSUAL

THERE IS GOOD NEWS from the West. A federal appeals court recently ruled that a convicted murderer doing life in a Nevada prison was correct when he claimed in a suit that a cellmate's smoking was cruel and unusual punishment.

The court served notice on all prisons that they had to set up separate but equal facilities for puffers and nonpuffers, just as the toniest restaurants do. Secondhand smoking has always been a problem for people locked up, but so far prison authorities have refused to pay any attention to the complaints.

The State of Nevada and its attorney general have argued that once you give in to prisoners such as Mr. William McKinney who complain about smoking, pretty soon you'll have to deal with gripes on everything, including the quality of prison wine.

But now, like most states, Nevada may be forced to comply with the decision of the court of appeals. Unfortunately, the judges did not spell out how the ruling should be administered.

Joseph Kleinbaum, Butt Professor at the Stonewall School of Jurisprudence, said, "The worst part of the decision is that now when prisoners are sentenced, we will have to ask them whether they prefer a smoking or nonsmoking institution."

325

"What a mess!" I exclaimed.

"My question is: Since we know that smoking shortens your life, should a judge mete out a lesser sentence to someone who uses cigarettes than to someone who doesn't?"

"If I was on the bench, I'd give secondary smokers a pardon just because they've suffered at the hands of those who don't give a damn about polluting the air. Why not solve the problem by putting all smokers into solitary confinement?" I suggested.

"That would be unconstitutional. You can't punish people for smoking—at least not yet. The state has to provide places where smokers can do time even if it costs the taxpayers a bundle."

"Do smokers tend to be more criminal than nonsmokers?"

"We don't have the figures on that, but we do know that smokers *look* more criminal than nonsmokers."

I then asked, "How are the tobacco people handling the appeals court decision?"

"They're mad as hell. Prisoners are among their best customers, and they even use cigarettes as currency. The tobacco industry says, 'If forcing nonsmokers to share cells with smokers is cruel and unusual punishment, then what's wrong with cruel and unusual government?' "

"I would hate to be in a prison with nothing but smokers," I said.

"The law is the law," Kleinbaum replied. "Maybe if a nonsmoking criminal knew that he might be sent to a smoking institution, he would think twice about committing a crime."

SPRING PRACTICE IN L.A.

THE LOS ANGELES POLICE DEPARTMENT started spring training early this year. I went out to the park to see them work out.

"How are you hitting 'em?" I asked a policeman swinging several bats.

"Not bad," he replied, spitting out a wad of tobacco. "It takes a little time to get into condition. But it doesn't take long to become a slugger."

"What's that guy doing over there?" I inquired.

"He's hitting foul balls with a cattle prod. It's his way of keeping his eye on the ball."

"Are people still trying out for the team?" I wanted to know. "Or are all the slots full?"

"We always have room for a few good players. This is a tough league and the men burn out very fast."

"I saw some of the team at play on the evening news," I said. "Talk about batting practice."

The policeman sounded angry. "That videotape of our practice should never have been shown. We were just horsing around and people thought we were playing for real."

"I must admit it looked as if you were playing for keeps," I said. "As a matter of fact, I heard them yelling something like 'Kill the ump!' but it wasn't the ump they wanted to kill."

Now the policeman's face was livid. "You can't even have

private practice anymore without someone crashing the ball park. The guy who took that tape ought to be yoked."

"Why is that?"

"He didn't have a license to carry a video camera."

"I didn't know you needed a license to own a camcorder in Los Angeles."

"Not officially. We have been trying for years to have people in this town register their cameras. We're also trying to get them to wait seven days before they can purchase one. The man who took those pictures is a menace to society because he gave the L.A. Police Department team a bad name."

"Your guys really put their heart into the sport," I said with admiration. "I've never seen anyone play such hardball."

"We have a saying on this team that if you can't stand the heat from the fans, don't show up in uniform for the game."

"I'd like to ask this," I said. "Are there as many foul balls on this team as everyone says?"

He swung his club at an imaginary jaw. "Heck, no. There are no more foul balls here than there are in any sport. The fact that we hit better than most cops means we attract all the attention."

"Do you think you'll see the scandal die down?"

"It always does. Look, you can't play in this league without someone getting hurt. After all, everyone knows that this is a contact sport. The only reason we're getting a bad press is that some people can't tell the difference on videotape between a strike and a hit."

"What about your manager, Daryl Gates? How does he feel about the team's being suspended?"

"Not good at all."

CLIMB EVERY MOUNTAIN

THE NEW FIGURE for the savings and loan bailout is $500 billion. For those who are unable to comprehend this amount, just put half a trillion dollars on your kitchen table.

There are some people who say that $500 billion isn't what it used to be, but for the lower middle class it's still a sum not to be sneezed at.

You can build five hundred Taj Mahals in Atlantic City for $500 billion. For $500 billion, Donald Trump can even make a reasonable divorce settlement with his wife. It will also buy you one of Imelda Marcos's buildings in New York City, or two orchestra seats to any Broadway musical.

While Nervous Nellies think of the $500 billion as a debt, others look at it as nothing more than a tall mountain of paper that reaches up to the sky.

Cleveland Franklin, who specializes in bailouts, invited me to climb the largest mountain of bad paper that the country has ever seen. It's located in what is now known as the "Vale of Greed."

He tied a rope around me and handed me some grappling hooks.

"Follow me up," he shouted. "The base of the mountain is made of junk bonds. Above the clouds it's all real estate loans."

"It sure stinks," I said. "How could this country build such a tall stack of debt in such a short time?"

"The banks just kept making loans, and every time someone couldn't repay a loan, the S&L rolled the loan papers up into a ball and tossed it on the pile."

"But it's awesome!"

"You have no idea how many bad loans they made. I'm going to pull you up onto this ledge. It's very famous."

"What is it called?"

"The Grotto of the Gang of Five. Legend has it that five senators met with a savings and loan medicine man on this very outcropping and blew smoke at each other. This kept evil spirits from hurting the medicine man, and in exchange he showered gifts on the senators."

"Is he still alive?" I asked.

"Yes, but all the deadbeat paper on the next two levels belongs to him."

Both of us struggled on upward. Cleveland handed me an oxygen mask.

"You can get a good view from here," he said, as we tied ourselves to another ledge. "You see those carcasses down there?"

"There are a lot of them."

"They are all dead S&Ls. They were abandoned by their avaricious owners."

"The S&Ls deserved better than that."

"We're almost to the top. You can never say that you have reached the summit of an S&L debt, because tomorrow it's bound to be higher."

I was excited. "I never thought that one day I would be standing on top of five hundred billion dollars' worth of red ink."

"This mountain represents more than lost causes," Cleveland told me. "This debt has become an environmental hazard.

It smells all the way from New Jersey to Texas. Someday it's going to smother California."

"Can we go back down? I'm beginning to feel nervous. There could be an avalanche of fresh debt at any time."

"Don't worry. You can't get hurt. It's only paper."

WHERE THE MONEY WENT

NOW THAT THE Persian Gulf war is over, we have all returned to our favorite subject at the dinner table: children.

It started when someone raised the question, What do we do with our money?

"Ours," said Zeigfield, "goes for taxes and children."

Bloomgarden said, "It's different in our family. Our money goes to the children, and whatever's in miscellaneous is for taxes."

Debbie Dawson told us, "After paying for rock concerts, we're lucky to have any money left over for Cheerios."

Bloomgarden said, "I wonder if any of our children appreciate the fact that because of them we have no money for ourselves."

"They probably would," Sagebrush told him, "if they weren't so engrossed in their Nintendo games."

Debbie Dawson said, "Our kids are in college. They are certain that their tuition is paid for by the Easter Bunny."

I didn't want to be left out of the conversation. "I mentioned to mine that money doesn't grow on trees, and you can't believe how shocked they were. One even asked, 'Are you sure?' "

It turned out that all the members of our group were in hock because of their children.

"Why do we deprive ourselves of so much to enable our children to have everything?"

Paul Lopatin explained, "We do it because they might think less of us if we didn't. How can any of us look into the teary eyes of a child and say no when he or she asks for a Sony Walkman? Lilly and I made a vow when we got married that we would go to the poorhouse rather than let one of our flesh and blood cry for even a minute of their lives."

"We had to redo Alice's room from top to bottom because she just discovered pink," Brumbecker said.

Susan Pepper wanted to know, "Do you think that someday they'll realize we didn't spend any money on ourselves so that they could have it *all*?"

I replied, "How could they know?"

Maurice Sislen said, "We've been very lucky. Our kids don't ask for money—only things."

I laughed. "What kinds of things?"

"For example, last week my son asked for a motorcycle. I explained to him that the only spare cash we have has been set aside for a trip to visit his grandmother in Iowa. He said that he didn't want to pressure us, but most of his friends' parents had canceled their trips to buy Harley-Davidsons for their children."

"At least when we grow old," I mused, "we can sit in a wheelchair in a nursing home and know that we did right by our children. We never deprived them of whatever they felt they had coming to them."

"Yes," Susan Pepper said, sighing, "but the question is, Will they come to visit us in the nursing home?"

Debbie Dawson said, "Why should they, if they have everything already?"

WOOF!

I WAS HAVING dinner in a Washington restaurant with Belberg. He had a large piece of steak on his plate, and he called the waiter over to our table. "Would you put this in a doggie bag for me, please?" he said.

"Yes, sir."

When the waiter disappeared, I whispered to Belberg, "You do that every time we go out to eat."

"Do what?"

"Ask them to put your leftovers in a doggie bag. There's nothing wrong with this, except that you haven't got a dog."

"They don't know that," Belberg said.

"It's not the point. By asking for a doggie bag, you're living a lie."

"I'm doing it because the restaurant help are much nicer to you if they think you're a dog owner. I suspect that most of them have dogs. Besides, when I ask for a bag it makes them feel that the food is not going to waste."

"I don't know if I should trust someone who gets food wrapped for a dog he doesn't even own."

"Who's getting hurt?" Belberg wanted to know. "Look, the restaurant is happy to get rid of the food, everyone thinks that I'm a real good guy, and when I leave I'm carrying a package that a French poodle would kill for."

"What do you do with the food?"

"I usually dump it in the trashcan next to my apartment house."

"Why don't you give it to a dog?" I shouted at him.

"I don't want any canines in my building to become dependent on me. As a matter of fact, that's why I don't own a dog. They're always expecting you to bring home the leftovers when you go to a restaurant."

"I'm glad there are not many people like you who are chiseling dog scraps from the management."

"What difference does it make what I do with my leftovers? I'm paying for them."

"What happens if an employee asks you your dog's name?"

"I tell them it's Czar Nicholas, and his breed originated in Rasputin's monastery."

"Well, at least you give them a good story."

"For a guy who never had a dog, I'm the best. Sometimes after I finish a story the waiter goes back into the kitchen and throws in a couple of bones."

"This doesn't shame you?"

"Not really. Look, I didn't start life lying about being a dog owner. It came to me one night at a restaurant when everyone else at the table asked for a doggie bag. The waiter assumed that I wanted one as well and handed me a silver-foil swan. When I thanked him and told him Czar Nicholas would go crazy, he took the leftovers from the next table and handed me them too."

I said, "I want you to know that I think you're weird."

The waiter returned with the bag and a big smile on his face. Belberg handed him a dollar, "You're sending joy to a dog who has been doing nothing but guarding sheep for twenty-four hours."

The waiter was so impressed that he validated Belberg's parking ticket three times.

PLAY BALL!

As the baseball season begins, the voice of salaries can be heard throughout the land.

Never have players been paid as much, nor revenues from product endorsements been as high. The numbers are so large that many newspapers are seriously considering taking baseball off the sports pages and covering it in their business section instead.

Has big money changed the game? You better believe it. Just listen in on the conversation from the dugout of the Los Angeles Bandits.

Jim Akers, the manager, tells his team, "Everyone be sharp today. The Fatfree Diet Powder Company is going to do a TV commercial in the dugout, and I don't want any screwing up while my contract renewal is on the table."

He looks down at the players, "McMurtry, you're first at bat."

"I can't, boss. I have to see my broker this afternoon. He wants me to get out of treasury notes and into something more comfortable."

"Damn it, McMurtry, you should have done that this morning."

"I was buying apartment houses this morning. Heck, I only have two hands."

335

"Boss, my lawyer wants to know if he can stand next to me at shortstop to discuss a suit we're filing against a thrift that went bankrupt last weekend."

"That's a stupid question, Bowditch, and you know it. Lawyers aren't allowed on the field during the game."

"Not even if there's no one on the bases?"

"Okay, I want heads-up ball. Merrill Lynch is thinking of building an entire advertising campaign around the team, and all their big shots are in the stands to make sure that we're bullish on America."

"Rickleberg, there's a little kid out here who wants your autograph on a baseball card."

"Tell him it will cost him twenty-five dollars, and I don't take personal checks."

Brad Taicher turns to Potsdam sitting next to him and says, "This is a big day for me. PaineWebber is going to take me public."

"You mean you're being listed on the stock market!" Potsdam exclaims.

"A clause in my contract with the team says that if I hit forty home runs, they have to make me one of the Fortune Five Hundred."

Potsdam says, "I'm only batting two-twenty on the Dow Jones average. I should never have listened to my brother-in-law when he advised me to invest in Iraqi war bonds."

"PaineWebber wants me to merge my steakhouse chain with the Kansas City Royals," Taicher tells him. "They say that with our combined assets we could be the largest steak-baseball conglomerate in the league."

"Where's the designated hitter?" Akers yells.

"He's down here reading *The Wall Street Journal*."

"Babalew, you're up."

"I lost a bundle on IBM. How can you expect me to hit the ball?"

"Shut up and get on base."

"That's easy for you to say. Don't you ever think of anything besides baseball?"

FEAR ITSELF

THE SATURDAY-AFTERNOON GANG was sitting around quaffing beer when the subject of fear came up. Colfax spoke first.

"I'm afraid of making love with a married woman, and then when it's over she'll ask me to kill her husband."

Delmonte said, "My fear is that I will disappear into a Washington, D.C., pothole and no one will know where I am."

Littlefield joined in. "I am most afraid of being bitten by my father-in-law's pit bull."

It was Wendel's turn. He took a sip of beer and then confided, "My nightmare is getting a speeding ticket in Los Angeles."

"What's so scary about that?" I asked him.

"Suppose there is nobody around with a video camera?"

"You're fearful for no reason. There is *always* someone around with a camera."

Wendel confessed that he was still frightened. "What if they make me get out of the car?"

"They won't do that just to give you a speeding ticket. What kind of police do you think they have in Los Angeles?"

"Suppose the cop who stops me forces me to lie down on my

stomach with my hands behind my back, and my legs spread out?"

"He wouldn't dare," I assured him.

"Why not?"

"Because Chief of Police Gates wouldn't stand for it."

"In my dream he does."

"Wendel," Delmonte said, "people have speeding-ticket nightmares in every large city in this country, but nothing ever really happens. My guess is that if you were stopped by a policeman in Los Angeles for speeding, he would salute smartly and let you off with a stern warning."

"Is this your nightmare or mine?" Wendel wanted to know.

"It's mine."

"Well, in my dream I'm surrounded by ten cops and they're playing hockey puck with me."

We all laughed.

I said, "Maybe in Soweto, but never in America. You should watch what you eat before you go to sleep."

Wendel didn't speak for a few minutes, and then he added, "I wasn't speeding."

"Everyone tells the cops the same thing," I told him. "That's why they make you stretch out on the pavement, and put a stun gun around your neck. The police hate liars."

"In my nightmare they whack the hell out of me for no reason at all."

"The Los Angeles police don't whack people without a reason. Maybe they don't like your haircut."

"I have a nice haircut," Wendel protested.

"To you perhaps, but when the police see you, it may not be to their liking."

Wendel continued: "In my nightmare I need twenty stitches in my head."

Colfax said, "Come on. You look as if they'd hardly laid a glove on you."

COME FLY WITH ME

For his sake, I hope they don't make John Sununu fly on commercial airlines just because of the recent White House regulations about his pleasure trips in government planes.

If they do, he is going to be in for a big surprise.

Let's imagine that he has to go to New Hampshire to see his dentist: .

Sununu must first get in line with fifty other passengers, including a man at the counter who is changing his ticket from a direct flight to Karachi to a flight with side trips to Muscat and Oman, Bogotá, Vancouver and the Solomon Islands.

The chief of staff finally gets to the head of the line and informs the ticket agent at the computer, "I wish to go to Manchester, New Hampshire."

She starts to hit the computer keyboard. "Business or pleasure?" she asks.

"What difference does it make?"

"We have a twenty-percent discount for White House aides traveling for pleasure—you get nothing if you're on business."

"I hope to go skiing in Squaw Valley afterward," Sununu says.

"Skiers are entitled to a ten-percent discount, but there is a surcharge of fifteen percent for their skis."

Sununu responds, "What if I was traveling on business for the

339

president to handle a matter that could affect the entire fate of our new beginnings in the Middle East?"

The agent hit the computer keys again. "Is Vice-President Quayle going with you on this trip?"

"No, he isn't."

"That's too bad," she tells him. "If you are accompanied by the vice-president of the United States, you both travel at half fare."

"I'm going to miss my plane. Please give me a ticket."

The ticket agent asks Sununu, "Why didn't you inform us three months ago that you wanted to go to Manchester? We would have given you a thirty-percent discount and you could have stayed at a veterans' hospital for the weekend."

"At the time I didn't know that I was going. It's terribly important that I get on that plane."

"Why?"

"Because it has a telephone and I have to keep in constant touch with the president."

"The telephone is in first class, and you're buying a coach ticket. How do you expect to use it?"

"Can't a coach person use the first-class phone?"

"You must be joking. First-class passengers would never stand for people in tourist class getting their filthy fingers on *their* phone."

"All right, then, upgrade me to first."

"We can't do that unless we have letters from two members of the Democratic Party attesting to your good character."

"I'm a benevolent man, and everyone in Washington loves me."

The agent replies, "That's not what it says in the computer."

WELCOME HOME

I WATCHED A television show called *Welcome Home America*.
It was a tribute to the USO and our boys who fought in Desert
Storm. There were 4,500 troops in the audience as well as three
presidents: Bush, Ford and Reagan. Nothing could have been
more heartwarming or patriotic.

But as the program went on I noticed something very
strange, so I turned to my loyal Republican friend Cloister and
said, "There are no Democrats in the tribute."

"Why would you want to feature Democrats?"

"Didn't the Democrats have anything to do with Desert
Storm?"

"Heck, no." He chuckled. "This was a Republican war from
start to finish. It was produced by a Republican president,
directed by a Republican secretary of defense, orchestrated by
a Republican secretary of state, and every officer worth anything was on the GOP side."

I was aghast but not surprised. "What about the Army, Navy,
Air Force and Marines? They couldn't *all* have been Republicans."

Cloister said, "Damn near all of them were. If there was a
Democrat in the ranks, the word never got back to Washington."

"I didn't know any of this."

"Why do you think the Republicans are staging all the welcome-home celebrations? It was our military, and we paid for it."

"Cloister, is it just possible that the Republicans are trying to cash in on Desert Storm for political reasons?"

"What makes you say that?"

"It's so obvious in this show. It's not entertainment. It looks more like a GOP rally in a presidential election year."

"You are insulting our fighting men and women. Do you think they would be here if they thought they were being used?"

"What else is there for them to do on a Sunday night? Don't get me wrong. The people who took part in Desert Storm deserve everything they can get, except a third-rate TV show decorated by three Republican presidents."

I know that I got through to Cloister, because he was choking on his beer. "Why don't the Democrats have their own program instead of crying foul when we put one on?"

"Because Desert Storm was not a Republican war or a Democratic war."

"What kind of war was it?"

"It was a great war if you don't ask the Kurds," I told him.

He looked at me with disgust. "You hate America, don't you?"

"No. Why do you think so?"

"Anyone who criticizes a show starring Debbie Allen, Tony Danza, the Pointer Sisters, Kenny Rogers and Tom Selleck, plus three Republican presidents, has no right to stand up for America."

A Star Is Born

As we enter the new world of communications, the telephone company is firing more and more live operators and replacing them with recorded announcements.

It's now so bad that a person considers himself lucky if he is still speaking to a warm body. What the public doesn't know is that the telephone company takes great care in selecting the women to do recorded announcements. Since their voices will remain on computer tapes forever, phone executives can't afford to miscast someone for the part.

I attended an audition for a new voice to represent one of the principal retail outlets. It was held in a large theater on Broadway in New York City. There must have been 150 hopefuls waiting to try out.

Onstage were blondes, brunettes and redheads, dressed in everything from dirndl skirts to leather pants. Many were warming up their voices with arias from *Aida*. Others were kicking their legs in the air, and still others were seated on their chairs shaking with fright.

The director, Cam Funkhouser, came out onstage and said, "I'm glad that you could all come. What we're looking for today is someone who can handle long-distance as well as wrong-number calls. Ever since we changed the area codes, customers have been making stupid mistakes. Your voice has to keep them on track, not only by informing them that they made an error, but also by making sure that they don't do it again.

"Now this is the kind of situation you have to react to: A girl in college is calling her parents, collect. She's desperate because she has run out of funds and has lost her dog all in the same day. At this moment she wants to hear a compassionate voice she can trust, and one that sounds as if the phone company gives a damn. Most of all she wants to hear, 'Thank you for using AT&T.' Okay, I'm going into the orchestra seats, so belt it out."

Cam sat next to me. A girl came up to the microphone, her hands on her hips. Winking at Funkhouser she said, "Thank you for using AT&T."

"No, no, no," Cam shouted. "You're not inviting a guy up to your place for the evening. Thank you very much."

The next young woman was quivering. She said something but we couldn't understand a word.

"We can't hear you," Cam yelled. "Your voice is going to go to Tokyo and Zambia. If we can't hear you in the orchestra, how can they hear you in Sydney, Australia? We'll call you."

A lady in a black leotard came forward and started dancing.

"What are you doing?" Cam asked.

"I can say more with my body than with my voice."

We had listened to almost all the contestants, and Cam was about to give up, when a girl in an ankle-length peasant dress and a straw hat stepped forward. Without a pause, she stretched out her arms and belted out, "Thank you for using AT&T."

Cam jumped out of his seat. "By Jove, she's got it. I believe she's got it." Then he grabbed me and started to dance in the aisle. "The phone of Cohen is mainly made of chrome. The phone of Cohen is mainly made of chrome. Made of chrome, made of chrome, Cohen's phone is mainly made of chrome."

Cam ran up onto the stage and told her, "Repeat after me, 'We're sorry, but you must press "one" before calling your number.' "

She did it, and Funkhouser hugged her and said, "Baby, Ma Bell is going to make you a star."